Hidden Heroes

Of

Easter Week

Memories of Volunteers from England who joined the 1916 Easter Rising

Robin Stocks

Published by Robin Stocks

First published in 2015 by
Robin Stocks
Wakefield Road
Denby Dale HD8 8QD
UK

Text © Robin Stocks 2015

ISBN: 978-0-9934399-0-2

Printed and bound in Great Britain by
CPI Group (UK) Ltd, Croydon CR0 4YY

Acknowledgements

I have been trying to track down the Manchester 1916 Volunteers for so long that I fear I will be unable to thank all those people who helped me. There have been so many. I'm sorry if I've missed you out.

Without the patience and kindness of family members who have been unfailingly helpful in response to my persistent questioning over many years, this story would never have been told. Thank you, Bernadette Wall, Bill Earle, Carol Schofield, Carol Lewkowicz, Christopher Wall, Donald Newton, Doreen Mottram, Joe Arlt, Joe Farrance, Julia Earle, Kate Hayes, Lilian Earle, Marion Farrance, Shirley Jepson, and Vera Clark.

As I had very little relevant historical knowledge when I started, I have incessantly tried to pick the brains of so many who knew more than me. Without their generous help I would have spent far longer trailing up dead ends. In particular, Gerry Kavanagh has been unstinting in his help, as have Aindrias Ó Cathasaigh and Mick O'Connor. Many have shared their knowledge with me, particularly Alan Brooke, Alex Ward, Brian Kennedy, Charlie McGuire, Cyril Pearce, Dave Harker, David Moore, Derek Scott, Joe Flynn, John Lowry, John O'Gorman, Liam Harte, Martin Dowling, Mary Walsh, Mervyn Busteed, Michael Herbert, Neil Doolin, Dr Sandra Moss, Martin Millar and Tomas Maconmara.

This part of our history would have remained hidden without the considerable labour and help from the staff at the Bureau of Military history. Those who work in archives offices and libraries are the real heroes of most historians. I have been particularly helped by those at University College Dublin, National Library of Ireland, and its photographic archive, National Archives Kew, New York Municipal Archives, US National Archives, Doncaster Archives, Working Class Movement Library, Marx Memorial Library, and Leeds, Manchester, Huddersfield, and Denby Dale Public Libraries. I am also very grateful to the Association of the Ragged Trousered, North Cheshire Family History Society, The National Museum of Ireland and Manchester Irish world Heritage Centre.

I would like to thank Richard Nicholls for patiently guiding me through the process of publication.

I am very grateful for those who have given their permission for the use of copyright images. These are credited at the end of the book. If I have inadvertently used any images without permission, please may I apologise.

Above all, I'd like to thank Julia who has put up with me and spent untold hours with me in cemeteries, archives offices and family meetings in the quest to find the truth about her cousin, once removed, Liam Parr.

Dublin in 1916

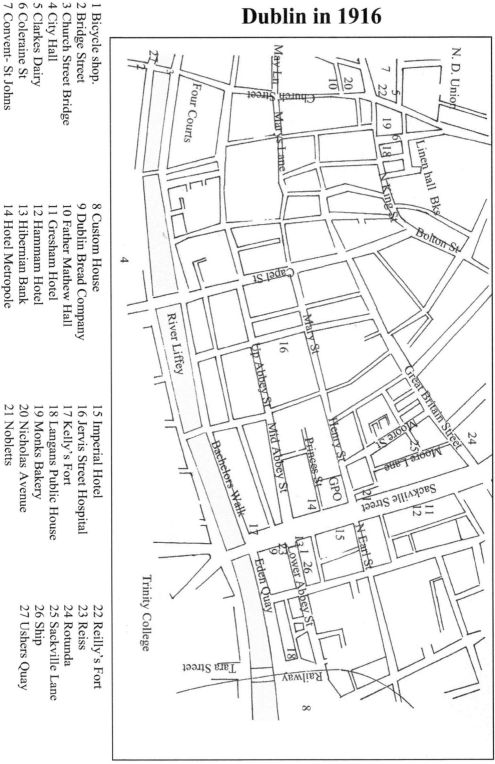

1 Bicycle shop.
2 Bridge Street
3 Church Street Bridge
4 City Hall
5 Clarkes Dairy
6 Coleraine St
7 Convent- St Johns

8 Custom House
9 Dublin Bread Company
10 Father Mathew Hall
11 Gresham Hotel
12 Hammam Hotel
13 Hibernian Bank
14 Hotel Metropole

15 Imperial Hotel
16 Jervis Street Hospital
17 Kelly's Fort
18 Langans Public House
19 Monks Bakery
20 Nicholas Avenue
21 Nobletts

22 Reilly's Fort
23 Reiss
24 Rotunda
25 Sackville Lane
26 Ship
27 Ushers Quay

Contents

Prologue i

Introduction iii

Chapter One: Liam Parr's childhood in Dublin 1

Chapter Two: Liam's introduction to the pipes and Irish Nationalism 17

Chapter Three: Liam Parr moving to Stockport 33

Chapter Four: Gilbert Lynch and industrial unrest 45

Chapter Five: The Irish crisis develops 69

Chapter Six: Early 1916. The Manchester Volunteers travelling to Dublin 79

Chapter Seven: Saturday 22nd April 1916 95

Chapter Eight: Sunday 23rd April 1916 97

Chapter Nine: Easter Monday 24th April 1916 - The Rising begins 101

Chapter Ten: Tuesday 25th April 123

Chapter Eleven: Wednesday 26 April 133

Chapter Twelve: Thursday 27 April 145

Chapter Thirteen: Friday 28 April 155

Chapter Fourteen: Saturday 29th April 169

Chapter Fifteen: Sunday 30 April 1916 179

Chapter Sixteen: Monday May 1st 189

Appendix: Liam Parr learning the pipes 193

Sources, Books and Websites 197

Picture Credits 203

Index 205

Prologue
Easter Saturday – 1916 - Dublin

Gilbert is standing guard in a safe house in North Frederick Street. This is a secret hideout for English and Scottish Volunteers waiting for the planned rebellion. They had heard rumours that the building was due to be raided by the police and the men had resolved to resist with arms if this happened. Gilbert had arrived from Stockport only a few days before, carrying a smuggled load of weapons. He had missed the planned pickup and been left alone in a city he didn't know. He had left his bag in a hotel room which was raided, and most of the arms captured, only escaping by being sent to this refuge by Michael Collins.

Here he is met by his old friend Liam, a Dubliner who had been living in Manchester. Liam has been in hiding, in the Plunkett family's mill, also waiting for the uprising. He introduces Gilbert to Sheila, a family friend who is organising her squad of women ready for 'the day'. Together the three of them go to a ceilidh that night where Gilbert and Sheila dance till dawn. Gilbert said: "I kissed Miss O'Hanlon and got my face well smacked for it" (they were to become sweethearts and marry after the rising.)

Within two days all three were to be under fire behind barricades in the midst of an insurrection that was to change the course of Irish history.

This is their story, and that of the other Manchester Volunteers.

Introduction

During the early months of 1916 nearly a hundred Irish rebels secretly left the cities of England and Scotland in ones and twos and travelled to Ireland. They had heard that the uprising, for which they had planned and hoped, finally seemed to be approaching.

Several dozen caught ferries from Liverpool and Glasgow and slightly fewer went from London. The histories of some of these are well known - the most famous traveller from London being the ex post office clerk Michael Collins. The stories of most of the others are more obscure. Until now the histories have made no mention at all of any contingent going from Manchester or Stockport.

This has always seemed hard to understand. My father in law used to tell stories of his cousin from Stockport who was in the Dublin GPO during the Easter Rising. The stories also claimed that this man, Willie Parr, played the pipes for de Valera, that he died young as a result of hiding in ditches and that the IRA came to his funeral and turned it into such a major event that some family members were astonished, and not pleased.

For a long time we were tempted to dismiss this as an unfounded family fantasy. However, recent access to Irish Government pension files has shown that four men from the Manchester area actually did take part in the Rising, one of whom was Willie Parr.

This account is his story and that of his three comrades.

In January 2014 the Irish military archives began releasing the files of those who had applied for government pensions claimed for the parts they had played in Easter Rising and the War of Independence. A very interesting document was included in the first batch of documents to be made public. This was a report on republican activities in the Manchester area between 1913 and 1922, written by Patrick O'Donoghue. He compiled the information in about 1937, and was writing from detailed personal knowledge, having been the very active leader of the Irish Republican Army in Manchester. He was arrested in 1921 and sentenced to 15 years hard labour for 'felony treason'.

The report begins, "The first Company of the volunteers was formed in Manchester in November 1913, and a second Company in February 1914. Both Companies drilled in St Wilfred's Catholic Schools, Hulme, Manchester. As far as is known the following took part in the Rising of 1916: Larry Ryan (now dead); William Parr and Gilbert Lynch and O'Dwyer of Brook Street (formerly of Co. Tipperary)".[1]

The same release of documents included a list of those who were part of Kimmage Garrison in the weeks before the Rising and who paraded to Beresford Place (Liberty Hall) and the GPO on 24/4/1916. Named on the list are: Lynch,

Gilbert, from Manchester, now of 164 Crumlin Road; Liam Parr of Manchester (Decd), and Laurence Ryan of Manchester, also Decd.[2] (William Parr is referred to as Liam.)

In addition, the Military Archives have made public the pension files of most of this group.[3] Liam Parr's file has been copied to his relatives.[4] Although the identity of O'Dwyer remains elusive, we have discovered another Manchester Volunteer, Redmond Cox who was omitted from O'Donoghue's list.[5]

There has proved to be considerable difficulty in the naming of these participants as they used Irish and English versions of their names as well as using aliases. For simplicity in this study, I have used the forms most commonly used in the person's lifetime, although I have noted the other names when they occur.

This book therefore tells the tale of Liam Parr, Gilbert Lynch, Larry Ryan and Redmond Cox. In addition, included is the story of Sheila O'Hanlon, whose life and experiences played an equally important part in the making of history. Sheila served throughout the Rising, the War of Independence and the Civil War as a member of Cumann na mBan (the women's organisation parallel to the Volunteers). Sheila was also a close family friend of Liam Parr. Sheila met Gilbert Lynch during Easter week, and later married him.

Most of these people have left us no memoirs, diaries or reminiscences to help us to chronicle their lives. This is usually the case with members of the working classes, and is one reason why their place in the making of history is so often forgotten. It is a tragedy that there are so few published biographies of the ordinary rebels or soldiers to set amidst the shelves of those of the leaders.

In this case, though, we are very fortunate. All the people studied here applied for Irish Government pensions, so that their service in the independence struggle has been recorded and confirmed. In addition, many hundreds of the Volunteers had their memories transcribed in witness statements, which were preserved by the Irish Bureau of Military History. The witness statements have now been released, and provide an unparalleled archive of grass roots memories of a twentieth century revolution. Many of these statements were written by people who were standing shoulder to shoulder with the Manchester Volunteers. This has meant that I can use their statements to illustrate the experiences they shared with the Manchester Volunteers.

The resulting story is told by the rank and file participants in their own words. It is not an analysis of the strategy of the leadership as examined by a twenty-first century historian. I hope that this book captures some of the emotions, excitement, fear and exhilaration of those who participated in such momentous times. These were people who made history, but whose role was subsequently completely forgotten. This is an attempt to return a few of the extraordinary 'ordinary' people to their rightful place in the chronicle of the Twentieth Century.

I hope it does them justice after all these years and that this attempt to portray the hitherto forgotten experiences of the Manchester Volunteers will bring to light further information and other stories. It is possible that family members will have been told about their relatives, perhaps tales that they did not know whether to believe. If these tales are anything like ours then they may well be largely true and should be preserved, shared and investigated. I look forward to hearing new information or stories which could lead to a fuller understanding of the lives of the Manchester Volunteers. Likewise I welcome any information which could correct errors occurring from the limitations of the sources available at present.

1 Bureau of Military History. Military service pensions collection. Manchester battalion. MA/MSPC/RO/608

2 Bureau of Military History. Military service pensions collection. Kimmage Garrison 1916. MA/MSPC/RO/607

3 Bureau of Military History. Military service pensions collection. Gilbert Lynch,MSP34REF41334;Sheila Lynch,MSP34REF2399; Laurence Ryan, DP6862

4 Bureau of Military History. Military service pensions collection. William Parr-DP 9542, and also Margaret Parr II/RB/4077

5 Bureau of Military History. Military service pensions collection. Redmond Cox, MSP34REF1983

Chapter One
Liam Parr's Childhood in Dublin

Of the four members of the Irish community who travelled from Manchester in 1916, only two of them had been born in the area. Gilbert Lynch was born in Stockport in 1892 and Laurence (Larry) Ryan was born in Salford in 1894. Redmond Cox was born in Boyle County Roscommon in 1893, but came to Cheetham in Manchester as a youth.

Liam Parr, on the other hand was born in the centre of Dublin in 1891. He spent his childhood and youth there and only moved to Manchester in about 1910 when he was about 19. Liam Parr was therefore a witness to all the changes and developing tensions that led to the 1916 uprising in which he and his comrades took part. He was not just an eye witness who did nothing but passively watch what was happening around him. On the contrary, he took an active part and played his part in making history.

William George Francis Parr was born on the Oct 8th 1891 at 45 High St Dublin. Although he was registered as William, he was known for most of his life as Liam (or sometimes as Willie or Billy). He was the first child of young parents who had married the year before, and were still only nineteen and twenty. His father, Christopher, was a brass finisher, which is a term used to describe a variety of trades in the brass working industry. Most brass finishing involved the filing and buffing of castings using abrasives and rouge. At this time it usually resulted in dangerous working conditions, and buffers often developed lung illnesses. Christopher's parents had been living in Inchicore near the railway works in the West of Dublin so it is likely that he would have been employed and trained by the Great Southern and Western Railway Company. This was the biggest employer in the area, with a huge works covering 75 acres and employed 1200 people in 1875, including 80 apprentices. The company built railway engines and rolling stock. In 1885, the company had built a complete seven carriage train used for a royal visit.[1]

Liam's mother's maiden name was Mary Costello. Mary's family came from Gardiner Place in the centre of Dublin.[2] Her parents were both Irish, but had met and married in America where her father had been recovering after being wounded whilst fighting in the American Civil War. The American Government had awarded him an injury pension which he received all his life. Around the time that Liam was born, Mary's parents had moved with their two younger children to England to settle in Stockport.

Liam's childhood was spent in 'The Liberties', just south of the river in Dublin. By the time Liam was nine, the family had moved a short distance to a three room tenement flat at 17 Upper Exchange Street. This address housed six families with a total of 32 people. He now had four brothers and sisters and the family were quite lucky in the amount of space they had. Many of their neighbours, with families just as big, had to make do with only one room. By this time, Liam's father was a tradesman, a plumber, and so perhaps they weren't as near destitution as some of their neighbours.[3]

"Although the census described this as a tenement, it was considered a desirable working class address. It is a small street off Parliament Street, which is no more than two hundred yards long, itself".[4]

Families like their neighbours, who had only had one room, would divide it by hanging up a blanket at night to separate the sexes. Cooking was usually all done on an open fire. At this time, Dublin could claim that it had the worst housing conditions in Europe and an infant death rate that only rivalled Calcutta in the British Empire.

A century and a half before Liam was born Dublin had been a capital city with its own parliament, centres of government and administration within the United Kingdom. Because decisions were made in Dublin, the city had attracted the wealthy classes of Ireland who had elegantly proportioned Georgian town houses constructed in the centre of the city in addition to the stately homes they had on their country estates. The town houses were often built on wide avenues, or squares, and had very large rooms with high ceilings and enormous ornamental fireplaces.

Some of this prosperity filtered through to the working population, particularly in Dublin. At this time, some of the Costello ancestors of Liam Parr worked as coach makers in Dublin, and succeeded in surviving in the trade for several generations, living in what was then called Great Britain Street. The Costello's were not one of the bigger coach makers in Dublin, but were well enough respected to be mentioned in a letter discussing business aspects of coach making which was sent by a Thomas Viny to Benjamin Franklin (in Paris in 1785). At the time, Franklin had been a United States diplomat to the French Court, and a few years later he was to sign the American Constitution and write a treatise opposing slavery.[5]

The prosperity of Dublin, and the Costello family, was not to last. Following the unsuccessful United Irishmen Rebellion of 1798, the British Government abolished the Dublin parliament, and with it most of the role of the Dublin administration.

Very soon after that, the Irish wealthy and prominent citizens decided they had no need to live in Dublin as most of the important decisions were now made in London, which is where they now located their city homes. The lavish, resplendent Georgian houses in Dublin were now rented out by landlords, who sub-let them to anyone who would take them. A generation or two later and houses that had been bought in 1791 for £8000 were sold for a mere £500.[6]

At the same time, Dublin's economy all but collapsed as it lost the market and the stimulus provided by the demands of the wealthy. The coach building industry is a good example of how this affected local manufacturing. In 1800 there had been more than 40 coach factories in Dublin, together employing up to 2000 workers. By 1855 the number of firms had reduced to ten, and the total employment was only about 200.[7] The Costello family suffered with the rest and were no longer able to carry on as coach makers after this time, their business probably failing during the early decades of the nineteenth Century in the period after the abolition of the parliament. The workers would have had to try to find work with other employers. Liam's grandfather had taken his skills with him, and used them in America.

Dublin was a city with very little other industry apart from the docks and brewing. In this it was very unlike cities of the north of Ireland, like Belfast, which had other employments such as ship building, and linen. In fact, Ireland, excluding the industrialised north, was treated by Britain as a producer of food for industrial mainland Britain. This left it with few other sources of work, or income, when the potato blight struck with particular severity in the 1840s. The failed potato harvest, coupled with a series of particularly disastrous decisions made by the authorities in London and Dublin, resulted in the loss of two thirds of the population of Ireland to death and emigration.

Of course, the famine did not only affect those living in the countryside, but had profound effects on those living in Dublin. Huge numbers of people moved into the city, and added to those already squeezed into an overcrowded housing stock. Although some lived in the terraces we are so familiar with, a huge proportion lived in the classically proportioned town houses of the eighteenth century aristocracy, which had been converted into tenements by 'profiteering landlords'. These were not very practical houses for ordinary people to live in, particularly as many families could not even aspire to live in a whole room, but sometimes had to share. For example, one family might live in each corner of a once elegant dining room.

In 1911, an official report into housing in Dublin announced that 66% of the city's working class population of 128,000 was living in substandard housing, and almost all of these were living in just 5,000 tenement houses.

James Connolly wrote about this report saying: "We knew that Dublin had a far higher percentage of single-room tenements than any other city in the Kingdom. We did not know that nearly twenty eight thousand of our fellow citizens live in buildings that even the Corporation admits to be unfit for human habitation. We had suspected the difficulty of decent living in the slums; this report proves the impossibility of it. Nearly a third of our population so live that from dawn to dark and from dark to dawn it is without cleanliness, privacy and self-respect. The sanitary conditions are revolting, even the ordinary standards of savage morality can hardly be maintained. To condemn a young child to an upbringing in the Dublin slums is to condemn it to physical degradation and to an appalling precocity in vice".[8]

Liam's family were one of these working class families living in a tenement. Their tenements might not have been among the worst, but the first two addresses where he lived have been long demolished in clearance programmes.

A French aristocratic visitor wrote about her visit to the Liberties in 1889, two years before Liam was born. "To see the abject squalor of Dublin in its very depths one has only to walk along by St Patrick's, and particularly the street which joins the two cathedrals - a street consisting of two rows of tumbledown, mouldy-looking houses, reeking of dirt, and oozing with the disgusting smell of accumulated filth of many generations, with old petticoats hung up instead of curtains, and very often instead of glass in the dilapidated windows. On each ground floor, shops with overhanging roofs, and resembling dirty cellars, expose for sale sides of rancid bacon, bundles of candles and jars of treacle - a delicacy as much sought after as soap is neglected - greens, cauliflowers, musty turnips and bad potatoes; while at every three doors is a tavern, which in the midst of these hovels resembles a palace. Every other house is an old-clothes' shop, where the sale of the above-mentioned rags is combined with money-lending at large interest. Shoes that are taken out of pawn there on Saturday night for Sunday mass are pledged again on Monday morning".[9]

Liam's father, Christopher Parr, was fortunate in being a skilled worker, and this probably explains why the family lived in slightly better conditions than some. However his 'fortune' was dependent on being able to find regular skilled work and there were few industries employing skilled workers. There were plenty of immigrants arriving from the country desperate for work. It was a boss's market and wages were kept ruthlessly low. A very large proportion of the working classes were employed as casual labourers at very low wages, and these were a group that had traditionally been ignored by the trade unions.

Although Liam's childhood friends would have come from the working class tenement dwellers like himself, Dublin had a very complex hierarchy of those who were more comfortably off.

"In the towns tuppence-ha'penny looked down on tuppence, and throughout the country the grades in social difference were as numerous as the layers of an onion".[10]

In Dublin, of course, at the top of the pyramid was the British imperial establishment, who were largely English and Protestant. Below this level, in a predominantly Catholic city, was a large middle class who had long tended to support some sort of calls for more home rule for Ireland.

A contemporary observer, C.S. Andrews, caustically described the Catholic hierarchy in Dublin in his book, Men of No Property. "At the top were the upper class or Castle Catholics, such as medical specialists, barristers, and wholesale merchants who had dinner in the evening and dressed for it... "Their accents were indistinguishable from those of the Dublin protestants who held the flattering belief that they spoke the best English in the world." The middle middle classes such as medical doctors hoped their children would become Castle Catholics. "They had their dinner in the middle of the day and entertained themselves at musical evenings".

The lower middle class Catholics lived over their business premises and were people like publicans or grocers who "ate mid-day dinner, wore night shirts rather than pyjamas and slept in feather beds. They took no holidays and seldom entertained".

"Beneath all these were the labourers and domestic servants who took no interest in politics because "their main concern was to provide food and lodging for their children; they frequently failed to do either… They amused themselves, in good times, in the pubs, and when times were hard, they accepted misery as the will of god, to be accepted with fortitude, and to be rewarded in the next life".[11]

The prospect of being rewarded in the next life was not just an abstract verbal cliché; the odds of actually leaving this life early were considerably higher than in the rest of the British Isles. James Connolly quoted the most up to date statistics in 1915: "Let us get to facts. According to the latest returns, the death rate in Dublin was 27.7 per 1000. This was the highest of any city in Europe, as given in the Registrar Generals list, the next highest being Moscow - 26.3 per 1000. In Calcutta, in the presence of plague and cholera, the rate was only 27 per 1000". Even more significant is the difference between the classes in infant mortality. He quotes official figures from 1903 which gave the death rates per 1000 of those under 5 years. This figure was 0.9 for the 'professional and independent classes' , 2.7 for the 'middle class' and 27.7 for 'artisan's and pretty shopkeepers' class'. Connolly described this as "ceaseless slaughter of human life… and it is upon the poor that the main burden of such slaughter falls".[12]

During this first decade of the century, Liam's mother had 8 more children, two of whom had died before 1911. This suggests that Liam Parr would have had a childhood which, while not characterised by the most abject poverty, would not have been easy. We have no reason to believe his life was very different from countless other working class children living in the centre of Dublin at the time. Unfortunately, hardly any memories of Liam or his family have survived to be handed down to us, but it is a great consolation that the reminiscences of some others have been preserved, and their experiences are probably broadly similar to those of Liam and his brothers and sisters.

Nancy Cullen was a few years younger than Liam Parr, but her recorded memories of living in Cook Street, in the early decades of the twentieth century, are describing a way of life that was probably little different from that of the turn of the century. Cook Street was in the Liberties only a couple of roads distant from High Street, where Liam was born, and no further from Upper Exchange Street where he was living when he was nine.

"...and there used to be a barrel organ-grinder man and another man with an ice cream cart and you could buy a cone. He had a cart with two shafts on it and two legs and then he stopped and he'd have a bugle and he'd blow his bugle. And, of course, naturally, when the bugle went all the kids went out".

"Children used to go around running in their bare feet, no shoes, and most of them would have stone bruises. And I remember if a kid fell and hurt himself and it was badly cut they'd shove him into a pram - no matter how big he was - and push him to the hospital".

"There was very little for children then. But you could go around and pick up bricks and build a house up to maybe here (three feet high) and get four or five bricks and build it up and make a table or chair and put paper on it. And maybe you'd have a brick for a doll. You know, make a doll out of a brick, get a bit of coloured paper and put it around it for a bonnet..."

"We went to High Street School, a National School and Catholic. Very small school, two rooms..."

"Now there was a house next to ours and it always had the name of being a haunted house... always. And we used to go up there on a winter's evening and we'd bring a candle and sit on the stairs and tell haunted stories. We'd be about nine or ten. And we'd be sitting there telling haunted stories for ages and everyone afraid to move. And then everybody'd scramble down the stairs! Everyone'd run together. And then the kids had to go upstairs to their own house and the hallways were very dark, no light whatsoever on the stairs. Pitch dark and you had to feel your way. And we'd stand at the door and say, 'watch for the banshee' - frightening them. But that was the fun of it".

"There was people and they'd say, 'Oh, I heard the banshee last night, there's going to be a death.' And surely there would be! Or somebody'd say, 'I heard three knocks.' See, three knocks, that was a sign of death..."

"To me, all the women back then looked the same. They were dressed the same as an old person... shapeless. Wore long, heavy shapeless skirts down to their ankles and underneath the skirts a petticoat. And shawls..."

"At that time when we were kids there was an awful lot of poverty on the street. I didn't think much of it then but it was only since I got older that I realised that it was terrible poverty... and I remember one day saying to me mother, 'Why are the men sitting there and my dad has to go to work?' I thought it was terrible that he had to go to work. And she was explaining to me that there was just no work for them. They'd be playing cards there for ages, only just for buttons. And then they might get up to play a game of football and the football would be a roll of paper maybe put in an old sock. In them times many of the men was idle but very seldom you seen a man with a dirty shirt or a dirty collar on his shirt. They were always very clean..." [13]

Another person who wrote about a working class Dublin childhood was Sean O'Casey. He was a few years older than Liam Parr and was brought up a Protestant, but played with children of both religions.

"Let's have Ball in the Decker, first", said Johnny, "an' afterwards, Duck on the Grawnshee; an' I'll be last in both for the sake of the game".

Then they all laid their caps in a row at an angle against the wall of a house. They took turns, Touhy first and Johnny last, trying to roll a ball into one of the caps, the player doing his best to avoid rolling it into his own. When the ball rolled into a cap, the owner ran over to his cap, the rest scattering in flight, caught the ball up, and flung it at a boy nearest and easiest to hit. If he missed, a pebble was put in his cap, but if he hit a boy, then a pebble was put in the cap of the boy the ball had struck. The game went on till a boy had six pebbles or more (the number being decided at the beginning of the game). Then the boy with the six pebbles in his cap had to stand by the wall, and stretch out his arm, and press the back of his hand firm against the bricks. Then each boy, with a hard half-solid ball, had six shots at the outstretched hand; each aiming at hitting it as hard as he could, and enjoying the start of pain appearing on a boy's face whenever the hard ball crashed into the palm of his hand. Each boy had to go through the ordeal, the number of blows being the same as the number of pebbles in his cap. Johnny liked the ordeal; his hands were small and firm and hard, and the impact of the ball stung his hand far less than it stung the softer and larger hands of his comrades. So the game went on till they were tired, and many eyes were blinking back the tears from the smart of hands that were red, and stung fiercely.

Then followed Duck on the Grawnshee, in which a marble was placed in a slight depression, making it look like a squatting duck. Round the resting marble, a chalk circle was drawn. The boy who owned the duck on the grawnshee stood, with one foot within the chalk circle, watching the other boys who shot their marbles from the kerb, trying to knock the duck off the grawnshee. If a boy failed to knock it off, he had to gather up his marble again without letting himself be touched by the boy who was doing the duck on the grawnshee; if he was touched by the duck, with a foot in the circle, after lifting or touching his marble, then the touched boy became the duck, and the other joined the rest who were trying to knock the duck from the grawnshee. When the marbles thrown had stopped so near the duck that the outstretched hand of the boy who guarded the grawnshee could easily touch any who ventured to pick up a marble, the owners had to stand still, and depend on one who was a good shot to send the duck flying from the grawnshee, for when the duck was off the grawnshee the touch lost its magic, and the boys could seize their marbles and run off without danger, till the owner of the duck had replaced it on the grawnshee. So Johnny shot his marble at the duck on the grawnshee, or stood, watchful and alert, with one foot in the ring, ready to touch any boy within reach who made to get his marble lying motionless on the ground near the grawnshee; shouting, laughing as he did so, for hunger was forgotten, time had stopped, and his joy was full".

"Or, best of all, when the boys had come back from school; when they had done their home lessons, and had come out into the street to get what fun they could: some of them, with suitable sticks, would start a game of hurley; others would rush away, to return with old legs of chairs, ashplants with crooked ends, walking-sticks, or a rib of a big box, pared at one end to give a grip. Opposing sides would be chosen, and the real game would start - one group striking the ball up, the other group striking the ball down the street - pushing and cursing when the game went against them; and shouting and cheering when a goal was scored. And Johnny, with his long hair growing into his eyes; his bandage thrust like a wad into his pocket; his face flushed and wet with sweat, rushed here, rushed there, swinging Archie's ashplant, cursing, shouting, cheering with the best of them, pucking the ball viciously when it came his way, slashing at any shin that came too near the ball, his own legs trickling with blood from blows received from others, feeling no pain; for alive with energy, hunger was forgotten, time had stopped, and his voice rang loud in the chorus of the song of the street".[14]

Sean O'Casey was brought up a Protestant in a predominantly Catholic city. His parents had been lower middle class, but when Sean was six, his father died and the family progressively slipped into poverty, bringing him closer to the experience of the working class Catholics around him. Liam's childhood is likely to have been similarly short, as he was introduced to the trade of plumbing which was to become his occupation for most of his life. He worked as a journeyman plumber in later life and would probably have either been apprenticed, or taught by his father, who was himself described as a plumber in the census of 1901. [15] [16]

The only story that has been passed down about Liam's childhood is that all the children in the family were taught by the Costellos (his mother's family) to spit on the statue of William of Orange.[17]

The statue of William III, the victor of the Battle of the Boyne of 1701, stood on College Green outside Trinity College. It depicted William on a horse poised on a high plinth and had been for generations a loathed symbol of everything the Catholic and nationalist community hated. It had been used as a focal point for demonstrations of loyalist sentiment since the eighteenth century, particularly on the anniversary of the battle of the Boyne and on royal birthdays so had become an equally a potent symbol of nationalist opposition.

It is significant that this is the only memory of a Dublin childhood that has survived a century of being handed down in the family. This suggests that a powerful emotion was attached to the action, perhaps also associated with a fear of punishment by the authorities. In any case it firmly locates Liam and his family within the nationalist section of the community.

I wonder how they responded to the visit of Queen Victoria in 1900? This was opposed by many nationalists such as Maud Gonne, who saw it as a visit by Victoria Hanover, Queen of England, to stimulate the recruitment of Irish volunteers to join the British Army to fight in the Boer war. The whole visit drew the wrath from a wide alliance of nationalist figures who still saw Victoria as the 'Famine Queen". The official Dublin Castle authorities laid on a 'treat' in Phoenix Park for 15,000 children. This precipitated, in response, the creation of a loose committee of women who organised a 'Patriotic Children's treat' to reward those who didn't cheer Victoria. This included a parade of 30,000 children, and was marshalled by young men from the Gaelic Athletic Association. Liam was nine at the time, so he may well have taken part considering the family's nationalist sympathies.

The group of women initially came together as an ad hoc body to organise the treat, but afterwards many of them continued working together and created a nationalist organisation, called Inghinidhe na hÉireann (daughters of Ireland), specifically for women. Its president was Maud Gonne. Their objects were predominantly to encourage the Irish language and culture, and often the women ran very large classes for children in Irish history and Celtic mythology. In June 1901 they took Dublin children on an outing to Wolfe Tone's grave in Sallins, County Kildare.

"On the journey there, the children carried various Irish and Boer flags, and to the delight of their patrons, booed and hissed all British soldiers who crossed their paths".[18]

Inghínídhe was busy with 'anti British work', but also with what they called 'constructive work' such as trying to organise school meals for children. They agitated by trying to pressurise bodies such as Dublin Corporation to provide school meals, "and by giving practical demonstration of how to do this by starting ourselves and giving school dinners... In the National Schools in High Street and Johns Lane (districts which sorely needed such an innovation) we got the sympathy and help of both the managers and the teachers."

This was the area where Liam lived as a child.

"The meal was good Irish stew made with meat and vegetables, or milk puddings and jam... All idea of pauperism was kept out of the scheme, as every child who could pay paid their penny to the teachers, (and sometimes it was only a halfpenny) but no one was allowed to know who paid and who did not".[19]

Catholicism and Irish culture

The 1901 census stated that all the Parr family were Roman Catholic. The British government who organised the census asked about the religion of the residents as well as whether they could speak Irish. They were using the census to try to gauge the strength of nationalist feeling in a time of increasing agitation for home rule. In this, the Parrs were similar to nearly all their neighbours in the street in that none told the census enumerator that they could speak Irish. The vast majority of people in Dublin only spoke English.

Traditionally the only Irish speakers in the city were those who had recently arrived from the most deprived, 'backward' and poverty stricken areas of the far west and south of the country. Since the mid-nineteenth century, many nationalists had been noting the decline of the Irish language and had feared that it might be irreversible unless something was done urgently. In the 1891 census only 14% of the population of Ireland were bilingual and 85% said they spoke only English.[20] This, however, was changing as now the country was in the middle of an 'Irish cultural revival'. In the past, speaking Irish had often been seen as an embarrassing sign of an individual's peasant roots. Now there were more and more Gaelic classes scattered around the city to meet the needs of those keen to learn from scratch. The motivation for most people to attend classes in Irish language and culture was a commitment to Irish nationalism.

The long-standing nationalist movements were still in existence, but were seen by many, at around this time, to have become moribund, stuck in ruts, and lacking in imagination. The Irish Parliamentary Party, led by John Redmond, was supported by practically everyone who had the vote. It sent MPs to Westminster who tried to work deals there to negotiate some form of home rule for Ireland. This was probably the policy that was supported by most 'respectable people with common sense'. These were also the class of wealthy people who dominated the Dublin elected authorities, and were already infamous for the corrupt way they managed the city.

There was also the 'physical force' tradition of Irish nationalism which held that Ireland would never be free without some sort of an uprising for which they had to work initially in secret, through an 'oath bound' society called the Irish Republican Brotherhood (IRB). This organisation had been more popularly known as the Fenians, but by the beginning of the twentieth century, they too had become something of an uninspiring stagnating organisation to many.[21]

At the beginning of the century many felt that that the energy, that previous generations had put into political campaigns for home rule, was better spent on protecting and reviving Irish culture.

"A 'cultural turn' in Irish politics followed , creating a milieu in which, as Terry Eagleton has written, 'cultural practices did not so much displace political activity proper as continue it by other means'".[22]

These cultural practices took many forms. There was the Gaelic Athletic Association, which organised its members to play Gaelic football and hurling and strictly prohibited them from ever playing any imported English games such as cricket, tennis, polo or football. As early as 1890 it had involved 50,000 young Irish males. Some branches of the GAA were ferociously patriotic, and soon developed unofficial links with the secret Irish Republican Brotherhood.

The nationalism of some of the other activities was more understated. There were classes in spoken Irish, archaeology, Irish legend and music. W B Yeats travelled round the west studying and giving talks on Gaelic folklore. This was the time when there was an upsurge in the energy and vibrancy of the Irish literary scene. Although it would be hard to generalise about a group of figures as diverse as Oscar Wilde, George Bernard Shaw, James Joyce and J M Synge, all were described as being part of the "Irish Literary Revival". Most wrote in English, and many moved away from Ireland, but there was a tendency for much new writing to be influenced by a new appreciation of Irish cultural nationalism.

Much new writing exalted the lives and traditions of the peasants of the far west of Ireland, and discovered a haven of Gaelic culture. Many collected and preserved folk tales and traditions, a practice that was criticised by James Joyce as collecting from a person with a "feeble and sleepy mind". He talked of the "fullness of the senility" of the "folk ways". Despite Joyce's admonitions, there was an audience for what he would have seen as an over sentimental and idealised version of the Irish tradition. When this was coupled with a repressive attitude to sexual matters, it led to a near riot at the premiere of Synge's play, 'A Playboy of the Western World' in 1907 at the Abbey Theatre. Protestors physically assaulted the actors for creating "an unmitigated, protracted libel upon Irish peasant men, and worse still upon Irish girlhood".

The Irish cultural revival also applied to dance and music. In 1892 Douglas Hyde had made a speech on the necessity for de-anglicising Ireland in which he said, "Our music, too, has become anglicised to an alarming extent. Not only has the national instrument, the harp… become extinct, but even the Irish pipes are threatened with the same fate. In the place of pipers and fiddlers, who even twenty years ago were comparatively common, we are now in many places menaced by the German band and the barrel organ… For the present, then, I must hope that the revival of our Irish music must go hand with the revival of Irish ideas and Celtic modes of thought which our Society is seeking to bring about, and that people may be brought to love the purity of 'Siubhail, Siubhail' or the fun of 'Maureen Ruadh' in preference to 'Get your hair cut' or 'Over the garden wall' or, even, if it is not asking too much, of 'Ta-ra-ra-boom-de-ay'".[23]

In response to this, the Feis Ceoil Association was formed with the objects of: ensuring that Irish music was performed and collected, and to encourage 'the rise of a New Irish School of composers, who by their works, may prove that it is possible for Irish musicians to be as truly National in their art as Dvorák and Grieg have been.'[24]

Meanwhile the Gaelic League began organising its own cultural festival, an tOireachtas, the first of which was held in May 1897. The Gaelic League Wexford Feis in 1905 included competitions for Brass bands, pipes, figure dancing, coronet solo, step dancing, fife and drum bands, jigging, whistling, flute, fiddle, solo singing, quartets, harp and choirs. E.T Kent (Éamonn Ceannt) was one of the adjudicators, presumably for pipes. [25]

These organisations were trying to preserve and revive Irish culture of all kinds, and the pipes were an essential part of this. Later photos of Liam show him wearing a piper's uniform and playing the Irish war pipes which were large, mouth blown pipes rather than the more common uilleann pipes. There was a continuing tradition of uilleann pipe playing in Ireland at the time but mouth blown pipes had become extinct, despite there being documentary evidence of their existence in the past. Cultural links were cited between Scotland and Ireland, and the structural similarities between the illustrations of the Irish war pipes and the great highland pipes were emphasised. Citing these links as a justification, pipe enthusiasts began to use highland pipes to play a distinctly Irish repertoire. War pipes produced a more dramatic, louder sound, more suitable for outdoor playing and playing in a group than the more gentle uilleann pipes. The Irish war pipes proved to be particularly well suited to lead marches and parades and so most martial organisations would use a pipe band to lead them on ceremonial occasions. Eventually the Volunteers, the Citizen Army and the Fianna Éireann all marched to the sound of bands of Irish war pipers.

All the pipers and the republicans seemed to move in the same small circle. An example was the St Laurence O'Toole Pipe Band which was formed in 1910 by a group which included many figures later to become famous, including Padraic Pearse. The secretary was Sean O'Casey and the veteran nationalist Tom Clarke became President. The band was to lead workers' marches during the Dublin lockout in 1913 when they were set upon by the mounted police and some of the members were injured and had their instruments broken. [26]

There was to be a massive overlap between the personnel of the band and members of the Irish Volunteers. In 1916 William Daly, a London Volunteer, travelled to Dublin and enrolled in E company of the 2nd battalion which was led by Tom Weafer. Daly said that practically every member of the band was also a member of the same company of the volunteers.

"The club had also a pipers' band composed of its members who, when the time arrived, laid aside the pipes and took up the rifle in the sterner times".[27]

As part of this cultural nationalism Liam probably began using the Irish form of his name at about this time. From now on he was more commonly Liam de Paor rather than William Parr. It is also pretty likely that Liam learnt Irish at this time as speaking the language was considered an integral part of the activities of so many Irish nationalist organisations. When his wife Margaret wrote about him in 1939, she said "…he could speak Gaelic but could not read or write it. He felt he could not get down to study when there was so many other things to do and that the language could not thrive while the country was ruled over by a foreigner and he devoted his whole time to that end". [28]

Liam and the Bonhams

Liam probably had learnt to speak Irish before 1911, but this was not recorded in the census of that year as he had moved to England, where one's proficiency in Irish was not one of the required questions. In Dublin, although the 1911 census does not record any of his immediate family speaking Irish, it does record that his cousin, Alice Bonham, could speak both English and Irish.[29] (Alice was technically Liam's first cousin once removed).

Alice was eight years older than Liam and I assume they must have known each other to some extent, but we can't tell how closely. She lived with her parents in Rathmines. Alice's mother was the sister of Liam's Grandma, Mary Costello (Nee Murphy). Her father ran an ironmongers and building suppliers in Dublin, and was quite comfortably off. He was elected to be on the board of governors of the South Dublin Workhouse. Liam's father was a plumber so there was a significant class difference, but there is likely to have been some connection between the men if only as a customer and a supplier. The Bonhams remained in contact with Liam's grandparents, the Costellos, and visited them in Stockport. [30]

The Bonham family lived in the reasonably prosperous suburban district of Rathmines, just outside the Dublin city boundary. Gus Bonham was not just a workhouse guardian, but also stood for election as a councillor on Dublin Council. At this time the corporation of Dublin was controlled by businessmen who usually stood for the moderate Irish Party, but to many they were infamous for the venality of their corruption. It was generally believed that the reason why the Dublin Corporation took no effective measures to deal with the city's slums was that so many of the councillors were themselves landlords of class three tenement housing. A letter from a well-educated catholic in 1912 on the possibility of some form of limited home rule stated,

"The whole scheme of the present Bill is calculated to push the power into the hands of the most dangerous and inefficient class in the country. All the indicators are that the Irish Parliament will be similar in character to the present Dublin Corporation, which is shunned by all decent men and instead of being an object of pride is an object of contempt to the citizens". [31]

There is no reason to implicate Gus Bonham in any of this, and it is uncertain whether he was ever elected to the Council, but he was a poor law guardian of the South Dublin Workhouse in 1911. The Poor Law system in Ireland had been set up by the British Authorities on the same lines as that on the mainland, but since local government had been reorganised in 1898 it had come under the control of the local respectable middle classes. Not that this improved the lot of the inmates.

"Now that the native Irish were in charge of their own insane, they were no more generous than the ascendancy governors who had for so long based their parsimonious management of the asylums on the just rights of property and on the belief that, in any event, institutions for pauper patients should reflect the grimness and discomforts of poverty. Reports of early twentieth century meetings of the new committees reveal a preoccupation with financial matters, opposition to wage increases, questioning of expenditure and a remarkable lack of concern for the living conditions of the patients themselves". [32]

1 Inchicore. Info website accessed Jan 2015 http://www.inchicore.info/history/

2 William George Parr birth cert, 1891.

Christopher Parr, Mary Costello marriage cert, general register office Dublin. 1890.

3 1901 census, Christopher Parr. Dublin Ireland

4 Kavanagh, Gerard personal communication 7 feb 2014

5 Tomas Viny, letter to Benjamin Franklin. May 6th 1785, in Franklin papers website accessed March 2015. franklinpapers.org/franklin/yale?vol=43&page=099

6 Kearns, Kevin, C. Dublin tenement life. Gill and Macmillan. Dublin. 1994

7 Bielenberg, Andrew, Coach Building. In Connolly, SJ ed The oxford companion to Irish history. Oxford University Press, Oxford. 2002.

8 Connolly, James. The reconquest of Ireland. 1913 in Callow, John. Labour and the reconquest of Ireland. Evans Mitchell books London 2013

9 De Bovet, Anne, Three months in Ireland, London 1891, quoted in Pakenham, Thomas and Valerie; A traveller's companion to Dublin, Robinson, London, 2003.

10 O'Malley, Ernie. On another man's wound. Mercier press. Cork. 2013

11 Andrews, C S; Dublin Made me. The Lilliput press, Dublin 2001

12 Connolly, James, The Reconquest of Ireland, in Callow, John, James Connolly and the Reconquest of Ireland. Evans Mitchell Books London 2013

13 Kearns, Kevin, C. Dublin tenement life. An oral history, Gill and Macmillan Dublin 1994

14 O'Casey, Sean, Autobiographies 1. Papermac London 1992.

15 William Parr described as plumber. Birth Certificate of Bernadette Parr 1931 and Fintan 1928. UK gen register office.;

Application for Irish pension form AP51, in DP.9542, Pension administration section. Department of defence. Ireland;

William Parr death certificate. Manchester South registration district. UK General register office;

Sinn Fein rebellion Handbook, Weekly Irish times, Dublin. 1917,

16 1901 and 1911 census. Christopher Parr, Dublin. Ireland

17 Personal communication from members of Earle family…

18 Lawlor, Damian; Na Fianna Éireann and the Irish Revolution-1909 to 1923, Coalite Books, Rhode, undated.

19 Molony, Helena, witness statement WS 391

20 Ó Muiri, Pol; Look West in Dublin review of books, Issue 69, July 2015

21 Lyons S L. Ireland since the famine, Fontana, 1973, quoted in website accessed 21.
Nov.2014 http://en.wikipedia.org/wiki/Irish_Republican_Brotherhood

22 Dowling, Martin. Traditional Music in Irish Society - Historical perspectives. Ashgate. Farnham, Surrey. 2014

23 Hyde, Douglas, quoted in Dowling, Martin. Traditional music in Irish Society - Historical perspectives. Ashgate, Farnham, Surrey. 2014

24 Secretaries of Feis general Committee. quoted in Dowling, Martin. Traditional music in Irish Society - Historical perspectives. Ashgate, Farnham, Surrey. 2014

25 Dowling, Martin. Traditional music in Irish Society - Historical perspectives. Ashgate, Farnham, Surrey. 2014

26 SLOT website accessed April 2015 at https://web.archive.org/web/20130616042956/http://www.slotpb.com/history.shtml

27 Daly, William, witness statement WS 291

28 Parr William Pension application Pension administration section. Department of defence. Ireland. Documents re Parr DP9542
Letter to de Valera

29 1911 Dublin Census. Augustine Bonham and family

30 Documents provided by US national archives re George Costello American Civil War pension application

31 John Moynihan in Ferriter, Diarmaid- Ireland 1900-2000 Profile books. London 2004

32 Robins,Joseph, Fools and Mad, in Ferriter, Diarmaid- Ireland 1900-2000 Profile books. London 2004

Chapter Two
Liam's introduction to the pipes and Irish Nationalism

In the middle of the first decade of the century Liam was aged about fourteen, living with his parents and brothers and sisters and probably training to be a plumber. He had finished school and was leaving his childhood behind and beginning to find his own identity, going through a period that would later be described as the teenage years. It is during this period that Liam is most likely to have learnt to play the Irish war pipes, and embraced a culture of 'advanced nationalism'. Within a decade, Liam was a committed radical, ready to take up arms, and also an accomplished pipe player. Unfortunately, there are no documents describing how this happened. The evidence suggests the most credible scenario is that he had some involvement with Fianna Éireann during the period between 1909 and about 1911, and played pipes with some of its members. (Appendix 1 discusses the evidence.)

Éamonn Ceannt and the Dublin Pipers' Club
At some time in the first decade of the twentieth century, the Parr family moved from the 3-roomed tenement flat in Upper Exchange Street to a 2- roomed house in Herberton Lane.[1] Although this was a smaller home, it was in a more respectable area and perhaps it would have been considered a step up the social ladder. Herberton Lane was then on the edge of the city limits.[2] A few doors away lived Éamonn Ceannt, a clerical officer working for Dublin Corporation.[3] Ceannt remained at this address until 1915 or 1916, when he moved the short distance to the South Circular Road at Dolphin's Barn.[4] Ceannt was an accomplished bagpiper, secretary of the Dublin Pipers' Club, and teacher of Irish. His wife Aine, was also a piper and a nationalist. Before Aine was married, she had been the club's treasurer.[5] Ceannt was also an active trade unionist and nationalist who joined Sinn Féin in 1907 and the Irish Republican Brotherhood in 1912.[6]

Ceannt had been an Irish nationalist long before this. In 1900, when he was 18, he hoisted a Boer flag in his parents' garden although it was soon removed by his father. His father was a policeman and Éamonn's brother was in the British Army, so this is not surprising. The Ceannt family was not unusual in having such divided opinions within the family. Sean O'Casey was in a similar situation, as his brother was in the British army while he was moving towards radical nationalism.

"Ireland had become a place of stormy argument, with Dublin at its centre. Every man, woman and child fought battles hour by hour, either for the British or for the Boers. Transvaal flags were in everyone's hand. At times spontaneous processions formed in the streets, marched through the city, booing every redcoat that passed, and often coming into collision with the irritated police… A Transvaal committee had been formed, with Arthur Griffith and some Irish members of parliament, to help the brave Boers to an Irish ambulance".[7]

Despite the proximity of their addresses, there is no evidence that Ceannt taught Liam to play the pipes, and Liam's name does not appear in any of the records of the Dublin Pipers' Club. Nevertheless, it would be strange if they hadn't had some contact with each other.[8] Both Parr and Ceannt were living in the midst of a vibrant ferment of musicians, political activists, nationalists and artists in the comparatively small city of Dublin at this time and, I'm sure, everyone knew who everyone was. This probably meant that there were plenty of people to help if a young man had shown enthusiasm to learn the pipes.

Another reason why Liam and Ceannt might have known each other is that Éamonn Ceannt was a good friend of James O'Hanlon who lived at Dolphins Barn.[9] The O'Hanlons were also friends with Liam's parents and all three families produced staunch republicans who were to fight in 1916.

The Baden Powell Boy Scouts

By 1909 Baden Powell's idea of Boy Scouts had spread to Ireland. In that year, it was announced that there was to be a major rally of the Boys Brigade and the Baden Powell Scouts in Dublin, at a ceremony overseen by the British Lord Lieutenant of Ireland. Republicans were presented with the prospect of seeing large numbers of enthusiastic Irish boys parading before the Imperial hierarchy waving Union Jacks.

Constance Markievicz said, "I could see these children growing to manhood and gaily enlisting into the British army or police forces, and being used to batter their own class into submission in a class war at home, or giving their lives in an Imperial war made to hold Ireland as a slave state within the British empire, fighting always the battles of the international financier to hold in subjugation India and Egypt and to fight other capitalist empires and states for the right to steal their valuable properties belonging to defenceless and undeveloped peoples.

Yet another thing was troubling my mind. Already I had sensed the coming war with Germany. War with Germany must bring troubles in its train for England. The words, 'England's difficulty is Ireland's opportunity' kept beating in my brain, and the question ever arose, how are we to profit by this opportunity: will it slip by as did the Boer War with no man ready to strike a blow for Ireland's freedom?" [10]

Constance Markievicz was to be one of the leading figures involved in setting up a republican alternative, called Na Fianna Éireann.

Constance Markievicz

Markievicz had been born Constance Gore Booth into the Anglo Irish landowning class in Sligo. Here she spent her youth as a skilful and fearless horsewoman. When she wasn't on horseback, she spent her time doing all the things that an aristocratic daughter was supposed to do. She was educated by governesses and took part in the rituals of being presented at court as a debutante. However she never settled into the role expected of her, instead remaining happier outdoors shooting animals, (as was normal for the time and class) or drawing and sketching.

During this time a young WB Yeats visited Constance and her family in Sligo; he introduced them to Gaelic culture and mythology which they previously "had not thought existed". For a time he decided he had fallen in love with Constance's sister Eva, but without her showing any interest. Constance concentrated on art and Eva wrote poetry while both began developing a social commitment. They campaigned for votes for women in Sligo, and then the sisters left Ireland, Eva moving to Manchester and Constance to London. In her twenties, Constance attended the Slade School of Art in London and studied art in Paris. She returned with an impecunious, aristocratic Polish artist who became her husband. A member of the Anglo-Irish ascendancy had become a Polish Countess. They had set up an artistic and bohemian household in Rathgar where they were part of establishing the Dublin Arts Club in 1905, which included W B Yeats, J M Synge and Percy French. They had met James Joyce the previous year before he settled in Paris.

Meanwhile, Constance's sister Eva had been living in Manchester and had been co-secretary of the Manchester and Salford Women's Trade Union Council since 1900. With her partner Esther Roper, she had been working for working class women's rights as well as women's suffrage.[11]

In 1908 Eva campaigned on behalf of the rights of barmaids in the parliamentary campaign against the Liberal candidate, Winston Churchill. She enlisted the help of her sister, who assisted with an effective publicity stunt. The press provided considerable coverage. The Manchester Guardian reported:

"A coach of olden times was driven about Manchester yesterday to advertise the political agitation on behalf of barmaids. It was drawn by four white horses and the 'whip' was Countess Markievicz, sister of Eva Gore Booth. In all parts of the city the coach and its passengers excited general interest and in the NW division especially, the cause of the barmaids was made known not only by demonstration but by speeches and personal interviews".[12]

Another candidate at the same election was Dan Irving of the Social Democratic Federation who enlisted the help of his friend Walter Hampson, otherwise known as 'Casey the Fiddler'. Hampson was a travelling musician who gave humorous lecture recitals on music and socialism. During the election, he paraded the streets of Manchester with a sandwich board bearing the slogan 'Fiddle and I speak for Socialism'.[13]

The Formation of the Fianna Éireann

In 1906, Markievics had rented a small, two-roomed cottage near Balally, at Barnacullia, close to the Three Rock Mountain in South Dublin. She had been looking for somewhere where she could paint, walk and write somewhere quiet and close to Dublin. In the cottage, she discovered some 'Sinn Féin' magazines, which had been left by a previous occupant. She was inspired by her first contact with 'advanced nationalism.' It is therefore not surprising that she went first to Arthur Griffith, the originator of Sinn Féin, with her idea for a nationalist alternative to the Baden Powell scouts.

Griffith's newspaper was called 'Sinn Féin' (loosely translated as 'ourselves alone') and had been launched several years before. It was gaining some support among those nationalists who wished to look for a way forward that avoided embracing 'physical force nationalism'.

"Griffith believed Fenian-style reliance on armed rebellion had failed and the effective tactic was passive resistance. This would involve a withdrawal from Westminster and the establishment of a national assembly in Ireland, refusing to pay British taxes, creating independent Irish courts and an Irish civil service, taking control of local authorities and boycotting British products. He wanted Ireland as part of a dual monarchy under the British crown and developing into an industrialized country".[14]

Helena Molony of Inghinidhe na hÉireann was not impressed. She seemed to feel that they were a bit 'dull'.

"We thought that Sinn Féin was a movement to attract the 'moderate' nationalists, and the Anglicised or more peace-loving section of our people.

The social ideal of Sinn Féin did not appeal to us. They wished to see Irish society (as their official organ once expressed it) 'a progressive and enlightened aristocracy, a prosperous middle class, and a happy and contented working class.' It all sounded dull, and a little bit vulgar to us, and certainly a big come down from the Gaelic Ireland of Maedhbh, Cuchullaín and the Red Branch Knights, which was the sort of society we wished to revive".[15]

Arthur Griffith was also politically of the right, being notably anti-socialist, anti-communist and pro-monarchist. Molony had already cut her political teeth in the women's organisations, such as Inghínidhe, which were more socially free thinking in many ways than some of the IRB influenced nationalist organisations. She had been in contact with James Connolly while he was still in America, and she was later to take part in the Rising with the Irish Citizen Army.

"I was more or less political mentor to the Countess at that time, she was groping at first. She read, and read, and read... The Countess Markievicz attended a big meeting in the Rotunda, for the establishment of Sinn Féin; and then Griffith told her to join the Gaelic league. She asked him, 'How could I work for Ireland?'

'He said join the Gaelic league.'… but it was not enough. She found what she wanted in the Inghínindhe. Then it seemed the right thing, to her direct mind, to begin founding an army of boys who would grow up to know what they were fighting for".

At about the same time, Markievicz discovered the politics of Jim Larkin and described her experience of hearing him in 1910: "Sitting there listening to Larkin I realised that I was in the presence of something that I had never come across before, some great primeval force rather than a man. A tornado, a storm-driven wave, the rush into life of spring, and the blasting breath of autumn, all seemed to emanate from the power that spoke. It seemed as if his personality caught up, assimilated, and threw back to that vast crowd that surrounded him every emotion that swayed them, every pain and joy that they had ever felt made articulate and sanctified. Only the great elemental force that is in all crowds had passed into his nature for ever. Taller than most men, every line of him was in harmony with his personality. Not so much working man as primeval man…a Titan who might have been moulded by Michelangelo or Rodin…"[16]

Markievicz, getting no support from Arthur Griffith for her plans, decided to go ahead alone. During the summer of 1909, she set up a nationalist scout group called the Red Branch Knights, with boys from Brunswick Street National School. They had a first, slightly chaotic camp in the Dublin Hills. Previously to that, Bulmer Hobson, who had been brought up a Quaker in Belfast but had been sworn into the IRB in 1904, had set up a boys' organisation which he called Na Fianna Éireann. It was named after mythical Irish warriors and its objects were to: "serve as a junior hurling league; to promote the study of the Irish language and the make the boys sound nationally".[17] Although it no longer existed in 1909, Na Fianna Eireann had lasted successfully in Belfast for some years after its formation in 1902.

In August 1909, Markeivicz and Hobson decided to come together to create the new Fianna and the first meeting was advertised in the Gaelic league newspaper, as well as in others.[18] When Hobson told Markievicz that there would be a problem paying for a meeting room, she volunteered to pay the weekly rent of 34 Lower Camden Street, a building that had previously been used by the Irish National Theatre Society.[19]

In August 1909, the first public meeting of Fianna Eireann was held in Lower Camden Street, Dublin. (This was very close to the house where Liam's grandparents had lived 30 years previously.) About a hundred boys attended the candle-lit meeting which was addressed by both Hobson and Markievicz. He said that the organisation's ultimate aim was the complete independence of Ireland.

Na Fianna Éireann's rules were:

> Object: To establish the independence of Ireland.
>
> Means: The training of the youth of Ireland mentally and physically by scouting and military exercises, Irish history and language.
>
> Declaration: "I promise to work for the independence of Ireland, never to join England's armed forces, and to obey my superior officers".

Markievicz told the boys that they would choose their own executive council at that first meeting, but this resulted in many refusing to give her a place on the committee. Hobson wrote: "When the election of officers was taking place at the meeting, there was obviously a certain reluctance among the boys against the election of the Countess to office, principally on the grounds that she was a woman... The feeling against the presence of a woman in the organisation continued in varying degrees of intensity for many years and probably never completely disappeared. [20]

Hobson was elected president, but returned to Belfast a few weeks after the foundation, leaving Markievicz to provide much of the organisation in the first year, not to mention finance.[21] Among others on the committee were Helena Molony and Tom O'Donoghue. There must have been a wide range of ages at those first meetings, ranging from Andy Dunne, who was about 10 or 11, to a group of boys in their early twenties. Seamus Kavanagh was 13, who later listed Brian Callendar, of Johnsons Court, as one of a number of young men in their early twenties. Another was Peadar Kearney. Both were to be active in the Fianna pipe band- Kearney also writing 'The Soldiers Song'. If Liam was there at some of those early meetings, or was in contact with the older boys who were setting up the pipe band, he would have been aged 17 at the time. This suggests that Liam could have been as much a helper as a member, the bulk of the members being much younger. Kavanagh described how he was persuaded to go to that first meeting when he was working in a shop:

"A lady customer entered the shop one day and purchased a shape and ribbons for the purpose of making a lady's hat. She spoke with, as I thought, an English accent, and it was the first time I had ever seen a lady smoke a cigarette... the lady addressed me. "Little boy," she asked, "What is your name?" I told her it was James Kavanagh, and she asked me, "would not 'Seamus' sound nicer?". I said I thought it would. I thought to myself that it was peculiar for a person with an English accent to be asking me a question like that, at that time. She said, "Will you promise me that you will never answer to any other name but "Seamus" in future?" She followed that by asking me did I ever hear of Wolfe Tone, Robert Emmet, the Manchester Martyrs, and '98.

I said I did. She asked would I not like to be like one of them. I said I think I would… She informed me that the National Boy Scouts were being formed and that the reason for their formation was to counteract the influence of the Baden Powell scouts which existed mainly as an adjunct of British imperialism in the country… After she had left the shop, I learnt that she was Countess Markievicz". [22]

The Fianna were similar to the Baden Powell Boy Scouts in that they took city boys to the country, but differed by spending time teaching them to fire guns. Markievicz made use of a legal exemption to the prohibition on the use of firearms allowing a householder to use them 'inside his own compound'. Accordingly, she felt permitted to openly teach the boys to shoot in the land around her cottage at Barnacullia.[23] The Fianna was therefore one of the first organisations that began training with firearms before the formation of the Citizen Army, Irish volunteers, or even the Ulster Volunteers. At first this was very ad hoc, probably growing naturally from Markievicz's country woman's ease with guns. It was probably coupled with an attraction, on her part, for taking risks and showing off. She would take pleasure in carefully and strictly instructing the boys in the skills of using her own fire arms; she was well known as a particularly good shot herself. She began with Winchester rifles and then moved to service rifles and revolvers. The boys were taught how to carry, handle and clean guns. It was said that if she caught a Fianna boy pointing a gun at another, even in fun, she 'so clouted his ears that he never did it again'.[24]

"The Fianna were trained to shoot by Madame Markievicz with a small Lee Enfield rifle when out of doors and a large air rifle when in doors".[25]

Although they learnt woodcraft and tracking in the countryside, they concentrated on using their knowledge of the city and its back alleys to dodge police, carry messages and at times create disruption. The target for the disruption was often their rivals, the Baden Powell scouts. The greatest source of pride among a Fianna boy was to have got the hat 'in honourable combat' from the head of an 'English' scout.

"She knew they were the sons of men who'd had the superiority of Englishmen preached at them from their earliest days, men who had behind them failure and defeat, who'd been taught to believe that the Irish went forth to battle but they always fell. Those victories counted much in the training of the boys… after all, they learned their own strength". [26]

The first Fianna group, or sluagh, remained based in the hall in Lower Camden Street where they first met. Here Con Colbert instructed them in drill, as well as Irish history. Some also attended classes in Irish, taught by Pádraig Pearse. Soon other Fianna sluagh were formed, but this one always remained the Fianna sluagh that Markevicz was involved in, the one for whose rent she paid out of her own pocket. It cost her ten shillings a week[27] (different witness statements quote different sums).

One of its first activities was a dramatic group which put on 'the Saxon Shilling' by Padraig Colum. In the Fianna players were: Madame Markievicz, Andy Dunne and Helena Molony among others. The Camden Street branch also had a pipe band from quite an early date. Gary O'Holahan, who joined the Sluagh Emmet in 1910, remembered, "The Camden Street branch wore jerseys and kilts, and had a pipe band."[28]

This branch was known as An Céad Sluagh (the first branch) of the Fianna, and it became the rallying point for most Fianna parades and demonstrations. Its members included Liam Mellows, and his brother Barney, as well as Tom O'Donoghue and others, who would later form the Fianna Pipe Band.[29]

The Fianna was far from being a dull and earnest organisation in those early days. "One contemporary remembered the boys 'tearing down union jacks, swarming up lamp posts to paste up anti-recruiting bills, ragging Baden Powell scouts', and playing off tricks on pompous British officials, and attributes their spirit to the mischievous, boyish presence of the Countess".[30]

The Fianna Pipers

One of the early activities of the Camden Street branch (or sluagh) of the Fianna was to set up a pipe band and it is very likely that Liam was either a member or had some involvement with it (the evidence for this is discussed in the Appendix - Liam Parr learning the pipes).

The Fianna boys were spending much of their time drilling, marching and parading, and they must have realised the benefit in having their own pipe band to lead them. Music was an important part of the Irish national revival and the Fianna were only one of a number of groups in Dublin starting pipe bands. This branch (sluagh) also had a choir during the first winter of its existence.[31]

One of the first members of the Fianna was Andy Dunne, who was particularly well known as a musician; practically every mention of him in a witness statement refers to him singing so he was probably in the choir. Liam's involvement in the Fianna must have brought him in contact with Dunne if he didn't already know him. The Dunne family are likely to have been connected by their Church and neighbourhood with the O'Hanlon family who were close friends of Liam's parents, so Liam might already have known Andy.

The first Fianna band was organised by Brian Callendar and recruited about a dozen members including several who were to be prominent in the future. One was Tom O'Donoghue who would become pipe major of the James Connolly pipe band which Liam would join in later years.[32] Another piper was Peadar Kearney.

"Among the pipers was Peadar Kearney, the writer of 'A Soldier Song' which it was hoped, would become the marching song of the Fianna, but other people asked Brian O'Higgins to write 'The Marching Song of the Fianna' instead".[33]

A witness wrote that the members of the Fianna Pipers were Brian Callender, Brian Reynolds, Barney Murphy, Peadar Kearney and about eight others. It seems highly likely that Liam and Andy Dunne would have been involved with this Band, if not members.[34]

There are no records telling us how long this band lasted, but it may have folded by 1912 because, in that year, Fianna musicians were the core of players for a new band being set up by the Chairman of No 16 Branch of the Irish Transport and General Workers Union, Robert De Coeur. Jim Larkin had given them £25 to buy instruments and equipment to set up a band attached to the union. In fact an early mention of the band described it as 'sluagh James Fintan Lalor', of Fianna Éireann, and its first pipe major was Tom O' O'Donoghue. The band became very active during the 1913 lockout leading the workers' marches, and it is from that time that the band came to be led by a bodyguard with hurleys, who came to be part of the Citizen Army.[35]

By August 1914 the Fianna Pipers needed re-launching and there were three sets of pipes left from a previous band. A group of boys were sent to a Mr. McKenzie in Bolton Street to learn the war pipes.[36] Their leading drummer was Andy Dunne so he is likely to have been a member of the previous incarnations of the band.[37]

Although Dunne drummed for the Fianna Pipers, he was primarily a singer. Those who remember him from this time seem to most commonly remember Dunne for having a very fine tenor voice, (as well as for his role in dealing with smuggling weapons which arrived unexpectedly at Markievicz' house shortly before the uprising).[38] It was highly likely that Andy Dunne would have sung with Liam as he also was known as a singer with a 'fine tenor voice'. Liam was so well known as a singer that Larry Ginnell used to call him either 'the Minstrel Boy, or 'the Bard of Armagh' from the songs he often sung. Perhaps 'The Minstrel Boy' had added significance for Liam as it was one of the Irish songs sung by his grandfather's regiment during the American Civil War.

The Camden Street Sluagh would use its room for regular socials and ceilidhs. With the educational courses in language and history, as well as the military and scouting training and the music, the Fianna must have provided a busy life for a young lad. Even route marches seem to have provided occupation for a musician.

"These marches gave us great scope for exercising our limbs and our lungs. More often they provided the opportunity to sing the songs of the Gael, as swinging in martial tread we let our voices ring, sometimes to the accompaniment of mouth organ, bagpipe, or even the modest tin whistle".[39] Andy Dunne was noticed as a singer by Markievicz, who was often noted as encouraging him to take singing lessons. She wrote a poem, called 'The Battle Hymn' for him to sing.[40] She retained her concern for him after the Rising when she was in Aylesbury Prison, and wrote in a letter to her sister Eva:

"Give all the crew my love. Tell Andy Dunn to go on singing. Peroly will know where to find him. I often think of the 'click' and the refugees and our kitchen teas. Tell Andy that later on we'll try to get someone to teach him…" In the same letter, she also mentioned 'Mr P' with 'nice brown eyes' in Manchester, but I have been unable to identify who this person is, so there is no reason to suppose it might be Liam.[41]

Andy Dunne did not limit his performances to the Fianna Hall in Camden Street, but was a regular singer at Liberty Hall.

"Another way of maintaining the morale of the Irish Citizen Army and their friends was the holding of concerts every Sunday night at Liberty Hall. Some of these concerts were built around plays from the Abbey Theatre repertoire and were performed by the Liberty Players… For the concert items among some of the singers were generally the names… Andy Dunne, Joe Connolly, Connie O'Hanlon… with Madame Markievicz often giving a recitation. One of the plays produced was one of James Connolly's entitled 'Under which flag?'."[42]

The other Fianna branches, or sluagh, set up around the city included one in a building owned by Jim Larkin's Irish Transport and General Workers Union. This branch, called Sluagh Emmett, was based in Beresford Place, an address made more famous later by being the address of Liberty Hall. Members of the Fianna often expressed very deep commitment to its principles. In the words of Sean Prendergast of Sluagh Emmett: "Here was a chance for me to show that I was Irish and that I longed to see Ireland free; 'The complete Independence of Ireland'. This was the Fianna ideal. It soon became mine, and found me responsive to everything it stood for and proclaimed… Was it not a labour of love to save for our uniforms of which we were so proud to wear? I think the first thing I secured was the haversack, next the belt, then the hat, and by the time I had these secured I was beginning to 'look up and take notice.'"[43]

Prendergast obviously enjoyed his route marches. "Distance seldom upset us as we boasted the fact that we were young and active. Besides we were always sure of a rest on the way for refreshments and a rest of sorts. Oh, the joy of spending our few coppers on minerals… then 'falling in' after our 'appetiser'; we would be safe for another few miles. When reaching our favoured haunts we set ourselves the task of lighting fires, and brewing tea, and enjoying an alfresco meal. This over, we engaged in many exercises, climbing the mountains, scouting, tracking etc. After a few hour spent in this fashion we would reform and prepare for the return journey. Now for the real thrill, now for the most exciting and truly invigorating part of the outing, downhill. It was poetry, music, romance to the soul, marching down the mountainside in the dusk of a fine summer evening, our steady tramp, tramp, tramp breaking the peace and quietude of the countryside. Below us nestled in a hollow, our own beloved Dublin, reflected in the red or crimson glow of the setting sun shining out in splendour..."[44]

He said that the sluagh was made up mainly of working class boys, with many apprentices to trades such as carpentry, plumbing, electrical and printing, so Liam certainly would not have felt out of place if he was in an environment like this.

By August 1910 the Fianna was sufficiently well established to be able to hold its first Ard Fheis (annual conference) at the mansion House in Dublin with delegates from Limerick and Belfast, as well as Dublin. This was followed by a group photo and a céilidhe. Some of these photos have survived, but no names have been recorded making it impossible to identify individuals. It would be surprising if Andy was not there but we cannot tell whether Liam is pictured.

IRB and Fianna Éireann

The initial enthusiasm to launch Fianna had come from Markievicz, and she had been joined at the inaugural meeting by Bulmer Hobson. He was, at the time, only an ordinary member of the Irish Republican Brotherhood, and "whilst his involvement with the Fianna was entirely off his own bat, he 'harboured the idea of recruiting suitable candidates from the Fianna to help bolster the IRB'".[45] The IRB began recruiting Fianna members in 1911, and many, such as Liam Mellows were sworn in when they reached the age of seventeen. The IRB circle within the Fianna was given the innocuous sounding cover name of 'The John Mitchel Literary and Debating Society', and Con Colbert was elected its first leader, or centre. Each year it arranged a circle meeting on the night before the Ard Fheis to discuss what line to take on motions to be presented. In this way they usually secured a majority for their preferred policies.

Since the turn of the century, when it had seemed to the IRB that there was little prospect of an armed revolt in Ireland, their energies had been concentrated on building up influence in other nationalist organisations, such as the Gaelic League, Gaelic Athletic Association, and now, Na Fianna Éireann. As a secret, conspiratorial organisation this was necessary, as so many Irish uprisings in the past had been defeated because the authorities had breached their security, but it left them open to accusations of infiltration and undemocratic manipulation. Markievicz had always argued 'against the influence of secret societies, claiming they were a danger to the nation's health...'[46] - however a Fianna IRB member described her as 'a person completely without guile', which I suspect was meant as an insult!

Eventually a group of the Fianna boys came to be known as 'Madam's boys' or the 'Surrey House clique' from their habit of spending so much time at the Markievicz house that she had moved to in about 1911. She enjoyed the role of being at the centre of a very large and shifting community of young lads, intellectuals, actors, artists, socialists and radicals of all sorts. One of the members of this clique was Andy Dunne.[47]   When the Easter Rising came, Markievicz, Molony and Dunne chose to fight with the Citizen Army rather than with the Volunteers.[48] Perhaps they felt more attuned with the politics and attitudes of James Connolly than that of the Irish Republican Brotherhood.

For a start, Connolly believed in the equality of the sexes, rather than the glorification of 'woman' in her traditional role.

He said: "The worker is the slave of capitalist society; the female worker is the slave of that slave. In Ireland that female worker had hitherto exhibited in her martyrdom, an almost damnable patience. She has toiled on the farms from her earliest childhood, attaining usually to the age of ripe womanhood without ever being vouchsafed the right to claim as her own a single penny of the money earned by her labour, and knowing that all her toil and privation would not earn her that right to the farm which would go without question to the most worthless member of the family, if that member chanced to be the eldest son.

The daughters of the Irish peasantry have been the cheapest slaves in existence - slaves to their own family, who were in turn, slaves to all the social parasites of a landlord and gombeen ridden community".[49]

Connolly was also calling for more than a change from English to Irish rulers in Dublin Castle. "We mean to be free and in every enemy of tyranny we recognise a brother, wherever be his birthplace: in every enemy of freedom we also recognise our enemy, though he were as Irish as our hills…"

The objective was the "whole of Ireland for the people of Ireland - their public property, to be owned and operated as a national heritage, by the labour of free men in a free country… we do not call for a 'united nation'. No nation can be united whilst capitalism and landlordism exists. The system divides society into two warring sections - the robbers and the robbed, the idlers and the workers, the rich and the poor, the men of property and the men of no property".

He said that the success of the Irish should be measured "upon their progress towards the mastery of those factories and farms upon which a people's bread and liberties depend".[50]

The Fianna at Belcamp Park and Surrey House

Markievics had rented a house at Belcamp Park, in Raheny, between July 1910 and July 1911, and attempted to make the enterprise self-supporting by market gardening. The project was not a financial success though the Fianna enjoyed it. Some Fianna boys went there for camps in about 1911, while some lived there the whole time.[51] When it had to be abandoned, Markievicz moved into furnished rooms in Lower Mount Street, and in 1912, she moved to Surrey House in Rathmines.[52] Liam is likely to have been in Dublin for some of this time so may have been there.

The O'Hanlons

The O'Hanlons were family friends of the Parrs. The oldest daughter, Julia - usually known as Sheila, or Sighle, (spellings vary) - was 15 in 1911. She was working as a seamstress and dressmaker and was a few years younger than Liam and Gilbert. When Sheila was born in 1895, her father had been a builder and the family were living at 26 Holles Street. In 1899, Andrew Dunne was born in Cumberland Street, which was a neighbouring street. This was the Andy Dunne who Liam Parr knew, probably through Fianna Éireann, or through their common musical activities. It is very likely that there were family links between the O'Hanlon and the Dunne families, as Sheila's father and Andy's mother were both witnesses when Patrick Hanlon was christened in 1896, at St Andrew's RC Church. Patrick Hanlon's parents were living in the same street as Sheila's parents, but it has, so far, proved impossible to demonstrate a family connection between them. Nevertheless, given their proximity, the fact they had the same surname, attended the same church and one acted as god parent to the other's child, it appears very likely that they were related.[53]

By 1901, Sheila's parents and family had moved to St Joseph's Terrace in Dolphin's Barn, and her father, James, was working as a clerk for the railway. Ten years later he was still a clerk, and they had remained close to the same address at Dolphin's Barn. In 1911 the house they lived in must have been of a reasonable size as it had a rated value of £11.10 shillings. As well as the family accommodation, the first floor front room was let to a Michael Nolan as an office.[54] Andy Dunne's mother's maiden name was Nolan so this could suggest another family connection, or it may be a pure coincidence.[55] In any event, members of the O'Hanlon, Dunne and Parr family were all embarked on parallel paths that were leading towards the events of Easter week.

In 1911, the O'Hanlon family lived in Camac Place, overlooking Camac Bridge, at Dolphin's Barn in Dublin. Nearby, in Herberton Lane, lived their friends, the Parr family. (Herberton Bridge was the next bridge to Camac Bridge on the Grand Canal.) In 1911, at the address in Camac Place, lived James O'Hanlon, who was a commercial clerk, married to Rose (Rosanna) and their five children. James O'Hanlon, as noted previously, was also a great friend of Éamonn Ceannt.[56] The second daughter was Mary Margaret (usually known as Mollie) who was still at school.[57] The family were staunch nationalists, Mollie later saying that her father, sister and brothers had all been 'in the movement.' Both Mollie and her sister Sheila joined the Inghidhe branch of Cumann na mBan in 1915 when it was formed.[58] Margaret Kennedy, who was to be Sheila's commanding officer, joined the same branch at about the same time.

"It was Annie Keating - now Mrs. Gerry Boland - that first introduced me to Cumann na mBan. She invited me down to 32 Lower Camden Street, where the Fianna had a hall, which Cumann na mBan rented from them on Tuesday nights. We had the old Inghinidhe na hÉireann room for meetings in No. 6 Harcourt Street on Thursdays….. In Camden Street we were trained and exercised in drill, figure marching, stretcher-drill, signalling and rifle practice with a little rook rifle. We also went on route marches regularly on our own initiative in order to train the girls in marching and in taking control. We had two instructors from the Fianna for drill, signalling and rifle practice - Seamus Pounch and a man named Devereaux (I don't know his christian name). Uniform material was available on purchase, some of us got them made and wore them. We also bought haversacks and First Aid outfits.

Our branch was called the Inghinidhe na Éireann branch of the Cumann na mBan. In Harcourt Street we learned First Aid, Morse Code, Signalling, Dispatch Memorising, etc. Seamus Pounch insisted that we should be put on a military basis instead of being governed solely by a committee, and that officers should, therefore, be elected. Ours was the first Dublin branch to have officers. The two officers: elected were: Eily Walsh (now Mrs. Martin Murphy) as Commandant, and Miss. Rose McNamara as Vice- Commandant.

As we were the only branch on the south side we were attached to two battalions - the 3rd and 4th. On the big march past on St. Patrick's Day 1916, we were under orders to be ready as this might be the 'real thing', meaning, of course, the Rising. We all wore full equipment and carried rations for twelve hours. We continued our regular and intensive training up to Easter Week on the basis already outlined, on each Tuesday and Thursday night. Occasionally on Sundays we would go out to the Dublin Mountains with stretchers, etc. for training". [59]

In 1911, a Jack O'Hanlon was on the supreme Council of the Irish Republican Brotherhood. He resigned from the council that year over a dispute with Bulmer Hobson on the running of the IRB newspaper 'Irish Freedom'. I have been unable to ascertain whether there is any family relationship with the O'Hanlons that Liam's family knew. [60]

Liam Parr- Leaving Herberton Lane
In 1911, shortly before he was 19, Liam had left home and moved to England, to Stockport. Until then he was living with his parents at 11 Herberton Lane, New Kilmainham, Dublin. There were now 7 children there, 2 had left and 2 had died. This was a 2-roomed house with one window facing the front - a class 3 house, which was poor for the street. In 1911 there were 9 of them living in 2 rooms, which means they had less space and were living in poorer accommodation than 10 years previously, but in a much more prosperous and respectable neighbourhood. It is therefore hard to be certain whether the family would have felt this to have been a step up or down.

1 1911 census Ireland

2 Kavanagh, Gerard. Personal communication, 7 feb 2014

3 1911 census Dublin

4 Kenny, James. Witness statement WS174

5 Ceannt, Aine. Witness statement.WS264

6 Henry, William, Supreme sacrifice, the story of Éamonn Ceannt. Mercier press, Cork, 2005.

7 Pictures in a Hallway, from O'Casey, Sean, Autobiographies vol 1 papermac 1992 London

8 Parr's name does not appear in any of the records of the Dublin pipers' club so he might have learnt piping through other organisations, most likely Fianna. Personal communication by email from Mick O'Connor. 2 Oct 2013. For links between the O'Hanlons and the Parrs see later.

9 Hayes, Kate. Personal communication. 8 June 2015

10 Markievicz, Constance, Eire, June 9, 1923. Retrieved on 20 Nov 2014 from https://fiannaeireannhistory.wordpress.com/2014/05/18/countess-markievicz- recalls-the-founding-of-na-fianna-eireann-in-1909/

11 Tiernan, Sonja, Eva Gore-Booth, an image of such politics. Manchester University Press,. Manchester 2012

12 Manchester Guardian22 April 1908 quoted in Norman, Diana, Terrible Beauty- A life of Constance Markievicz. Poolbeg, Dublin 1988

13 Reid, Naomi; Hampson, Walter (Casey). In Bellamy, Joyce and Saville, John; Dictionary of Labour Biography. Vol VI; Macmillan. London 1982

14 Cavendish, Richard, the foundation of Sinn Féin. History Today. Vol 55. Iss.11. 2005

15 Molony, Helena, witness statement WS 391

16 Lissadell hall website. Accessed January 2015. At http://www.constancemarkievicz.ie/politics.php

17 Bulmer Hobson quoted in Lawlor, Damian; Na Fianna Éireann and the Irish Revolution 1909 to 1923.Caoillte books; Rhode, Ireland. undated

18 Hobson, Bulmer, witness statement WS 31

19 Hobson, Bulmer, witness statement WS 31

20 Hobson, Bulmer, witness statement WS 31

21 Lawlor, Damian; Na Fianna Éireann and the Irish Revolution 1909 to 1923.caoillte books; Rhode, Ireland. Undated

22 Kavanagh, Seamus witness statement WS 1670

23 Lissadel House website . Accessed January 2015. http://www.constancemarkievicz.ie/politics.php

24 Norman, Diana, Terrible Beauty, Hodder and Stoughton ,London,1987

25 Cashin , Seamus, witness statement WS 119

26 Colum. Padraic, quoted in Norman, Diana, A Terrible Beauty,. Hodder and Stoughton. London 1987

27 Pounch, Seamus. Witness statement WS 267

28 Holohan, Gary. Witness statement WS 328

29 Prendergast, Sean, witness statement.WS 755

30 Quoted in Watts, John R. Na Fianna Eireann, A case study of a political youth organisation. University of Glasgow 1981

31 Bean na hÉireann Jan 1910 quoted in Watts, John R. Na Fianna Eireann, A case study of a political youth organisation. University of Glasgow 1981

32 info on pipe bands from Mick O' Connor. Personal communication – email.2.10.2013

33 O'Donoghue,Thomas; Witness statement WS 1666

34 Cashin, Seamus. Witness statement WS 0008

35 O'Donoghue,Thomas; Witness statement WS 1666

36 Christian, William; Witness Statement, WS646

37 Christian, William; witness statement.WS 646

38 Witness statements mentioning Dunne and music and an important member of Fianna are: Robbins, Frank WS 585: Prendergast, Sean,WS 755; Reader, Seamus, WS 1767; Cashin, Seamus, WS 0008

39 Prendergast, Sean, witness statement.WS 755

40 Prendergast, Sean, witness statement WS 755

41 Markievicz, Constance, letter to Eva Gore Booth , from Aylesbury Prison dated 21 1916; D4131/K/7/3; Public record office Northern Ireland.

42 Robbins, Frank, witness statement WS 585

43 Prendergast, Sean, witness statement WS 755

44 Prendergast, Sean. Witness statement WS 755

45 Lawlor, Damian; Na Fianna Éireann and the Irish Revolution 1909 to 1923.caoillte books; Rhode, Ireland. Undated

46 Lawlor, Damian;Na Fianna Éireann and the Irish Revolution 1909 to 1923.caoillte books; Rhode, Ireland. Undated

47 Pounch, Seamus. Witness statement WS 267

48 Kavanagh, Seamus, Witness statement WS 1670

49 Connolly, James. The reconquest of Ireland 1915, in James Connolly and the reconquest of Ireland , Callow, john; Evans Mitchell Books, London 2013

50 Connolly quoted in James Connolly and the reconquest of Ireland , Callow, john; Evans Mitchell Books, London 2013

51 Kavanagh, Seamus, witness statement WS 1670

52 Lissadell House website. Accessed jan 2015. http://www.constancemarkievicz.ie/politics.php

53 Irish genealogy.ie website accessed march 2015 at http://churchrecords.irishgenealogy.ie/churchrecords/

54 1908 electoral register…1911 census of Dublin

55 Dublin St Andrews parish records. Irish genealogy ie website accessed march 2015 at http://churchrecords.irishgenealogy.ie/churchrecords/

56 Personal communication Kate Hayes 2015

57 1911 census.

58 O'Hanlon, Mollie. Pension application. MSP34REF43514

59 Kennedy, Margaret witness statement WS 185

60 Hobson, Bulmer. Witness statement. WS 30

Chapter Three
Liam Parr moving to Stockport

In about 1910 or 1911, Liam left the family home in Dublin and moved to England to live with the Earles, his aunt and uncle, at 22 Tintern Avenue, West Didsbury, Manchester. Although, later, his widow said that he moved in 1913, he is on the 1911 census living with William Earle, and working as a porter in a grocery business.[1] [2] We do not know why he moved, though it was common for young Irishmen to move to England at the time, usually in search of work, freedom or better prospects. However, Liam's great uncle, Hannibal Ernest Earle, had a stroke at about this time, so it is possible that Liam had gone to help him, and his wife, in their shop doing the heavy portering jobs.

Hannibal Earle and Ellen Martin

Hannibal Earle was usually known as Ernest. There is a photo of the shop with the family standing outside, taken about 1905, when Ernest and Ellen were about 50. Ernest usually worked as a mechanic, but when he had the stroke, around the time of the photo, he gave up his main employment and joined his wife in her shop.

Ernest had started work in the cotton mills of Stockport, working as a 17 year old cotton piecer, but spent the rest of his working life as a mechanic, describing himself also as a turner, fitter and mechanical engineer. His wife Ellen ran a smallware shop from the house at 88 Turncroft Lane Stockport where they moved in about 1904. Family tradition describes Ernest as a more jovial individual than his wife.

"Ernest Hannibal was a real character," said William Earle his grandson. "He was a gas engineer who not only drank heavily but treated the whole pub as well. Ellen *(his wife)* used to post a ten bob note through the door when they went on holiday to Blackpool because she knew they would have nothing to carry on with on their return". She must have been surreptitiously posting it through her own front door to await their penniless homecoming. "Hannibal is known to have sent his daughter-in -law, Florence, a post card from Blackpool one year. The sum total of his text reads:

'Dear Flo, Funds are low

And Ellen's tight!'

(Presumably hoping that she would come to the rescue)[3]

Ernest (Hannibal) Earle died in August 1913. We do not know whether Ellen continued the shop with the help of Liam. Florence Earle was the auntie who Liam was presumably still living with at this time.

William Earle and Florence Costello

At the time when Liam moved in with him, his uncle, William Earle was a 31 year old electrical engineer working for the board of governors in Nell Lane Hospital, Manchester. This was a hospital set up as part of the workhouse system, and William Earle's job was to convert the lighting from gas to electricity. William's wife, Florence, was, of course, the sister of Liam's mother. She had been born 33 years before, as Florence Costello in Dublin near the Grand Canal but had left Ireland with her parents when she was about 20. Her family say that she had worked for Faulder's Chocolate Works by day and Stockport Theatre Royal in the evenings. Also living in the house were their two small children and a boarder who was a cook for the board of guardians.

George Costello and Mary Murphy

Soon after Liam arrived in Manchester he would have visited his grandparents, George and Mary Costello, and his sister who was staying with them. George and Mary had left Ireland when Liam was a child so this would have been the first time he had lived in the same town, or even same country, as his grandparents since he was a small child. He is likely to have known them from family visits between England and Ireland. In 1911 George and Mary were living at 156 Highfields Terrace, Stockport with Liam's 16 year old sister Mary, and three boarders. Mary Parr was working as a 'Lixol' maker in the book binding industry. The three boarders were two elementary school teachers and a bookbinder's sewer. All were young women from Ireland, so perhaps the boarder in the bookbinding industry had got Mary the job. George and Mary Costello were both around 70 years old, and George told the census enumerator that he was a 'retired army pensioner USA', so would probably have been grateful for the income from the boarders.[4]

Although George and Mary were at this address on census day 1911, the family remember them living in a succession of houses in Stockport, the frequency of the moves being due to them being prone to 'flitting from their landlords.' Whichever house they were in was said to always have had red linen blinds, by which their relatives could tell where they had moved to, and a policeman's helmet hanging up. The helmet is very hard to explain…

Mary was remembered as always wearing a cloak, bonnet, and long black skirt and needing to push George in a wheel chair whenever he went out. George was disabled as a result of injuries he sustained fighting in the American Civil War and requiring regular medical assessments to assess his eligibility for a pension. The assessments were designed to ascertain whether he had a genuine disability, and to decide whether his health problems were caused by his war service or were self-induced by alcohol or syphilis. In George's case, they did eventually rule these out, though in 1897 the doctor had written, "He says that he is strictly temperate, but admits to taking both beer and rum, and I am of the opinion he at times takes more than is good for him".

By 1906 he was unable to walk to attend his medical assessment and the doctor had to see him in his house.[5] George was eventually allowed a pension of $12 a month. Mary was in better health than George, and used to fetch his pension from the US embassy or consulate in Manchester, travelling from Tiviot Dale station, Stockport. She sometimes took one of her granddaughters with her who remembers, as a little girl, Mary calling into a pub they passed on the way back for 'a small port'.

As Liam was young and fit, it is very likely that he would have been one of the family members who would have pushed George about in his chair. Liam would certainly have heard the stories of George's exploits in America, probably from George himself. His grandparents must have seemed exotic and exciting to Liam with their history of living in America through the Civil War. The family remember that George fired "…guns out of the window - he had a pair of silver six shooters inscribed and presented to colonel or something Costello for his services in the civil war. Granny was worried that he would shoot someone so she went to Stockport police station with the guns and asked them to take them but they refused because he had a licence. So on the way back she dropped them in the Mersey… I expect they'd find them if they dredged it".[6]

I can imagine Liam listening avidly to George's tales of taking up arms for a cause.

George had left Dublin when he was 24 to sail to America. His father had been a shopkeeper in Dublin but, previous to that, the whole family had been connected with coach building, having played some part in the building of the royal coach which is still used in the state opening of the British parliament. George himself had probably worked in that industry, as he carried the skills to New York and worked in harness making and related trades when he was there.

This was in 1862 and 1863, during the early years of the American Civil War so he was able to find work, but it can't have been very remunerative as he could only afford to live close to the 'Five Points' neighbourhood, one of the roughest and most poverty stricken neighbourhoods of the Lower East Side. This was one of the districts depicted in the film 'Gangs of New York'. The film, of course, was not historically accurate but it does show that the streets were not paved with gold for the new immigrants. George's brother Alfred and his wife also moved to America a few months later and settled in Brooklyn. They were perhaps more fortunate than George as Alfred later moved to New Jersey, and had some success, opening a photographic business.

George was living in New York at the time of the New York Draft riots in 1863. In New York the Irish and the blacks had been living, crammed into the most overcrowded slums and both doing the worst paid jobs. Generally speaking people got along reasonably well when they were in the poorest mixed communities, but there had been occasions when one group was played off against the other to break strikes or keep down wages, and there had sometimes been riots and bloodshed. During the first couple of years of the American Civil War, the North, which included New York, was embarrassingly unsuccessful in militarily beating back the slave-holding rebels of the South. The war exacerbated the poverty in New York as prices rose, but wages didn't keep up and huge profits were made by military suppliers. The war was unpopular in New York, particularly with sections of the Irish who feared that if slavery ended they would lose their jobs to even lower-paid black workers released from slavery. When conscription was introduced to New York, it led to rioting. At first this was against the unfairness of the draft, as those with enough money could buy their way out of the army, but then it degenerated into a race riot against black people during which 11 black men were lynched. There is no reason to believe that George had been involved; the area where he lived had quite good race relations and his name is not mentioned in any arrest reports. George would not have been at risk of conscription as he had not applied to become an American citizen. When the riots had been put down, at the cost of 1000 dead, George volunteered to join the Union Army. This might have been because they were now offering cash payment of nearly $1000 for anyone who would sign up.

I don't know what happened to the money, but George went off to fight with a regiment of New York Irishmen. This was the 42nd New York Infantry, a regiment that already had fought for two years, most recently at Gettysburg, and had already sustained heavy losses. The regiment was proud of its Irish identity, and 176 of its members had recently made a collection of nearly $500 to avert starvation in Ireland. Most significantly, they sent the money to the Bishop Keane of Cloyne saying: "We hope it may contribute, if only in a small degree, to stop the stream of Irish emigration, and to keep our friends from starvation, so that, this war in which we are engaged being ended, there may be some of our race left at home whom we can aid in placing beyond fear of recurrence both the miseries of famine and the horrors of landlordism. Rt. Rev. Dr. Keane - we select him as the dispenser of our contribution towards the immediate relief of our suffering kindred in Ireland".[7]

They sent the money to Bishop Keane because they applauded him for his action in 'being the first to acknowledge, by his reception of the remains of the patriot McManus, the right of the exile to a resting-place with his kindred in the land for which he struggled'.[8] Terence MacManus had been one of the participants in the 1848 Young Irelander Rebellion who had been transported to Australia by the British courts. The national feelings of the soldiers were also demonstrated by the songs they were heard singing , and one of those most often noted was 'the Minstrel Boy'. This was an Irish nationalist song that had been carried across the Atlantic with Irish emigrants. It is appropriate that it was to be one of Liam's favourite songs, to the extent that the Sinn Fein MP Larry Ginnell would use 'Minstrel Boy' as a nickname for Liam during the next few years in Ireland.

Fortunately for George, when he entered the army and was sent to Virginia, it was too late in the year for much fighting because the roads became impassably muddy in the winter, so he was fairly safe until the next May. However, his safety was only relative as more soldiers died of a combination of fever, dysentery and syphilis than were killed by enemy action. In May 1864, George was part of an army of nearly 100,000 in Virginia under General Ulysses S Grant facing a slightly smaller army of Confederate rebel soldiers under General Robert E Lee. The two armies fought for nearly a month in thick forest with rifles and cannons, without any conclusive result except leaving half of George's comrades as casualties. This was when George was injured when a bullet went through his hand during the battle of Spotsylvania. He was sent to hospital in Washington and then Newark, New Jersey, and managed to avoid fighting again for the rest of the war. In New Jersey he became a ward master (orderly), a role intended as light work for recuperating soldiers. This is probably where he met Mary Murphy who was an Irish woman living in Brooklyn, who must have been visiting the hospital for some reason. Family tradition says she was a nurse, but the hospital only employed male nurses. Mary had emigrated from Ireland to America at a similar time to George. She was the sister of Gus Bonham's wife. George and Mary married in Brooklyn, and his brother and wife were their witnesses.

After the wedding George was put in the Veterans reserve corps, a body of soldiers who were not fully fit and were given light duties away from the fighting. George's section was stationed in Washington DC as the war was ending. He was in Washington when Abraham Lincoln was assassinated, but there is no way of knowing exactly what his role was. However there is a family tradition that he was supposed to be guarding Lincoln but left the theatre, perhaps for a drink, at the time of the shooting.

George, with the rest of the soldiers, was not demobbed at the end of the fighting, and many, including George, didn't bother waiting. There is some evidence that George was accused of deserting at this time, but the claims were abandoned. I think it was so common for soldiers to simply go home at the end of the war without waiting for permission that the authorities gave it up as a bad job.

After the war George and Mary sailed back to Ireland. Perhaps they hadn't found their "American Dream". In Dublin George worked again as a coach maker and he and Mary had fourteen children, but only four survived to adulthood. One of these was Mary/Stella, Liam's mother, who was born in 1871, and another was Florence who Liam was staying with. George's health began to deteriorate while he was in Dublin and he successfully claimed for a partial disability pension from the American authorities. They agreed that he was only fit for light work, though there was some doubt about what exactly was the medical diagnosis. In the early 1890s, George and Mary moved to Stockport but as George got older his disability increased, as did his pension.[9]

The Bonhams - Visiting Manchester

Margaret Bonham was Mary Costello's sister-both being called Murphy before they were married. Margaret, and her husband Gus Bonham, lived in Dublin where Gus was a plumbing equipment supplier. Their daughter, Alice, was learning Irish in Dublin. Mary and Margaret must have kept in good contact with one another because there are records of the Bonhams visiting the Costellos in Stockport.[10]

A story within the family was that Gus was the Lord Mayor of Dublin. This was not the case, but Gus Bonham was elected as a Poor Law Guardian for the South Dublin Workhouse. He was comfortably off-a retired builder living in a large house in the respectable suburb of Rathmines in south Dublin. He sailed to America to visit a cousin in New Jersey who was a mayor there at one time. There are a number of links to New Jersey. George Costello was in hospital and met Mary there, Gus Bonham's cousin lived there, and George's brother, Alfred, lived there. However it is not clear whether these are more than coincidences.

The Irish Community in Manchester in 1911

Manchester has long had a sizeable Irish community. Liam found his way into this community soon after arriving in the city. Throughout the nineteenth century all those who left Ireland would have landed in Liverpool, before the opening of the railway link to Holyhead over the Menai Bridge. Once in Liverpool, many, like Liam's grandfather, would have set off across the Atlantic, but large numbers settled in mainland Britain, particularly in Lancashire or London. Liverpool, of course is famed for the strength of its Irish community, but Manchester was the world's first city of the industrial revolution, and as such it sucked in huge numbers of workers to be often treated and housed abominably. Engels' 'Condition of the Working Class in England' is particularly descriptive of the living conditions in the Irish Communities of Manchester. In the 1861 census, taken after the years of the potato famine, about 13% of the population of Manchester were described as being born in Ireland. That doesn't tell us, however, how many people felt themselves to be Irish. There have always been so many Irish people working in England who have children here, but feel that they will one day return 'home', or would like to one day return 'home', that the concept of Irishness is hard to define. It is interesting to note how many of the important figures in the formation of the Irish state, and the Rising, were not actually born in Ireland. James Connolly, Jim Larkin, Tom Clarke and Liam Mellows were all born in England or Scotland.[11]

Liam Parr and Redmond Cox were born in Ireland, but Gilbert Lynch and

Laurence Ryan were both born in the Manchester area. In fact, neither of Lynch's parents were born in Ireland either, an example of how long- lasting a sense of national identity can be.

The local/national newspaper (the Manchester Guardian) chronicled the activities of the Irish community in Manchester, and what it reported reflected the changes going on in Ireland, with the gathering confidence and energy of organisations representing both cultural and political nationalism. In the period between 1900 and the Easter Rising, there are scattered news items telling us a little of the cultural activities of the Gaelic League, as well as the United Irish League, which acted as representatives of the Irish parliamentary party.

In the early years of the 20th century, the branches of the Gaelic league were only reported as campaigning in support of the teaching of the Irish language in Ireland, and of running classes in Irish in Manchester. Towards the end of the first decade, there are more reports of a wider concept of Irish culture such as music and dance. On the 13th April 1910, the Manchester Guardian reported a "soiree" put on by the Manchester City branch of the United Irish League, which included a performance from the O'Growney branch of the Gaelic league. "Last night's meeting of the Manchester City Branch of the United Irish League was the last of the session, and was given to Irish folklore. Mainly the subject was dealt with in song, recitations, and Irish dances but it was prefaced by an interesting explanation by Mr Delaunty, who told the audience that the study of folk-lore, which was begun in Germany sixty years ago, had already shown - that in their legends and folk-tales the various races were as closely related as the members of one family.

The rich store of Irish folk-lore was, he said, an ungathered harvest and he went on to point out its diversity, tales and songs that tell of lands of perpetual youth, of strange voyages, of ships that sail on land as well as sea, all characterised by a quality of glorious exaggeration.

"In all other literature," Mr Delaunty said, "there is a pessimism   which it may be given to us, as Irishmen, to withstand. In this love of the green earth and of the fair flowering of the Gaelic mind we have precisely the antidote for this disease".

Several songs were sung by Madame Lyons, Mr. James Foy, and Mr. J. M. Gibson, and recitations were given by Dr. F. J. Webb. The dances were very pretty, the Irish jig and reel were danced by the boys of St. Joseph's Industrial School, and the high cowl cap dance by members of the O'Growney Branch of the Gaelic League".[12]

The O'Growney Branch was the one that Liam Parr and Gilbert Lynch belonged to. It is impossible to be sure exactly when Liam moved from Dublin to Stockport, but it is possible that both Liam and Gilbert were at that meeting in 1910.

The United Irish league organised a similar event the following year consisting of a lecture on Irish folklore song and dance performed by (among others)

St Joseph's Industrial School, and the Gaelic League.[13]

The dancers of the Gaelic league were performing again within a couple of months, in the Free Trade Hall, at what the Guardian described as the fourth annual Irish concert. This suggests that there had been similar concerts since 1908, though they don't appear to have been reported in the Manchester Guardian.

"In the Free-trade Hall last night Mr. James Foy held his fourth annual Irish concert. The hall was crowded, and owing to repeated encores the programme was not finished until very late. From beginning to end the concert justified its description as 'A real Irish night', for all the songs were of Erin and the shamrock, of 'Macushia' or 'Mavourneen', and with the City Police Band playing Irish melodies the audience was always well entertained. Miss Agnes Tracy had a great reception when she sang 'Rich and Rare' and 'The Kerry Dance'. Mr. J. C. Doyle in 'The Colleen Bawn' and Mr. Foy himself in 'Men of the West' - were as popular as ever. Irish dances, the eight hand jig, hornpipes and reels were danced by Mr. Joseph Kenny and eight members of the O'Growney branch of the Gaelic league: Mr E. A. Carroll recited. Master Ignatius Wolshan played the piano, and Master John Dunne sang 'The Green Isle' and 'Old Ireland shall blossom again'. All the performers were enthusiastically recalled".[14]

In November 1910, WB Yeats came to Manchester and gave a series of lectures at the Memorial hall. The final lecture was extensively reported in the Manchester Guardian.

"At the Memorial Hall, Manchester, last night, Mr. W B. Yeats concluded his series of public lectures. Mr. Yeats said he was trying in these lectures, simply to give expression to some of the things he had thought and felt, as an artist, about beauty and truth and the meaning of human life. The artist, said Mr. Yeats, had no concern with morality, politics, humanitarianism, or philanthropy - all these had interest for him as a man, but as an artist his task was simply to pursue reality and set down the vision which revealed to him the meaning of life. This was the source of all great art, and he must resist the temptations which lured him away from it...

Irish national politics dated from the Young Ireland movement, when Thomas Davis and his friends had created by journalism a national ideal which was to take the place of national institutions. The images they had created of the ideal peasant and the charming colleen had spread wherever their race was to be found, creating something like a world-wide national consciousness, in which abstract virtues had taken the place of realities. Out of this consciousness arose the Gaelic movement; but by this time an industrial class had arisen, the first their country had ever seen and having neither leisure nor a traditional culture, its leaders were banded together only by political hatred and suspicion, so that their journalism was altering for the worse the imagination of the people...

It was for this cause that Lady Gregory and he himself had gone to the folklife of Ireland, for there only was the great imaginative tradition of the people to be found. In the imagination of the peasant lived the old Ireland of chivalry and nobility, which was a name of enchantment throughout Europe, but unless its imagination and its generosity could be called back, it lay at the door of death. It was because they knew this that the Gaelic League went to the cottage for the ancient legends, the imagination of the peasants and their attitude towards the world, an outlook personal, individual, and therefore, sincere... But besides an attitude towards life which was sincere, they got a language wonderfully expressive, a speech to be compared only with that of the England of Shakespeare – 'The most beautiful form of English now spoken on earth'.

It had been their dream to bring the imagination of the country back into the life of the town, not only its heroism and legend, but its wonderful comedy and humours of speech. Their success, so far as they had succeeded was due to the accident of his discovering J. M. Synge in Paris...

'Synge' said Mr. Yeats, 'was Ireland's Burns. Ireland was absorbed in politics, as Scotland in religion, and Synge was the only man I ever met who was absolutely incapable of political thought. He had been all over Europe, flying from organised life; he had lived amongst the poor without taking the slightest interest in poverty, yet he loved the poor, for he found their lives more artistic and beautiful than our lives'. Happiness came to Synge in the Aran Islands, where he escaped the nullity of the rich and the squalor of the poor, where he found a traditional courtesy and people living in the face of the great realities, death, childhood, and the affections...

After answering several questions Mr. Yeats was again asked to read some of his poems. A request that he would soon return to lecture in Manchester was much applauded by the crowded audience".[15]

It is possible that Liam or Gilbert attended Yeats talk in 1910 though it is impossible to know. Yeats was looking to traditional Irish culture as an aesthetic ideal, and was applauding Synge for being 'absolutely incapable of political thought' and for living 'amongst the poor without taking the slightest interest in poverty'. Although Yeats was 'much applauded' for his speech, I suspect many of the Irish had a more common-sense attitude to questions of poverty and the national question. Even at this time, a combination of poverty in the West of Ireland and a wish for a better standard of living was bringing more and more of the Irish to the towns of Ireland, as well as the cities of the rest of the world.

The national question must also have been a major concern for Yeats' audience, or at least for the Irish amongst them, and this was represented in Manchester during the first decade of the century by the United Irish League. Their policy was to support the strategy of John Redmond of the Irish parliamentary party to use their block of votes in the Westminster parliament to pressurise the Liberal party to grant "Home Rule" to Ireland. This appeared to be a productive policy when the Irish party held the balance of power in Westminster. While the Liberal party had been in opposition, they had claimed to support 'Home Rule' for Ireland. In the 1906 general election, the Conservatives had been replaced by Liberals as the majority in the Commons, and now the politically-conscious Irish community were waiting to see what they would deliver.

On St Patrick's Day that year, John Redmond came to the Free Trade Hall to address a 'great meeting of Irishmen and women'.

He said, "He was glad to be here to fulfil the duty of expressing in his own name, in the name of the Irish party, and in the name of Ireland, their thanks to the Irishmen of Great Britain for the magnificent loyalty, unity and discipline with which they acted during the recent election. (Cheers)... we have materially assisted - and I was glad to hear what was said about the elections in Manchester and this district - in driving that government from office and installing in office another Government which is friendly to Ireland, supported by a majority in the house of Commons - a government and a party who for the last twenty years have been pledged to the Principle of Home Rule (Cheers)... On this question of Home Rule, what is the immediate present attitude of the New Government? They have announced in the King's speech that they are engaged at this moment in considering plans - mark you, a pretty definite statement - for associating the people of Ireland with the government of their own country. Now I say that as we are not a nation of fools we will give the Government time to mature their plans. I do not say we will give them an indefinite time..." Mr Redmond ended his talk by saying, "...I sincerely hope that all the men and women and children in Manchester will support the Gaelic League movement, and in that way learn something of the poetry and the songs of our old country. I hope that in time the movement will rescue from the oblivion that was overtaking it the beautiful old language that the poets and saints and sages of our country thought and spoke and wrote in the past (Cheers).[16]

Liam Parr's parents moving to Stockport

Within a couple of years of Liam moving to Manchester, he was joined by his parents. They lived at various addresses including at 48 (or 49) Upper Brook Street. Liam met his future wife, Margaret Madden at the O'Growney Branch of the Gaelic league where she met Liam, her future husband. Later Margaret remembered: "their home in Stockport was the centre of everything Irish".[17]

Liam's daughter described the family in Manchester (though a bit later); "The whole family was fiercely Irish. They all adored my father, *(Liam)* and I was always introduced as 'Willie's girl', which brought a tender smile. When I came home after evacuation, I used to go over on my own, my two brothers also, and they were tremendously kind to us. They all worked so hard in the cotton mill, and the domestic work was done after midday on Saturday. They had great parties, with lots of music and fun and games, and it was open house at the Parr's..... Grandad Chris *(Liam's father)* had worked as a brass finisher. At the Parr home - 73 Hall Street - in front of a large fireplace, there was a very ornate brass fender the likes of which you would never see today. It was full of twists and scroll work, even hollow shaped acorns from which you could remove the lid. It used to fascinate me, but I couldn't understand as, when they told me grandad had made it, how a plumber could do it".[18]

Liam Parr meeting Gilbert Lynch in 1911

By the time that Liam Parr arrived in Stockport, Gilbert Lynch had probably already for some time been a member of both the Stockport United Irish League and the O'Growney branch of the Gaelic League. They would both have been about nineteen when they met.

1 1911 Manchester census

2 Pension application Pension administration section. Department of defence. Ireland. Documents re Parr DP9542

Letter to de Valera

3 Earle, William personal communication

4 1911 census

5 Us govt pension file for George Costello. In possession of the famly.

6 Family memory. Personal communication

7 Irish-American (newspaper) May 9 1863.

8 Irish-American (newspaper) May 9 1863.

9 Stocks, Robin, George Costello in America. Unpublished manuscript based mainly on George Costello's USA pension files, family memories and family history records.

10 Us govt pension file for George Costello. In possession of the family.

11 Herbert, Michael, the wearing of the Green, 2001, Irish in Britain representation Group,2001.

12 Manchester Guardian 13 April 1910

13 Manchester Guardian Mar 16 1910

14 Manchester Guardian May 16 1911

15 Manchester Guardian Nov 15 1910

16 Manchester Guardian Mar 19 1906

17 Margaret Parr in Parr, William pension file. DP9542.

18 Wall, Bernadette. Personal communication

Chapter Four
Gilbert Lynch and industrial unrest

Birth and Youth of Gilbert Lynch

Gilbert Lynch was six months younger than Liam. He had been born on 11th February 1892 at 11 David Street, Reddish, Stockport. Gilbert was the sixth child of a family of eight, six boys and two girls, and as he very conveniently tells us in his autobiography, his mother was born in Lancashire but greatly valued her Irish roots.

"She often told me that her mother was proud of the fact that her first cousin was Dr John McHale, Archbishop of Tuam, the Lion of Judah, the star of 42. She belonged to County Mayo, but like many other Irish families in Connacht were forced by economic determinism to seek a livelihood in some other country. As the cotton industry in Britain was expanding she came to Bolton, and found work in Bolton".[1]

Gilbert's father was orphaned when he was about 11, and was put in the St Joseph's Industrial School until he was old enough to work. Then he was started in the mill at Reddish. There was a policy of encouraging Irish culture at the school and groups of the boys appeared as dancers at Irish concerts in Manchester alongside the Gaelic league.

Gilbert himself eventually followed his father into the cotton mills, though he had had difficulties at school because of poor sight.

"My school days were very difficult because four of us were born like albinos - not true albinos because we had blue eyes not pink eyes, but we had white hair and we also had short vision, and although I was put in the front row if the teacher was putting on the blackboard vulgar fractions or small things like that, it was very difficult for me to see. But I had a wonderful memory and I did fairly well in the circumstances, but not as well as I would have liked, because I would have liked to have left school as early as some of the others in my class did to find work.

I did apply to go to labour and take what was called the Labour Examination, but when I got my arithmetic card - arithmetic was my strong point - most of the sums were in vulgar fractions. I asked the man who was in charge of the examination if he would mind reading them out to me, and he told me he couldn't do anything like that, that his function was only to see that nobody copied, nobody talked to one another or anything like that. Well, I failed on arithmetic. I had taken a copy of what I thought were the sums and had worked out the answers - they were all right according to the teacher's adding up, but it was evident I hadn't put the proper sums on the paper, [the man in charge] not being able to read them out".

When Gilbert was thirteen he started work part time for a relative who was a butcher. "I worked in the mornings from Monday till Friday, and on Tuesday evening after school I used to go to a place called Heaton Chapel and meet the drover who was bringing in the cattle from the Manchester market to Stockport, and on the way he would cut out whatever cattle were wanted for the various butchers, and he would cut out whatever sheep or beasts were in the drove for me and I used to bring them on to Reddish. I also worked all day on Saturdays. I think I earned the princely sum of four or five shillings a week".

When he was 14, he began work in the Reddish Spinning Company in the warehouse. "My job was to assist the man who weighed yarn that came down from the spinning rooms. It came down in skips - there were generally four skips from each pair of mules, and my job was to pull them up to the scales, put them on and take them off when he weighed them. After they were all weighed in the evening I took them all down to the conditioning cellar. It is necessary for cotton to be conditioned, and it is conditioned by steam. Each set of cops were left there for about five days, and when they had been in five days we brought them out in the morning. It generally took us up to near breakfast time. The hours were 55½ hours a week - from 6.00 to 8.30 and from 9.00 to 1.00 and from 2.00 to 5.30 Monday to Friday, Saturday from 6.00 to 8.30 and from 9.00 to 12.00. The wages were 9s 10d a week...

I worked at that job for two or three years and then a vacancy became available in the bale mixing department. According to the fineness of the yarn that was to be spun, the cotton had to be mixed for that fineness. If the yarn was coarse, say up to a hundred counts, we used American cotton. Finer yarn, there would be Egyptian cotton, and finer yarn still would be Sea Island cotton. The finer the yarn was, it required the cotton of a longer staple. My job also included picking off the tares, that is, the wrapper that was round the bales. I had to pick all the cotton off and tie all the tares up. I usually left these for Saturday afternoons, especially in the winter months, so that I could earn a few extra bob. I worked the other two and a half days as a packer in the warehouse, and I could make somewhere about an average of 21 shillings a week, which was a very good wage in those days. Eventually a vacancy came for a full packer in the packing department, and I applied for that job and got it. I still remained working as a packer until I left somewhere early in 1918".[2]

Gilbert's father was an important member of the local Liberal Association, being one of the 'two hundred', which was its executive, and at first Gilbert followed in his political footsteps. His first political memory is of being in his sitting room folding leaflets and putting them in envelopes. When he was older, Gilbert joined the National League of Young Liberals and attended conferences and lectures, particularly concerning the first national insurance act which the Liberal Government passed in 1911.

Gilbert Lynch becoming involved in Irish politics

Around 1908, Gilbert became involved in Irish politics. "During my association with the National Union of Young Liberals I met a man named Pat Kelly. He was the organiser for the United Irish League. He asked me was there a possibility of organising a branch of the United Irish League in Reddish, and I suggested that he should also contact a man named Mr Patrick McHugh who was employed as a clerk in the Manchester Corporation. Sometime previously he had married Miss O'Donoghue, who was one of the teachers in St Joseph's School. He eventually made the contact and I met Mr McHugh, and we did get the Irish and those of Irish extraction together and did form a branch of the United Irish League. We met in a rather unusual place, in a room belonging to the spiritualist! Eventually we decided we would have an open-air meeting on the question of Ireland, and it was decided I should act as chairman of the meeting and the meeting was to be held in Houldsworth Square. I don't remember the date of the meeting, but the whole incident is engraved on my memory. The meeting was held on the eve of the coming into canon law of the Old Age Pensions Act in Britain. I will never forget it – there was a fairly good crowd because it was the first open-air meeting of Irishmen, and there was a fairly large assemblage on Houldsworth Square.

I got up to speak, but the moment I got up the crowd vanished from my sight. I was stage-struck - it seemed a long time to me before I got my senses back, but I believe it was only a few seconds. I had got instructions that the duty of a chairman was to stand up, speak up and shut up, and not to keep the meeting too long and stand between them and the principal speaker. Just previous to that I had been reading Lecky's History of Ireland. Lecky was a Protestant, and therefore these things he wrote about could be used in good stead and it couldn't be argued that he was prejudiced in favour of the nationalists. Lecky's history showed how the trade of Ireland for a considerable number of years had been destroyed by regulations of the British government. Produce from Ireland could only be carried in British ships, it couldn't be carried in Irish ships or ships of any other nation...

I am afraid that the United Irish League did not last very long, but we did a certain amount of good work. But after the elections came round in 1910 it seemed to die off".

He was also a member of the Gaelic league, in the same branch that William Parr joined.

"I have already stated that the Masses in St Joseph's, Reddish were at 8.30 and 10.30. On one Sunday when we were coming out we found a man taking a collection for the Gaelic League. He asked me what time next mass was, and I told him 10.30 and as it was then only 9.15 he would have a long wait, and I suggested he should come to our house and have some breakfast, and he could come back then and collect at the 10.30 mass. He said he didn't like taking us so short like that, but I said my father was in the chapel and would be coming out in a minute and he would know whether there was enough in the pot to give him something. So when my father came out he insisted that he came along. His name was Peter Lavin, he was an employee of the Railway Company. He was a man who had met with an accident and had lost one arm. He was secretary of the O'Growney Branch of the Gaelic League which met in Booth Street, and he invited us to go down and meet them. We went down that evening after benediction and we met the whole crowd there.

I might say there were two branches of the Gaelic League in Manchester. One was the Craobh Oisìn which met in the centre of Manchester and the other, the O'Growney, which met near All Saints' of Booth Street East. The O'Growney Branch was looked upon and called 'the natives' because most of them in this branch were Irish of extraction, whereas in the Craobh Oisìn, the majority there were native Irish, most of them teachers, and they looked upon themselves as something superior to the Craobh Uì Ghramhnaigh".[3]

By about 1911, when Gilbert Lynch would have met Liam Parr, he had found his way from the young liberals to the Irish nationalism of the United Irish League. The league's role was to build support for the Irish party's policy of using the Westminster political system to gain some level of home rule for Ireland. Gilbert had also joined the Gaelic league, an organisation whose nationalism was much more complicated. It always saw its role as to strengthen and rebuild the traditional culture of Ireland, particularly the language, literature, music and dance. There had always been those who saw this purely in aesthetic or artistic terms without risking being sullied by politics. Yeats lecture reflects much of this attitude. Yet, in that first decade of the century, the cultural revival had become more and more intertwined with those seeking political change, and political change with methods and objectives more radical than those envisaged by the Irish party and its leader John Redmond.

The Fianna Éireann is a good example of this, with which Liam had been in contact in Dublin. Here was an organisation which combined the cultural and the nationalist with the political, and this was personified in its most remembered figurehead, Constance Markievicz. Her background was of the landed aristocracy and initially her interest was only in Irish Nationalism. However, like so many, she came in contact with James Connolly and Jim Larkin and her politics came closer to their conceptions of socialism.

Similarly Gilbert Lynch was developing towards a political understanding that involved him being more than a young liberal and an Irish nationalist but led to him becoming a prominent trade unionist and socialist. All his life he combined his politics with being a devout Catholic, as did Liam Parr.

Gilbert seems to have been a trade union member from a young age, so perhaps we can assume either this was encouraged by his parents, or he was working in a closed shop. In any case, he benefited from his first trades dispute.

"The first dispute I was involved in was in 1908. In the cotton industry, in the preparation and spinning end, there were two unions and two different classes of workers. In what was called the preparation end, i.e. the card and blowing rooms, the union membership consisted of about 95 per cent women and only 5 per cent men. But in the spinning end they were all men, and when wage negotiations took place they were generally carried out between the employers and the spinners, and the results were generally accepted by the card and blowing room members.

But when the negotiations took place in 1908 and an agreement was arrived at between the spinners and the employers, the women of the preparation end refused to accept whatever was agreed to, and said they were going to make their own agreement or not work at all, and the result was that all of the cotton trade was closed down. About 300,000 workers were thrown idle. We weren't involved directly in the dispute, but we were indirectly. As I explained previously, after the yarn had been weighed coming down from the spinners it was taken into the conditioning cellars for about five days. Well, we had to wait until all that was worked out and it took us about a week to work it off, and then we were laid off.

It proved a most interesting dispute to me because our mill had become part of the Fine Spinners combine, the management of which decided to pay all those who were not directly involved over 21 years of age twenty shillings a week and those under 21 years of age ten shillings a week. Therefore I was in receipt of ten shillings a week from the firm, and as I had already become a member of the Workers' Union, as I was locked out I received ten shillings a week from them. Therefore by working I got 9s 10d a week, but by being locked out I was in receipt of a pound a week. Furthermore, by this time my father had become a carder and my eldest brother an under-carder, and as both of these were on the staff they were in receipt of full wages. Therefore we did not find any economic stress from the dispute at all. We were also lucky as far as weather was concerned. During the seven weeks of the dispute the weather was glorious, no rain at all, and we enjoyed ourselves immensely".

It is interesting that the women workers were insistent on being represented in their own right, as workers, at a time when Eva Gore-Booth and her colleagues in the Manchester and Salford Womens' Trade Union Council were campaigning for just this to happen.

After this dispute, Gilbert became more active in the union himself. "…I still continued to be a member after the dispute, and succeeded in organising a number of my workmates. The branch used to meet once a fortnight in a public house called Ye Olde Tavern. In most towns at that time a number of public houses had club rooms, and these club rooms were let out to trade unions, football clubs and other organisations, and the rent from them was generally charged as beer.

I was elected a member of the branch committee, and I think my head swelled with importance with the fact of being elected. I thought they had appreciated my attributes and my usefulness to the movement, but it was about six months before I was disillusioned. We used to take in contributions from 7.30 till 8.30 on Saturday nights, and then afterwards we would have a branch meeting. I noticed that when the branch meeting started the waiter came up with about fifteen pints of beer. At that time mild beer was twopence a pint, but it was only after about six months I realised that this was the rent - the half-crown a week was fifteen pints of beer, and that my real cause of being elected was that I did not drink. There were about four more like me, and the more teetotallers on the committee, well, the less to drink the fifteen pints. I still, however, remained on the committee - this disillusionment didn't dismay me. I could still do work, and I continued to do it. I was subsequently elected as a delegate to the Stockport Trades and Labour Council and also to the district committee".[4]

1913 Dublin Lockout

On 26 August 1913 the Great Dublin Lockout began. The Irish community of Manchester must have all been talking about the news of a huge and dramatic strike in Dublin. It began when the owner of the Dublin tramways sacked 100 men for joining the Irish Transport and General Union which had been trying to unionise most of the unskilled workers in Dublin. Other bosses joined with the Tramways boss, William Murphy, and also sacked ITGWU members until 25,000 workers were locked out in Dublin. The dispute became even more polarized when police began violently attacking strikers' demonstrations, killing one man and injuring others.

The Dublin Transport workers strike was not seen as a distant and irrelevant item of news among the Irish community and trade union communities in Manchester. Most of the Irish in Manchester already knew too much about the levels of poverty in Dublin because that was usually what had driven them to come to England. Larkin was quite open in stating that he believed more changes were needed than just a minor pay rise. He knew that the dispute was as much about living conditions, and slum housing and poor public health as it was about low wages and long working hours. This was brought to a head when only a week into the strike two tenement houses in Church Street collapsed killing seven people. These were two adjoining four storey terrace houses with shops on the ground floor and a total of 16 rooms above. In these 16 rooms lived 10 families- 40 people. Only two months before, the owner had been warned to do repairs. The repairs had been completed to the satisfaction of Dublin Corporation, but the houses still collapsed. One tenant reported hearing a crack and seeing a marble fireplace move. One of the dead was a 17 year old worker at Jacobs Biscuits who was among those locked out. This was Eugene Sammon who had been trying to rescue his 4 year old sister. Public outrage led to the government setting up a public enquiry into 'The housing conditions of the working classes in the city of Dublin'. This showed that 118,461 people lived in tenements, including 13,800 who were living more than 9 to a room, and 1,560 who were living in cellars. It also discovered that the leading slum landlords included 17 councilors.

Public statistics also showed that the death rate in Dublin was the highest in the United Kingdom while the infant mortality rate was 160 per thousand compared to 106 in London.[5]

The Irish community in Manchester would have followed the fortunes of the Dublin workers, not only because most had close family links with Dublin, but also because the strike leaders came to Manchester to elicit support.

Parr, Lynch, Cox and Ryan were probably all in Manchester when huge numbers attended meetings in support of the workers. It would be surprising if they hadn't attended the meetings and taken part in the fund-raising to assist the Dublin workers. We certainly know that Gilbert Lynch attended the meetings because he described both being there and playing his part as one of the organisers. We don't know exactly what his role was, though as a trade Unionist of Irish descent he is likely to have taken part in any support organisation set up for the strikers, particularly as he was by now a delegate to Stockport Trades Council.

Jim Larkin in Manchester

The strike was led by Jim Larkin, a charismatic speaker who spoke both to galvanise support for the strike, and for socialism. On 14th of September he came to Manchester and addressed a meeting in Alexandra Park called by Manchester and Salford Trades Union Council.

"Mr. James Larkin, the champion of the transport workers of Dublin, paid a visit to Manchester yesterday and gave to a meeting of trade unionists and others in Alexandra Park an account of the origin and meaning of what he termed 'the new noun, Larkinism'. The visit was not quite unexpected, for an unofficial announcement that he would come had been made a day or two before, but officially, from the point of view of the Manchester and Salford Trades and Labour Council, who organised the meeting, his appearance was a surprise.

The meeting, the object of which was to protest against the Dublin 'atrocities', had been summoned for three o'clock in the afternoon, but a sudden heavy downpour of rain necessitated half-an-hour's postponement. Soon after the chairman, Councillor Tom Fox (president of the Trades and Labour Council), and the other speakers had mounted the platform Mr. Larkin, whose liking for the dramatic had already been sufficiently shown in his exploit on the balcony of the hotel in Sackville Street, pushed his way through the crowd. In spite of his latest disguise - a shaven upper lip - he was immediately recognised and invited to the platform. Already the Dublin Trades Council was represented there by Mr. Partridge, president of the Dublin branch of the Amalgamated Society of Engineers and a member of the Dublin City Council, and when it came to the speaking Mr. Partridge took precedence.

He decreed that the troubles in Dublin arose not from a strike or a simple lockout... but from a conspiracy between the representatives of the Government, and the employers to smash trade unionism. How necessary trade unionism was in Dublin he proved by citing the almost incredible case of a girl worker who after a week's work in a factory received ten pence in wages. He went on to denounce the 'drunken frenzy' of the police, and after mentioning specific cases of brutality produced from his breast pocket a broken truncheon. It had been shattered, he said, on the head of an unoffending citizen, and he added, grimly, that the man who used it would not need it again for some time to come.

Mr. Larkin began by apologising for his intrusion without notice, and adding that he was still, in the spirit, across the Channel. He was full of confidence. "When William Martin Murphy (he referred again and again to the head Of the Dublin United Tramway Company in this way) and his hired thugs set out to make good their boast that they will beat Larkinism, they will fail, because to beat Larkinism is to beat the race to which I belong". He was also full of defiance. "I care for no man," he said; "I have a divine mission to make men and women discontented, and no one can stop me carrying on the work for which I was born". In one comprehensive sweep he denounced "sweaters like Jacob," "murderers like Murphy," "Carson and his crew," "Redmond and his crew," a certain Nugent as a "Government spy," Lord Aberdeen as "the meanest thing that ever came from the land of the bannocks," the Trade Unions Congress delegates as persons who should be told to "go to hell" and everybody else he could think of at the moment. "I am out for revolution," he declared; "they can only kill me, and there are thousands more coming after me". From beginning to end the speech was packed with imprecations and abjurations of this kind.

A resolution protesting against the brutality of the Dublin police and demanding an inquiry into the responsibility for their conduct was carried with cheers. Mr. Larkin, as he left the meeting, said he was immediately going back to Dublin".[6]

There was extreme hardship in Dublin with 25,000 without wages, so a huge relief organization was set up from Liberty Hall, the union headquarters in the city, to feed the destitute families. Constance Markievicz was one of the helpers involved in this. Sympathy and support for the strikers must have been immense because on the 26th of September Larkin came to Manchester again to send off the steamer Hare with 250 tons of provisions collected locally. Another way that Larkin proposed that sympathisers outside Dublin could help the workers was by offering to put up the children of strikers. This would have meant that the union members would no longer be forced back to work by the moral pressure not to let their children starve. Strikers and their spouses found it much easier to countenance going hungry themselves than seeing their children without food. This is a scheme that had been used in disputes before, most successfully in 1912 in Lawrence, Massachusetts,

USA during a strike of mill workers led by Big Jim Haywood and the IWW. Here chaperoned children were sent to New York amid such press attention that there was a congressional hearing, the president was involved and the mill owners agreed to the worker's demands. Now, there was no shortage of volunteers, particularly in England and Scotland, to look after children, but the Dublin ITGWU did not reckon with the implacable opposition of large sections of the Irish Catholic hierarchy who saw Larkin as an atheist who was sending Catholic children to protestant households where they would be proselytised and be in danger of losing their faith.

The other ITGWU strike leader to speak in Manchester was James Connolly. He had been born in Edinburgh, of Irish parents, and had spent 7 years in the British Army. He had become an active trade unionist in America before returning to Dublin, where he set up the Irish Socialist Republican Party. Now he was helping Larkin run the strike. Connolly had no time for party politics, despising the Labour Party, believing that real power did not come from parliament but came from the power that workers had if they chose to take control of their work. He therefore believed that workers would only get a fair share of the cake when they joined "one big union" to demand workers control, strike to dispossess the owners and run the work places without the bosses. In this way the bosses and the state would be replaced. Syndicalist beliefs like these were becoming increasingly influential at this time when many union activists were becoming disillusioned by the compromise and corruptibility they saw in union and Labour party leaders.

On 16th November, Larkin again came to Manchester, this time with Connolly. First they went to the socialist Clarion café in Market Street where he was photographed with Big Bill Haywood and other supporters. Haywood was one of the American Trade Unionists who in 1905 had created the Industrial Workers of the World, or IWW, the legendary Wobblies. He said then, "We are here to confederate the workers of this country into a working-class movement that shall have for its purpose the emancipation of the working-class from the slave bondage of capitalism. The aims and objects of this organization shall be to put the working-class in possession of the economic power, the means of life, in control of the machinery of production and distribution, without regard to capitalist masters".[7]

Haywood was so hated and feared by the employers and powerful that he had been set up and arrested for a murder charge only 6 years before; to be acquitted after a famous trial in which his defense lawyer was Clarence Darrow.[8]

There were 5,000 supporters at the Free Trade Hall, while several thousand more, unable to get in, waited in the rain outside. The meeting included the Manchester Clarion Choir who probably opened the proceedings.[9] Connolly was the first speaker, and he told the crowded hall that the working class of Dublin was being slowly murdered.

"Mr James Connolly, of the Dublin Transport workers' union, said that there were in Dublin today, locked out or on strike, 20,000 men and women. Allowing an average of five persons to every adult, 100,000 men women and children, or something like a quarter of the entire population of Dublin, were being slowly and painfully but deliberately and callously starved in order to bend their neck to the yoke of slavery. But he could assure that meeting that now, in the twelfth week of their fight, they were as resolute and as confident as on the first day of the battle".[10]

Larkin then spoke for an hour. This is how the Manchester Guardian described it; "Larkin is something over forty years of age. His plentiful hair is a dusky grey, and over his forehead, until, disarranged by the straying of his fingers, it stands out like the peak of a cap… Standing with a light poise, turning sharply from side to side, gesticulating with outstretched arms frequently but with restraint, speaking with great vehemence and often with anger he carried the conviction of sincerity".

The Manchester Guardian reported the speech in considerable detail. It wrote that Larkin began by countering attacks from the Irish Catholic hierarchy that the union was planning to send the Catholic children of strikers to the families of Protestant supporters for holidays during which attempts would be made to undermine their faith. He then gave examples of attacks on strikers and police brutality, and ended by appealing for support from the British trade union movement in terms of industrial action rather than just sending money.

"It is time we woke up. If you are going to disgrace your unions and your labour by telling us you are friendly and are going to give us the money - damn you and your money. We don't want it. We want you to carry out the fundamentals of trade unionism. Don't scab on us as organised men. If the scabs handle goods in Dublin, are you going to handle them when they arrive here in Manchester or Liverpool? (Some cries of "No").

There is a man there, Mr. Ben Tillett; one of the pioneers of the trade union movement. They sacrificed 52,000 dockers to try to destroy him. They took stuff out of London and into London by trade union labour, and they left the poor dockers - the best men in the world - with their children starving. They got them beaten by a class that has neither soul to be saved nor body to be kicked. But whatever London struck at Dublin struck at. There never was a boat out of the port of London worked in Dublin during the strike. Now it has come our time in Dublin to be offered up as a sacrifice to Mammon, to capitalism. Are you going to allow it to go on? - (No). Then if you don't, send a message to the men who are your leaders and tell them – "We object. The employing class in Dublin will not get any help from this side of the water" - (Cheers).

I thank you. I hope you will appreciate that I am speaking under tremendous stress in this matter of feelings that you cannot understand.

Every man, woman, and child who is hungering in Dublin is sending into my soul a stab every minute, every hour I live. And the men and women who are lying in gaol in Dublin, I am with them, and I want them to get out. If you have any regard for me - you cheered me, but I know it is not for me; it is the things I stand for - send out tonight an apostle - go to your unions, you who are leaders, and tell them that this unholy compact with the capitalist class is to be broken down. We will no longer destroy ourselves by destroying our fellow trade unionists in Dublin. You send us money. We do not thank you for it. It is your duty. - (Cheers). If I were to attempt to thank you in the name of the Dublin workers you would feel insulted. You would do more if you could. You can do what I ask you; not hands in pockets alone - it is a good idea in one way - but get forward to your branch and hands up and vote for the men, women, and children in Dublin, and you will stand by them to the death. As Shelley says:-

Rise like lions after slumber
In unvanquishable number—
Shake your chains to earth like dew,
Which in sleep had fallen on you—
Ye are many—they are few.

We are many. The Murphys, the Guinnesses, the Jacob's are few. If I had time - on some other occasion - I would like to outline for you: the line of the new advance. What I suggest is co-operation in our unions and outside organisations; no rent in time of strike, and when once a strike is finished make the employer pay you for every hour you have been locked out or on strike. Now I am closing.

I felt that I ought to say these things to you. I hope you will make a resolution and carry it out - not a paper one, but one in the heart, - and put your whole soul and body into it. You women, don't forget what I told you about that girl in Hyde Park. Fight like you ought to fight. Fight like women. Good luck to you, until I see you again. - (Loud cheers)."[11]

After the meeting Larkin spoke in the street to several thousands more. Gilbert recounted his memories of seeing both James Connolly and Jim Larkin. "The meeting was held in the evening, just at knocking-off time. We had engaged the Free Trade Hall, but the hall was packed before either Jim Larkin or Connolly arrived. There was, however, a large open-air space in Peter Street. It was a kind of natural amphitheatre - there was a large open space in the centre, and then sliding sides. We decided to utilise this for the overflow meeting, and we were able to get hold of a lorry and put it in along with chairs.

James Connolly addressed this meeting, and that gave one an opportunity of seeing the difference between these two men. The crowd was all round the square, and James Connolly was a quiet, logical man, basing his speech on the rights of workers to organise in order to obtain a decent standard of life. He dealt with the

55

history of the dispute and the difficulties they were beset with. Eventually Jim Larkin came. One saw immediately that Jim Larkin was really the man they came to see, and he was entirely different to James Connolly. And as soon as he came in he called the crowd, and they all came round him. It was a tremendous meeting, one of wonderful enthusiasm, and no doubt the visit to Manchester was responsible for the sum of money that was raised in that city in the trade unions".[12]

The Manchester Guardian was at the same meeting. "The measure of the personality of Mr. Larkin was to be seen in the effect his appearance yesterday caused in the City. A wet and cold day revealed Manchester in a peculiarly disagreeable outdoor mood. Ordinarily the centre of the town would have been deserted. Yesterday it was filled. Even at noon there were strongly flowing currents of people, movements and shiftings of men and women, which increased hour by hour into a huge concourse which crowded the streets. Long before Mr. Larkin appeared the crowd had congregated as nearly as they could get to the Free Trade Hall. The hall itself could, of course, hold no more.

The first one saw in the street of Larkin himself was that of a man among a little group of half-a-dozen hurrying by way of a side street to the meeting. He was an easily distinguishable figure by his height and his carriage, taller than Mr. Haywood, even, 'Big Bill' of Idaho, more energetic apparently, than Mr. Ben Tillett who walked by his side.

The Peter Street pavements were thronged on both sides, and several thousands of people had congregated in the pit of a playground in Bridge Street. They had been waiting ever since the doors closed at the beginning of the meeting in the Free Trade Hall. Hundreds more followed him down to the open-air meeting. He was welcomed with a strident roar as the car stopped, and in a moment he stood on a wooden chair, pouring out passionate to pleadings coupled with denunciations. It was one of the strangest of scenes; a black mass of people, running down the rims of a sort of miry well surrounded by rows of old houses, whose rooms were lighted dimly by yellow lamps that shone through the open windows and showed obscure figures leaning out to catch what Mr. Larkin was saying. His voice in the open air had the quality of being directed to each separate person. Almost every sentence evoked responses; cries, encouragements, sometimes protests, that he answered as if he were standing at the spot from which each came. He asked the people never to believe that he an Irishman and a Catholic would take any part in the proselytising of children.

"Who am I?" he cried. "I am James Larkin, son of James Larkin, the son of Barney Larkin, of County Armagh. Ask my accusers for yourselves- Send them over to face me in Dublin". He went on in the darkness and the rain, and the people cheered to the last moment. They tramped off again through the rain after his car as it disappeared into the maze of old streets that lie behind Deansgate".[13]

It is very likely that Liam, Larry and Redmond would have been in the audience, as well as Gilbert Lynch, and would have seen Larkin and Connolly when they came to Manchester. I cannot imagine that anyone from Dublin, involved in Irish republicanism would have chosen to miss it.

End of the Lockout

Although supporters, and trade unions, all over Britain collected large sums for relief in Dublin, the trade union leadership never agreed to the sort of sympathy action that Larkin and Connolly were asking for. Increasingly during the winter of 1913 and 1914 the Dublin Trade Unionists were beginning to trickle back to work and admit defeat, having been starved into submission. Those who could get back into work accepted what conditions they could get, but many couldn't and remained on a blacklist. Many felt betrayed by the British TUC leadership, who they felt could have taken industrial action or 'blacked scab goods' in solidarity.

In March 1914 the Manchester Guardian drama and music section included, "Miss Delia Larkin, who is bringing the Irish Workers' Dramatic Company to the Cooperative Hall in Downing Street Manchester, on Monday, as a sister of Mr James Larkin, and all the members of her company are members of the Irish Transport and General Workers Union. Miss Larkin is popular in Dublin, where, in company with Countess Markievicz, she organised a food depot for the families of the strikers. This is the first time that members of a trade union have set up a theatrical company for the purpose of obtaining funds for the relief of strikers, but not the first on which help has been given to strikers by actors and actresses. The Abbey Theatre has already given a matinee in Dublin in aid of the strikers".[14]

The lock-out finally ended in early 1914, after widespread claims of police brutality against strikers. One result of this was that James Connolly, (Larkin's deputy) and Captain Jack White created the Irish Citizen Army to defend demonstrators from the police.[15] During the lockout, strikers felt the need to defend themselves against police violence, so they had set up a workers' militia. After the strike ended in 1914 it continued to drill and it became the Irish Citizen Army which was to play a significant part in the Easter Rising of 1916. Similarly, some pipe bands, such as the Fintan Lalor Pipe Band, subsequently felt the need to be protected by supporters with hurley sticks.[16]

The lockout also had a profound effect on the thinking of many of the nationalists making it impossible for them to ignore labour and class issues in their dreams of a free Ireland. While the hated boss, William Martin Murphy, was a Nationalist and had been an Irish Party MP, the lockout had a radicalising effect on many in the IRB, such as Tom Clarke and Padraig Pearse. Pearse contrasted the horrendous poverty of the workers as compared with the loafing of the elite; "after this he showed an inclination towards a cautious socialism, which - however naïve - gave Connolly an inkling of hope..."[17]

The 'Great Unrest' and Syndicalism

This strike was not an isolated occurrence in a time of peace and tranquility. There is a myth that Britons lived in an idyllic sepia 'summer of croquet on the lawn' and happy farm labourers, cheerfully gathering the harvest singing folk songs, until their comfortable lives were destroyed forever by the First World War. In fact, industrial discontent was so prevalent that many of the ruling class feared that a revolution was a possibility. Industrial unrest dominated the four or so years before the First World War and there was large growth in trade union membership. In 5 years, membership practically doubled, particularly for unions representing unskilled workers. Unions in the past had often been dominated by the skilled and comparatively better paid workers who were often intent on preserving their respectable positions. Now these were being superseded in the public eye by much larger organisations intent on getting a better deal for the poorer 'unskilled' workers.

Many of the more politically committed trade unionists were committed to the syndicalist belief that the emancipation of the working class must be achieved by their direct industrial action rather than by putting any faith in politicians, or union leaders. They campaigned for all workers to unify throughout each industry and confront their bosses using sympathetic strikes until control of the economy had been forced out of the hands of the owners and into those of the workers. They believed in workers' control as a way of replacing capitalism and running a new society rather than as something to be achieved within the existing society.

In 1911 there were national strikes among dockers, seamen and railway workers. In 1912 mine workers were striking, and in 1913 there was a strike of less skilled workers amongst the metal workers in the Black Country. In each of the 5 years leading up to war there were four times as many work- days lost through strikes than had been normal in the previous decade. Perhaps more significant than the number of people taking part in official disputes, were the number of strikes that were rank and file revolts against agreements signed by the trade union leaders with the employers. These were symptomatic of a growing mood of rebelliousness among a significant section of the working classes.

Partly this had been a response to a fall in real incomes for working people, as rises in wages failed to keep up with prices. However this did not explain the vehemence of so many of the strikes, or the fact that so many were taken against the advice of the union leaders. Although many of the industrial militants were affected by the ideas of syndicalism, this can hardly have been the case for the millions of workers who took part in strikes. George Dangerfield believed, "The workers did not want to be safe anymore: they had been repressed too long. And so the deepest impulse in the great strike movement of 1910 -1914 was an unconscious one, an enormous energy pressing up from the depths of the soul…"[18]

Lloyd George spoke in parliament on 8 May 1912 on the causes of the unrest. "First of all, or course, is the question of wages. Secondly, and I am not sure that it is almost as large a cause for unrest, there is the feeling that the conditions of life are not worthy of the dignity of men who are clamouring for improvement. And, thirdly, there is the feeling that they are not treated, under certain conditions, as if they were men possessing a mind of their own, but as if they were purely the creatures of the particular management..."[19]

A leading journalist Brian Gibbs described what the period felt like to him. "Underneath our gay social life with its pleasure and pageantry and sport - the Boat Race, the Epsom races, Henley, Ascot, Cowes, cricket at Lord's, the massed mobs at professional football matches, tennis tournaments, music and mirth at the White City - to all of which I went, not for fun, but as an observer and recorder of contemporary life with critical but not hostile eyes there were signs and sudden outbreaks of ugly conflict. The Welsh miners rioted at Tonypandy. I saw them marching down the Rhondda valley. I saw baton charges not pleasant to see. There was a general strike in Liverpool to which I was sent. It was as near to a revolution as anything I had seen in England. It started with a strike of the transport workers, and spread to other unions who declared sympathetic strikes. For many weeks - nearly three months - nothing moved in Liverpool. The dockers did not handle any cargoes. The railway porters came out. The tramway-men were idle. Even the road sweepers declined to work. Some troops were sent into the city to maintain order but increased disorder because they were stoned by the strikers and were not allowed to fire in self- defense. They had to retreat under showers of kidney stones with which the mob armed themselves. The situation was alarming and not without brutality among the strikers, whose passions were aroused".[20]

The government's chief negotiator George Askwith was in Hull during 1911 and he quoted a town councilor saying that, he had been in Paris during the Commune and had "never seen anything like this... he had not known there were such people in Hull - women with hair streaming and half nude, reeling through the streets, smashing and destroying". Ackwith said "There are only 80,000 troops available for the purpose, and the territorials cannot be trusted".[21]

"It is strange to have such experiences in England. We are living in a new world... More works are being closed down every day. More trains are being taken off the railways. The whole machinery of national life is slowly stopping..."[22]

"That the present unrest will cease I do not believe for a moment; it will increase, and probably increase with greater force. Within a comparatively short time there may be movements in this country coming to a head which recent events have been a small foreshadowing".[23]

Ernest Bevin, a Bristol dockers' activist at the time (later to be government minister), remembered those times, "It was a period which, if the war had not broken out, would have, I believe, seen one of the greatest industrial revolts the world would ever have seen".

Lloyd George had similar expectations. "In the summer of 1914 there was every sign that the autumn would witness a series of industrial disturbances without precedent. Trouble was threatening in the railways, mining, engineering, and building industries, disagreements were active not only between employers and employed, but in the internal organisations of workers. A strong 'rank-and-file' movement, keenly critical of the policies and methods of the official leaders of trade unionism, had sprung up and was gaining steadily in strength. Such was the state of the home front when the nation was plunged into war".[24]

Gilbert Lynch and Socialism

Political leaders and members of the wealthy establishment may have feared that revolt was in the air, but there must have been plenty of radical workers who hoped that they were right. This was a period characterized by a great upsurge in the popularity of Syndicalist and Socialist ideas, so it is entirely appropriate that this is about the time that Gilbert first became a socialist. In 1908 he had been a member of the National League of Young Liberals, but by 1916 he was planning on going to a Clarion national Easter meet, and in early 1917 he joined the Independent Labour Party.

It is hardly surprising that Gilbert became a socialist, being an active trade unionist, and living in times of such political ferment. In 1911 police armed with rifles had marched around Salford at the time of the dock strike[25] and his role on Stockport Trades Council must certainly have involved providing support for strikers. He must surely have taken part in the mass demonstrations in Manchester,[26] and we know he would help organise Connolly and Larkins' meetings during the Dublin lockout.

This is how he described the process. "About this time I made a change as far as my political outlook was concerned. I used to attend meetings in Mersey Square of the ILP. I was still a member of the National League of Young Liberals, but on one occasion the chairman of the meeting, a man named John Hill, who I afterwards knew very well - he was a plumber by profession - offered for sale a number of books. They were half a crown each, and he offered anyone who bought them, if they didn't consider they were good value, the return of the half-crown the following Sunday. I bought a book, but it was not for a considerable time after that I read it. One night when I had nothing to do I started reading it, and became so engrossed in it that I stayed up all night reading it. It was 'The Ragged Trousered Philanthropists' by Tressell. Tressell was a nom de plume, and the author was a house painter - a trestle is used by paper hangers. He told the story of a crowd of men working in a house. It was the most human document that I have ever read - I could laugh and cry while reading it…"[27]

The Ragged Trousered Philanthropists was first published in Britain in late 1914, so Gilbert must have been introduced to it after this date. The author had been born in Dublin, and before he settled in Hastings, had worked as a painter and decorator in South Africa during the 2nd Boer War where he had some involvement with the Irish Brigade which was fighting against the British.[28]

"This set me thinking, and eventually I became a member of the Independent Labour Party and subsequently became secretary of the Central Branch and propaganda secretary for the sub-federation".[29]

Gilbert Lynch put his socialism into words a decade later in terms which could almost have come out of 'The Ragged Trousered Philanthropists'. "Capitalism is nothing more nor nothing less than a huge book-keeping system by which a worker is robbed of the fruit of his labours. Labour creates the whole of the wealth, even the natural resources are only potential wealth until such times as labour power is expended upon it, and then it becomes real wealth. Thus, we claim that all those who render useful and necessary services are entitled to a fair share, not only of the necessities of life, but also the luxuries of life".[30]

By about 1914, Gilbert had discovered the three main ideas that he was to live by and combine for the rest of his life. He was always to be a devout Catholic, a socialist and an Irish nationalist. Larkin and Connolly also both combined Catholicism and political radicalism.

Gilbert explained his attitude in 1926; "Perhaps I will be forgiven if while kneeling there I let my thoughts wander a little from the ceremony to the world we are told was created by the same Christ for us all. I thought of the thousands, nay millions, of fellow beings, hungry for want of food, cold for want of clothing and boots to wear, and weary for somewhere to rest, and I thought of the shops and warehouses filled with enough to fill all those wants and leave a big surplus behind. Surely there is something wrong here... Oh God, when will these people lift the scales from their eyes and realise that the Architect of this Universe created these things of nature for us all and not for a privileged few".[31]

When Gilbert discovered socialism, politics was not simply a matter of putting a cross in a box every few years. To radicals it offered an entirely new understanding of the world, and a new culture, and a new series of activities and entertainments to fill up their leisure time. Perhaps the first of these that Gilbert came across were the Clarion clubs; Gilbert said that he was thinking of going with friends to the Clarion national meet over Easter 1916. The Clarion was a national socialist newspaper which was based on the teachings of Robert Blatchford, the author of Merrie England. Blatchford had begun by being apprenticed as a brush maker, but had made his living as a journalist, and had lived in Manchester, where he'd been convinced of the necessity of socialism by seeing poverty and reading books by William Morris and Henry Hyndman. He insisted that he'd never read Marx, and that his socialism is based on 'humanity and common sense'. He always took great pains to emphasise the Englishness of his writings; a tendency to jingoism that was never far from the surface. Nevertheless, he introduced socialism to probably more British people at the time than anyone else, and his clear jargon-free explanation of the workings of capitalism is a wonder to read. But the Clarion was much more than a newspaper. It launched a whole network of organisations, some of which still exist a century later. At the time there were the Clarion cycling clubs, Clarion scouts, vocal unions, fellowships, handicraft clubs, children's clubs and rambling clubs. There was also in Manchester a Clarion Café, at 50a Market Street, in which Larkin and Connolly were photographed in 1913. Stockport had had a Clarion Drama group running since 1910, which was still in existence in 1914.

The Clarion Cycling club was particularly active in the Manchester area. Harry Pollitt remembered his time with the Clarion Cyclists; "In my spare time I used to go out with the Openshaw Clarion Cycling club, and a grand bunch of comrades they were. I have heard a lot of scoffing at fellowship but in this club it was a reality which made hard poverty stricken young lives much brighter.

Every Sunday morning when I was not speaking, off we would go… It was mainly into the little Cheshire villages that we went, and just before dinner-time Harry Fisher would cry; 'All off, and give them ten minutes of the gospel'. Most of the Club members were also in the Margaret Street choir, and either Harry Fisher or Jim Crossley (who was always a kind of elder brother to me) would lead off the song, which was generally:

In youth as I lay dreaming, I saw a country fair,
Where plenty shed its blessings round
And all had equal share.
Where poverty's sad features
Were never, never seen,
And idlers in the brotherhood
Would meet with scant esteem.

This singing made people stop, and then I would give a ten minute speech. Very few ever stopped to listen, but we felt we had done our duty. We would wind up with 'England, Arise!', and on our way we'd go.

Returning in the evening, we would repeat the performance on another village green. Grand Times!" [32]

Clarion cyclists could extend their itineraries by staying out overnight at Clarion club houses such as the one at Handforth near Wilmslow which could accommodate 50 'Clarionettes' in four dormitories. Here, "Artists, lawyers, doctors rubbed shoulders with miners and little piecers, all linked by the common ideal and their faith in socialism".[33]

Stockport had a Communist Club with 'dainty, bright and charming' rooms at 18 Park Street, Hazel Grove, set up by anarchist communists who defined the communism they were advancing as; "the Free Society of Individuals - based upon the order of equality and liberty of expression, voluntary agreement and social service according to ability, desire and opportunity". Several of their members were to be imprisoned as conscientious objectors during the coming war.[34]

Gilbert was to join the Independent Labour Party (ILP), which also was a centre of a network of activities, and in fact had one of its most well-known figures, a local man, 'Casey the fiddler'. Gilbert must have seen Casey perform because he remembered what a wonderful evening's entertainment he produced with his playing and his talk.[35] I imagine he would have been something of a local celebrity among socialists - a Stockport resident, when he was at home, but usually on the road as a travelling musician, entertainer, humourist, and political lecturer. There are adverts for his performances in most weeks' issues of the ILP paper, the Labour Leader, in the years when Gilbert was discovering socialism. For example on the Sunday the 10th of January 1916, at 8 pm, 'CASEY' AND HIS FIDDLE- 'The Soul of Ireland in Music' was appearing at St Martin's Hall in Liverpool. It was organised by Liverpool Independent Labour Party. The tickets cost 6d and 3d. This was the evening entertainment to follow the General Meeting that took place in the afternoon in the Clarion Cafe.

A few weeks later Casey was in South Wales, with his regular accompanist Dolly, giving a lecture recital on music and politics. The review from the Merthyr Pioneer showed how successfully he had adapted the repertoire for the audience.

"Casey and Dolly - An appreciation.

Known throughout the country by repute (or as 'Casey' would say, by notoriety) these friends paid a visit to the I.L.P. Hall on Wednesday last, February 2nd, and were received by a crowd, which filled the hall to over flowing. Many had come undoubtedly out of curiosity, while some of the supposedly deeper thinkers had come to see what possible connection there could be between politics and music... With his racy delivery of his anecdotes, he, perhaps, clouds the serious truth that lies in his remarks, but listening to him while he traced the old folk songs of these islands to their fountain head, and found that these old strains were but the expression of a folk under oppression, me-thought I listened to a historian of the new or oldest age, where father and mother handed to their young the store of their acquired knowledge and experience. These thoughts came to me as I listened to his story, his introduction, and his quips and jests while he tuned his fiddle. But I wish to emphasise another side of this gaunt old hero who has fought his way through life with no ally save his inherent good humour. I wish to render him homage as a musician... Judged as a purely musical turn, it compared with the best and most refined product of our variety. Perhaps it could not be compared with some of our operatic productions, because it was not dry and stodgy enough, and, forsooth, 'Casey' is not of the class which is obliged to 'study' music; he lives it and makes it live... We had first a selection of fine loose ends of the 'birth period' of music, such as 'An Irish Lament', 'Emigrants' Song', 'Plough Whistle', and an 'Arran Island Song'. Developing from them came ballad selections and folk songs such as 'Jacobite Song', 'Erin the Teaa - and the Smile', some Welsh and Scottish Airs, Lillibullero and an Irish Rebel Song... His last three items would have satisfied even the most rigorous musical critic or professor... and let me say here that his last selection from Mendelssohn was extremely difficult, that he played from memory - and that he had his audience with him all through. There is one other thing I should like to touch upon that is the excellent, understanding between violinist and pianist... In a word, then the whole was in every way an excellent evening's entertainment; as a musical treat, as a political propaganda meeting, and as a pleasure giving turn it was par excellence".[36]

Casey was the stage name of Walter Hampson, who was a writer for the Labour Leader, the ILP newspaper. He had been born in Dublin in about 1865 and moved to Stockport with his parents when he was a child.[37]

He said that when he was eight, he had been started as a 'climbing boy' in his father's chimney-sweep business, often having to rise before four to clean chimneys before school. He wrote about climbing chimneys for his father and 'Old Snake'. "... it is now fifty years since my father, 'Old Snake' and myself went to work one night at my Lord Newton's mansion Lyme Hall, Disley. I was the hero of the evening. I was going to be initiated into the mysteries of the old hall chimneys. No one but my father and 'Old Snake' knew of the perils and dangers which the raw child must be taught. For three years had I climbed common people's chimneys, and the skill and ability acquired by years of practice were now to receive their reward...

My disciplinarian dad was determined that the final test of endurance must be the kitchen, and I dreaded it, because the old sweeps had told of men and boys in bygone days who had vanished into it, but never came out. 'Snake' put me down tenderly upon a large hob, and went back to the entrance hall to bring the cloths and brushes. As I sat on the hob I heard the hurried pattering of feet trotting down the corridor. Suddenly 'Snake's' voice roared out of the silent night, 'Jawl the loo! Duchess' (Climb the chimney, the dog is making for you). Duchess was a huge Lyme Hall dog which had worried scores of sheep, and was dreaded by every poacher from Macclesfield to Buxton. The hall porter, Bob Gosling had forgotten to lock her up. 'Snake's' warning came just in time, for the huge monster placed both paws on the bars and howled horribly. 'Snake' pulled the kitchen door to, locking us both in; but I was well out of reach. The hall porter came and took Duchess out of the room; and 'Snake' carried me down the chimney half dead".[38]

Although Casey did later combine working as a sweep with playing music, his first love was music, and that is how he chose to make a living for the rest of his life. "My first master was a thoroughly competent 'kerbstone' artist, or Paganini of the gutter. His stipend was sixpence per hour and refreshment de liquid. My dear old tutor would have been disqualified from joining the York ILP simply because he suffered from a 'Nabbit.' Oft when playing 'The moon Behind the Hill' he would completely spoil the effect by suddenly asking 'Have yez anny beer?'

Whenever I hear of a great artist producing liquid tones I always think of my old master and 'Have yez anny more beer?'"[39]

Casey evidently learnt his lessons well from the 'tutor with the 'nabbit' because he worked as a musician in various orchestras in the North of England, and was leader of the Stockport Theatre Royal Orchestra. This was the theatre where Liam's aunt had worked in the evenings. Casey was also sacked from various orchestras for demonstrating his politics with a sandwich board. In 1905 the Clarion announced that the 'Stockport fiddler and humourist' was to take to the road and give concerts and 'Socialist lantern lectures.' He continued travelling whilst writing for left publications for most of the rest of his life. At one point he had emigrated to Canada, and returned a year later at his mother's request. He played for marionette shows, and travelled to Scandinavia and South America. He was described as 'A lovable, whimsical, elfish character with a streak of genius, a kindly, generous, happy go lucky personality that one met in all sorts of strange places to who Socialism was not merely a matter of everyday politics but a striving towards the beautiful that was expressed in the philosophy of William Morris and Bruce Glasier'.[40]

Casey's writings and talks were a mixture of humour and serious politics in the same way that his shows balanced light and heavy music, entertainment, emotion and the lecture. He also expressed opposition to the war with a wry humour that, according to the reviewer, carried the audience with it.

"Casey's titbits between the selections were gems of genius… Herod, he regarded as a pioneer among rulers, because all the boys in Bethlehem were slayed before they reached their two years of age. Today the people fed and clothed, educated and loved them until they were eighteen when at the bid of our modern rulers they were sacrificed on the altar en mass".[41]

Gilbert Lynch and the Police

When he was about 17, and living in Stockport, Gilbert was awarded a medal by the police. "Another thing, when I was a young lad, about 17, the local policeman happened to be in trouble and was attacked by three burglars and I was passing and he called for assistance and I helped him and caught one of the burglars for the policeman; I got a a gold medal and chain then and on account of that I got more facilities than anybody else".[42] This gold watch was to prove very useful in the future.

1 Lynch, Gilbert; ed O Cathasaigh, Aindrias; The life and times of Gilbert Lynch; Irish Labour History society. 2011; Dublin

2 Lynch, Gilbert; ed O Cathasaigh, Aindrias; The life and times of Gilbert Lynch; Irish Labour History society. 2011; Dublin

3 Lynch, Gilbert; ed O Cathasaigh, Aindrias; The life and times of Gilbert Lynch; Irish Labour History society. 2011; Dublin

4 Lynch, Gilbert; ed O Cathasaigh, Aindrias; The life and times of Gilbert Lynch; Irish Labour History society. 2011; Dublin

5 Lockout centenary 1913-2013 website. Accessed Jan 2015. At http://www.lockout1913.ie/the-history

6 Manchester Guardian 13 Sept 1913

7 From Bill Haywood Wikipedia . accessed July 8 2015 at http://en.wikipedia.org/wiki/Bill_Haywood

8 Wikipedia article on Big Jim Haywood. http://en.wikipedia.org/wiki/Bill_Haywood

9 Salveson, Paul; Socialism with a Northern accent: Radical traditions for modern times. Lawrence and Wishart. London 2012.

10 Manchester Guardian 17 Nov 1913

11 Manchester Guardian 17 Nov 1913

12 Lynch, Gilbert; ed O Cathasaigh, Aindrias; The life and times of Gilbert Lynch; Irish Labour History society. 2011; Dublin

13 Manchester Guardian 17 Nov 1913

14 Manchester guardian March 21 1914.

15 Various histories of the lockout, its support in Manchester, and the citizen army. eg Newsinger, John, .Jim Larkin and the Great Dublin Lockout of 1913. Bookmarks, London 2013.; Herbert, Michael, The wearing of the green. A political history of the Irish in Manchester, Irish in Britain Representation Group. London 2001.

16 Fintan Lalor Pipe band, History. Web site. Not signed or dated. Retrieved Nov 2013 .at http://flpb.ie/index.php/history/

17 Townshend, Charles. Easter 1916, the Easter rebellion. Penguin London 2005

18 Dangerfield, George. The strange death of liberal England. Serif. London . 1912.

19 Lloyd George quoted in Brown, Geoff, intro. The industrial socialist. Spokesman books, Nottingham 1974

20 Gibbs,Philip, The pageant of the years. London 1946 quoted in Brown, Geoff, intro. The industrial syndicalist. Spokesman books. 1974 Nottingham,

21 Askwith, Lord, Industrial problems and disputes, London 1920 quoted in Brown, Geoff, ed. The industrial syndicalist. Spokesman books. 1974 Nottingham.

22 Chamberlain, Austen quoted in Brown, Geoff, ed. The industrial syndicalist. Spokesman books. 1974 Nottingham.

23 Askwith, Lord. Industrial problems and disputes, London 1920 quoted in Brown, Geoff, ed. The industrial syndicalist. Spokesman books. 1974 Nottingham.

24 Lloyd George, David quoted in Horton Jim. War on the home front- class struggles in Britain. Socialism today. Issue 180. July/Aug 2014

25 Photo at digital Salford. Accessed 8 Aug. 2015 at http://www.salford.photos/2015/06/armed-police-march-in-salford-1911/

26 Salveson, Paul; Socialism with a Northern accent: Radical traditions for modern times. Lawrence and Wishart. London 2012.

27 Lynch, Gilbert; ed O Cathasaigh, Aindrias; The life and times of Gilbert Lynch; Irish Labour History society. 2011; Dublin

28 There is disagreement as to whether he fought –see Harker, Dave. Tressell, the real story of the Ragged Trousered Philanthropists. Zeb book. London 2003

29 Lynch Gilbert ; ed O Cathasaigh, Aindrias; The life and times of Gilbert Lynch; Irish Labour History society. 2011; Dublin

30 Speech Lynch made in 1925, quoted on page 7 of Lynch, Gilbert;e d O Cathasaigh, Aindrias; The life and times of Gilbert Lynch; Irish Labour History society. 2011;Dublin

31 Article written by Lynch 1926, quoted on page 7 of Lynch, Gilbert;ed O Cathasaigh, Aindrias; The life and times of Gilbert Lynch; Irish Labour History society. 2011;Dublin

32 Pollitt, Harry. Serving my time. Laurence and Wishart. 1976. London.

33 Coates, Mabel and Colin. quoted in Salveson, Paul; Socialism with a Northern accent: Radical traditions for modern times. Lawrence and Wishart. London 2012.

34 Heath, Nick, Anarchists against World War I: two little known events- Abertillery and Stockport at libcom.org accessed 8 Aug 2015 at https://libcom.org/history/anarchists-against-world-war-one-two-little-known-events- abertillery-stockport

35 Lynch, Gilbert; ed O Cathasaigh, Aindrias; The life and times of Gilbert Lynch; Irish Labour History society. 2011;Dublin

36 Merthyr pioneer 5 feb 1916.

37 1881 and other censuses

38 Hampson, Walter (Casey) , Old Snake, in A wandering Minstrel I. 2nd ed Deveron Press, Turriff. Undated.

39 Hampson, Walter (Casey) , Fiddle- felicities, in A wandering Minstrel I. 2nd ed Deveron Press, Turriff. Undated.

40 Obituary of Casey form Forward quoted in Devine, Francis. Casey! Will the real Walter Hampson please stand up? Saothar Vol 33 (2008) pp 115-118

41 Merthyr pioneer 17 feb 1917

42 Gilbert Lynch pension application MSP34REF41334

.

1. Liam Parr

2. Tenement residents in Hoey's Court, 1901.

3. Eamonn Ceannt.

4. Constance Markievicz .

5. Fianna Eireann Council. Con Colbert front right.

6. Bulmer Hobson.

7. Sheila O'Hanlon.

8. Ernest and Ellen Earle outside their shop, probably with daughters May, Doris and Beatrice.

9. George Costello.

10. Maggie, Gus and Alice Bonham.

11. Gilbert Lynch as an older man.

12. *Manchester Clarion Café,1913. From right; James Connolly, Bill Haywood, Williams, Jim Larkin; 2nd from left Ben Tillett.*

13. *James Connolly.*

14. Jim Larkin.

*15. Robert Tressell-Robert Noonan
and Kathleen.*

16. Casey-Walter Hampson.

17. Larry Ryan.

18. Death and the profit ghouls; 'The workers of Europe are being slain in their thousands while devastation, famine and pestilence overshadow their families, in a war entirely directed for the benefit of wealthy exploiters'. From 'Forward', Aug 3rd, 1914.

19. Michael Collins.

20. Joe Plunkett and his wireless apparatus.

21. Annie Cooney.

22. Sackville Street before the rising.

Chapter Five
The Irish Crisis Develops

The Third Irish Home Rule Bill

After a stormy passage through Westminster, the British parliament finally passed the Third Irish Home Rule Bill in 1914. Home rule included a number of significant limitations. A large number of departments were to remain permanently in English hands, including Customs and Excise (about three quarters of the country's revenue), income tax, health insurance and old age pensions, The Board of Works, land annuities, factory and workshop control, the Post office, the police and the army. Irish MPs would remain in London and an English nominated Senate would have the power to delay Irish legislation. Redmond claimed that he had been assured that the legislation would be interpreted in a "friendly way".[1]

In addition opposition among Unionists particularly in the North of Ireland and amongst peers and Conservatives, made it appear less likely that even this level of independence would apply to the whole of Ireland. In September 1912 over two hundred thousand men in Ulster signed a 'Solemn League and Covenant to resist home rule', and a similar number of women pledged to support them. In January 1913, the pledge was made specific by the formation of the Ulster Volunteer Force, an organisation of 100,000 men prepared to fight against 'Home Rule', using arms if necessary. They began drilling with dummy guns, but managed to import considerable quantities of real arms, while the authorities appeared to turn a blind eye.

Nearly a year later, in November 1913, Nationalists in Dublin followed suit and launched the Irish Volunteers to safeguard the promise of Home Rule. Many of the moderate leadership of the Irish Volunteers believed their role was to merely encourage Westminster to keep to their promise of 'Home Rule'. However, many of the more radical Volunteers, particularly in the IRB, believed that London would never devolve meaningful power, and it would never apply to all Ireland, so they hoped the Volunteers could be the beginnings of an army of insurrection to achieve an Irish republic.

Foundation of the Manchester Volunteers

In 1914 Irish Nationalists in Manchester began to form a branch of the Irish Volunteers. It is through the Volunteers that Liam and Gilbert must have met Larry Ryan and Redmond Cox, if they didn't already know them.

Liam's wife Margaret said of Liam, "He was a great Gaelic Leaguer and worked hard for the O'Growney branch whilst here and helped to form the first company of volunteers with Liam Mc Mahon, Seamus Barrett and others".[2]

Liam McMahon was from Limerick but was working as a clerk in Manchester. He had previously lived in Liverpool where he had joined the Gaelic league and the

Gaelic Athletic Association, playing for Lancashire at Hurling. It was on returning to England on the ferry from an all-Ireland Hurling match in 1905, that he was invited to join the Irish Republican Brotherhood.

"When returning to Liverpool on the B. and I. boat I was approached by Paddy Lively. After a short conversation, during which he explained the aims and objects of the IRB, he asked me if I had any religious scruples about becoming a member. I said I had not. There and then, he administered the oath, as we stood by the rails looking out to sea…

About 1909... I was transferred to the Manchester Circle of the IRB. Matt Lawless was the Centre at the time. I also became associated with the Gaelic League and the GAA in Manchester. Sometime later we had a visit from Seán MacDermott about what we had to do. This was about 5 years before the Rising; and of course, his principle object at that time was getting the necessary war materials, and trying to spread the Circles of the Irish Republican Brotherhood. We met at the house of a man named Ó Ríain, in Seedley. There were about fourteen people present, of whom I can only remember Ó Ríain, his son Michael, and a Mr Newman. Of course we did what we could, as regards what Seán MacDermott wanted. From time to time we purchased war material - mostly revolvers and ammunition - and sent it across to Dublin".[3]

It seems pretty certain that the Ó Ríain that he refers to is the father of Larry Ryan, one of the four who would be going from Manchester to join the Easter Rising. We are fortunate that Miceál, the father, filled out a census form at about the same time that Seán MacDermott visited, as it demonstrates very clearly how he saw their identity. It shows a strong Irish Ireland commitment. Not only are all the names written fully and carefully in Irish (which is rare in England) but in the box which asked him to define himself as a British subject, he declined, instead writing 'resident'. The family were living at 13 Tootal Road, Seedley, and recorded are: 50 year old Miceál, his 48 year old wife Máire, 9 children and his 39 year old brother Stephen. Miceál and Stephen had both been born in Waterford Ireland, but Máire was from Liverpool and the children had been born close to where they were now living. Only three of the children were still of school age. Of the rest, one, the girl, was a domestic, three were clerks and one was a locomotive fireman on the Manchester Ship Canal. Miceál's brother was a labourer also on the Manchester Ship Canal. Miceál himself worked as a book keeper and had previously been a warehouseman. Perhaps he had encouraged his children to value numeracy and literacy, as it was unusual in a working class area for such a high proportion of the boys to have, what would now be termed, white collar jobs. Of course there is no mention of what work was done inside the home by Máire, who was looking after a household of 12.[4]

The fifth oldest child on the census was the 18 year old Labrán (otherwise known as Laurence or Larry) who was working as a clerk for a coal merchant. This is very likely to be the same coal merchant named as his employer on his pension application - J Roscoe and Sons - who had a canal haulage business on the Ashton canal. Their canal yard and wharf was situated on Meadow Street wharfs, Piccadilly, on the lower branch of the Ashdown Canal...[5] Larry's mother gave the address of his employer as Liverpool Street, Salford, so perhaps the company had an office on the main road half a mile further west. In either case, Roscoe's was a very small company, so Larry would have been very familiar with both the office and the canal wharf in those years when it was mainly involved with the canal carriage of coal in narrow boats on the Ashton canal.[6]

It is very likely that Larry joined the Manchester Irish Volunteers at the same time as Liam and Gilbert, in 1914.[7]

Gilbert Lynch described joining the first Manchester Company and their trips into the Pennines: "There were 2 coys formed in 1914, but as the two came along they kept strengthening, we were connected in the trafficking of arms over here".[8] [9]

"We used to go out to the surrounding country on Sundays to drill. The railways ran cheap excursions on Sundays, 6d (single) and 9d (return). We often went out in the moors and drilled there. When the war had almost approached, our drill instructor Phelim Kennedy suggested that if the war came the best thing would be to join up. The war wouldn't last more than three months, and in that three months we would all be fully trained soldiers and be of service to Ireland. None of the men accepted this, although many people in Britain were of the same opinion that the war would only last three months".[10]

Much of the volunteers' energies were devoted to acquiring weapons. Gilbert said, "I was collecting arms from 1915 and it was a dangerous job. I was living in Stockport where the local people joined up and at Ardley green, and got contact with local men of Irish extraction, and it was a difficult job because sometimes one had to wait night after night to make contact". He secured some arms through serving soldiers, and helped to get them sent over to Dublin. "Some girls brought some over; a Miss Cox brought some over. She is married at present to Sean Muirthuile".[11]

The Irish Republican Brotherhood in Manchester

The Irish Volunteers had been launched explicitly to safeguard the granting of Home Rule. Although the leader of the Volunteers, Eoin MacNeill, was a well-known moderate, there was, active in the background in the Volunteers, a heavy involvement of the Irish Republican Brotherhood. The IRB, of course, saw the Volunteers as a potential force for an insurrection. As a secret organisation it is hard to be sure who was a member, but Gilbert had sworn his oath and joined in 1913.[12]

The father of Larry Ryan was sworn into the IRB in 1909, by Liam

McMahon, so it would be surprising if his son was not a member by 1916. There appears to be no documentary evidence telling us whether other Manchester area volunteers were members of the IRB. It seems likely that the other volunteers, such as Liam, were politically close to those who were, even if they were not actual sworn members. Redmond Cox was probably a member - he knew to travel to the home of the Conlons in 1916, an address where he must have been privy to secret IRB activity.

1914-18 war begins

When war was declared in 1914 the local newspapers reported widespread enthusiasm, particularly for a war that would be over by Christmas. While it is true that papers can be criticised for having a pro-war axe to grind, and there were very large anti-war demonstrations in the weeks before the declaration, it is probably still reasonable to conclude that the vast majority of the people around Liam and Gilbert were very patriotic to the British cause, and many would have volunteered.

There were contrary voices speaking around Manchester. One of these was Harry Pollitt who had been active in the Clarion Cycling Club around the Openshaw Socialist Hall, and Manchester in general. It is possible that Gilbert might have met Pollitt, as both took part in Clarion activities in the area, but Pollitt's busiest time with the club might have been earlier than Gilbert's.

When Pollitt spoke out against the war, he did not meet with an enthusiastic response; "The Sunday that war was declared found me speaking for the Ashton-under-Lyne Branch of the B.S.P. Jim Crossley and I walked from Openshaw to Ashton, and Jim thought that there might be a little bother at the meeting, as Ashton was a barrack town and there would be plenty of soldiers about... I had never heard at that time anything about what the attitude of a revolutionary should be towards imperialist war; ...but I did understand what war meant, and knew that this war was not a war which the workers could support. I did realise that they ought not to be taken in by the fairy tale about the German eagle having twisted the lion's tail, an insult that only war could wipe out.

The meeting started. There was a fair on the Market Ground, and my platform consisted of a circus cart with high sides; and what a blessing those high sides were to prove before the meeting was finished! There was a big crowd - lots of red-coated soldiers in the audience. A lot of muttering could be heard, but whilst pretending to be blissfully unaware of it, I was only too conscious that a rough-house was in store. As my speech progressed, I became more and more open in my denunciation of the War, calling upon the workers to use the opportunity to make war on capitalism. After about three-quarters of an hour, a big fellow pushed his way to the front and yelled out: "Eh, you silly mugs, letting 'im get away with his gab. Can't you see he's spell-binding you. He sticks up for the Germans. Let's get him out of it! Let's get him off t'cart".

72

That started it. The Chairman and I armed ourselves with the two chairs in the cart, and in this way prevented the angry audience from climbing in to bash us. It was a real rough house while it lasted, and finally two policemen arrived on the spot. They escorted Jim and me to the Openshaw tram, with much fatherly advice not to be b***** young fools and come back again the next night, which was what I had promised the crowd I would do.

(That) meeting never took place. The crowd was there; ready to lynch me if I dared to say a word... The same policeman was there, and once again, gently but firmly, he led me to the tram with lots of advice about kids whose napkins were not yet dry trying to tell the world what it ought to do.

When the Moss Side Branch of the B.S.P. *(British Socialist Party)* proposed that a Liverpool comrade and I should address a meeting outside the Yeomanry Barracks at Brookes Bar, the meeting couldn't take place soon enough for me. When it started, however, it couldn't finish soon enough either!

With my most pleasant smile, I announced that I would say a few words about the War and what the workers ought to do. And those few words were all I did say, for the roar went up of "Bloody German! Pull him off!" etc. I tried to make myself heard above the din, but my eloquence was wafted away unheard on the evening breeze.

Then a young officer had the bright idea of forcing me to render 'God Save the King' as a solo... In my time I have cheerfully attempted 'Nellie Dean' and 'Sweet Adeline', but I was determined that if the heavens fell, God would never save the King in answer to any request of mine.

I was pinioned to the platform by soldiers. "Come on, you. You wanted to talk. Now sing instead". But never a note emerged. Then fists got to work, and some nice footwork which had never been provided for in the Queensberry rules. In the middle of the scrimmage, I noticed a woman forging through the crowd, making a way for herself by lashing out right and left with a very serviceable umbrella. She got through, seized hold of me, the soldiers being too much flabbergasted to interfere, and said, 'Come on, comrade. You come with me'. It has not usually been a practice of mine to heed the invitations of unknown women, but on this occasion I stuck to this one like a limpet, and we finally emerged from the fray. Meanwhile, 'God Save the King' was being lustily and fervently, if untunefully, sung, and my poor 'donkey's bedding' kicked all over the place.

When we got some distance away, the woman said, 'I'm a suffragette, and used to rough handling. Good night and good luck, comrade'".[13]

The 'donkey's bedding' had once been Pollitt's Sunday best straw hat. He was not alone in his opposition, the anarchist communists of the Stockport Communist Club of Hazel Grove were active in the No Conscription Fellowship and their premises were to be raided in 1916.

At the start of the war, John Redmond, the leader of the Irish Parliamentary Party, announced to the House of Commons that the English could count on Irish loyalty. "I will say that it is their duty, and should be their honour, to take their place in the firing line in this contest". The majority of his fellow countrymen agreed, perhaps feeling that a gesture of loyalty would guarantee home rule from a grateful English government.

In 1915 John Dillon, Redmond's deputy, came to Manchester to address a conference of Irish associations, from the South Lancashire area, on the subject of the war. Gilbert was there and discovered that it was really a recruiting meeting for the British army.

"Well, I had studied these pamphlets from the Union of Democratic Control *(written by E.D Morel)*, and after Mr Dillon had given his oration to the effect that we had to go and fight for the liberty of small nations, etc., the audience was asked if they had any comments to make. Well, I had a few lads with me and they asked me to say something. I did - I asked him about the freedom of small nations, the violation of treaties, etc., referring to the leased treaty of (Tsingtao) which had been invaded by the Japanese in support of the allies, and also about Shleswig-Holstein which had been taken from Denmark and so on. It wasn't long before myself and my pals were thrown out on the street, but it did one good thing - it did rally a number of Irishmen against being used for the war effort, and that was a good thing in itself".[14]

More than 90% of the Volunteers in Ireland voted to support their leader's policy, and in the early stages of the war there were large and enthusiastic meetings in support of the war.

The minority were, however, vociferous and active. Their ranks were drawn from either the politically-conscious socialists, or from the more extreme Irish Ireland nationalists. The rump of the volunteers stated that "Ireland cannot, with honour or safety, take part in foreign quarrels otherwise than through the free action of a National Government of its own." More directly, the Fianna scouts ran an anti-recruiting campaign involving upsetting the stages of recruiting posts and heckling recruiting sergeants. They papered Dublin with posters saying, 'Irishmen beware. Enlistment in England's armed forces is treachery to Ireland'.[15]

Connolly had long been predicting war, and when it came he asked, "What should be the attitude of the working class democracy of Ireland in the face of the present crisis...? I know of no foreign enemy in this country except the British Government... Should the working class of Europe, rather than slaughter each other for the benefit of kings and financiers, proceed tomorrow to erect barricades all over Europe, to break up bridges and destroy the transport service that war might be abolished, we should be perfectly justified in following such a glorious example, and contributing our aid to the final dethronement of the vulture classes that rule and rob the world… Starting thus, Ireland may yet set the torch to a European conflagration that will not burn out until the last throne and the last capitalist bond and debenture will be shrivelled on the funeral pyre of the last war lord". [16]

Cathal O'Shannon said that Connolly's first reaction to the news of the war was to say that a blow for Irish Independence must now be struck. This is the policy he persistently advocated until Easter 1916. "As an Irish worker I owe a duty to our class, counting no allegiance to the Empire… You have been told that you are not strong, that you have no rifles. Revolutions do not start with rifles; start first and get your rifles after. The curse is our belief in our weakness. We are not weak, we are strong. Make up your mind to strike before your opportunity goes". [17]

The IRB supreme Council had also decided that an uprising must happen while Britain's military forces were distracted by war. Accordingly they warned IRB circles in mainland Britain to be prepared. Cathal O'Shannon was sent to Glasgow around New Year in 1915. "He stated that the ground was being prepared for a rising in arms against the British Government and that we were to hold ourselves in readiness for any eventually; that as soon as the time was opportune a rising would take place". [18] It seems highly likely that IRB members in Manchester would have had a similar message.

Public opinion began to slip away from the war enthusiasts as the casualty numbers mounted. In addition, poverty increased as food and fuel prices began to rise rapidly at a time of a pay-freeze and continuing high unemployment. On top of this the Pope issued an encyclical in July 1915 calling on Christians to make peace, and denouncing the war as futile.

Conscription

For the first 18 months of the War, the manpower needs of the forces had been satisfied by recalling reservists and by exhorting volunteers to join up. Of course none of Liam Parr, Gilbert Lynch, Larry Ryan or Redmond Cox would have considered volunteering to fight for the British, but now they were at risk of being called up, as conscription was being introduced for single British (and Irish) men living on the mainland of Britain. It was not to apply in Ireland, although it had been considered. The law came into operation on 10th February 1916, so all four of them would be expecting their call up papers, if they hadn't already received them.

Many Irishmen, fearing conscription, simply sailed away from England, but some did not find it easy. In November 1915 the Cunard and White Star lines refused to allow 700 Irishmen to board ships in Liverpool bound for America. The ship owners felt it was their patriotic duty to refuse to carry men they felt should be at the front, and they were backed up by Redmond, the leader of the Irish Parliamentary Party, who said it was "very cowardly of them to try to emigrate". The men were defended by the Bishop of Limerick who defended the men's decision not to fight. "…they have no burning desire to die for Serbia… Their crime is that they are not ready to die for England. Why should they? What have they or their forebears ever got from England that they should die for her?"[19]

Many Irishmen were beginning to decide that it was going to get increasingly difficult to return home. Patrick Kelly was working in a tobacconist's in London, after being blacklisted for taking part in the 1913 lockout.

"In November 1915 conscription in England was almost a certainty. I had a friend in the LMS railway. He informed me one day that his company had received government instructions to hold themselves in readiness to refuse tickets to all men of military age who were attempting to leave the country. I took his tip and resigned my job and got a ticket to Dublin. As I approached Euston Station that evening I was approached by two recruiting officers. They asked me where I was bound for and why I was not in khaki. I said I had just resigned my job and was on my way home to Dublin for a short holiday before joining the Irish Guards. They wished me good luck".[20] On February 1st a warrant was taken out to raid the premises of the 'Workers Freedom Group or Anarchist Club' in Stockport, and pamphlets were seized with titles like 'Down with Conscription' and 'Apes and Patriotism'. [21]

1 O'Brolchain, Honor. Joseph Plunkett-16 Lives. The O'Brien Press.
2 Pension application, Pension administration section. Department of defence. Ireland. Documents re Parr DP9542. Letter to de Valera. Also family statement from his daughter Bernadette Wall that they met through Gaelic league.
3 McMahon, Liam, witness statement WS 274.
4 1911 UK census.
5 Whitehead, Peter J,; The industrial Heritage of Britain- the Ashton canal. Accessed 8 Aug 2015 at http://www.pittdixon.go-plus.net/ac-basin-ancoats/ac-basin-ancoats.htm
6 1911 UK census.; Ryan. Laurence, Pension application DP6862
7 Parr, Liam. Pension application. II/RB/4077
8 Lynch, Gilbert. Pension application MSP34REF41334
9 Letter from Joseph Gleeson dated 4 April 1938 in Gilbert Lynch pension application. MSP34REF41334
10 Lynch, Gilbert; ed O Cathasaigh, Aindrias; The life and times of Gilbert Lynch; Irish Labour History society. 2011; Dublin
11 Lynch, Gilbert, Pension application MSP34REF41334
12 . Lynch, Gilbert; ed O Cathasaigh, Aindrias; The life and times of Gilbert Lynch; Irish Labour History society. 2011; Dublin
13 Pollitt, Harry, serving my Time. Laurence and Wishart. London 1976
14 Lynch, Gilbert; ed O Cathasaigh, Aindrias; The life and times of Gilbert Lynch; Irish Labour History society. 2011; Dublin
15 Norman, Diana; Terrible Beauty, A life of Constance Markievicz. Hodder and Stoughton, London 1987
16 Connolly, James, Various quotes late 1914 from Greaves, C. Desmond. The life and times of James Connolly. Lawrence and Wishart . London 1986.
17 Connolly, James, Various quotes late 1914 from Greaves, C. Desmond. The life and times of James Connolly. Lawrence and Wishart . London 1986.
18 O'Flanagan, Michael. Witness statement . WS 800

19 Townshend, Charles. Easter 1916. The Irish rebellion. Penguin London 2005
20 Kelly, Patrick, witness statement. WS 781
21 Heath, Nick, Anarchists against World War I: two little known events- Abertillery and Stockport at libcom.org accessed 8 Aug 2015 at https://libcom.org/history/anarchists-against-world-war-one-two-little-known-events-abertillery-stockport

Chapter Six
Early 1916

The Manchester Volunteers travelling to Dublin

In Manchester, early in 1916, Liam Parr, Gilbert Lynch, Redmond Cox and Larry Ryan had either been told, or had suspected, that some sort of activity was likely to happen soon in Ireland. They were threatened with being called up to the British army, so had another reason to go to Ireland. If Gilbert had already turned to socialism by this point, then he would have rejected the calls to fight on political grounds. He might have said that this was a war in which worker was pitted against worker, to the benefit of nobody but the bosses- a war in which the bosses in the different capitalist countries squabbled with one another about the sharing of the spoils made from exploiting the colonies of Africa and the East. This was the attitude of many Socialists, particularly James Connolly. The Independent Labour Party, the party which Gilbert subsequently became very active in, was now campaigning vigorously in support of conscientious objectors to conscription. People who objected to being called up were now being sent to their local Military Service Panel to argue their case. The members were chosen usually from the local establishment, and had been briefed to 'recognise only genuine religious or moral convictions'. Men who refused to fight on Socialist grounds received very short shrift.[1] Those who refused on political grounds from Stockport were usually fined 40 shillings and handed over to the military authorities.[2]

Gilbert was very short sighted, but I don't know if that would have rendered him ineligible for military service.

We do not know exactly how and when the Manchester Volunteers were told that a rising was becoming imminent. William Daly described what happened in London. He said, "Conscription was in the air. How were we to circumvent it...?

Coming now to the meeting in January 1916, at St. George's Hall, specially convened for members and their friends. At the close of the meeting I was called in and told the result of it. It was decided that all single men were to go Dublin and await the Day, it being left to ourselves to decide when to travel, Michael Collins, Joe Cassidy and Joe O'Leary, assisting us with our fares &c".[3]

Many volunteers seem to have been members of the IRB and this is how they were informed that something was in the offing.

One of the first to leave was Redmond Cox, a 22 year native of Roscommon who had more recently been living with his sister in Warburton St, Cheetham and working as a grocer's assistant. According to his commanding officer, Cox had lived in Manchester for about nine or ten years when, in February, he returned to Dublin and joined F company of the First battalion.[4] He had probably stayed with Martin Conlon's family at 11 AltinureTerrace, Cabra Park; Mrs Conlon remembered him being there on Easter Monday morning. He didn't join the rest of the Mancunians at Kimmage or North Frederick Street, so he may already have had some acquaintance with the Conlons as they had family in Manchester. [5][6][7]

The next to leave Manchester (as far as we know) was Liam Parr. He caught the train on 25th February 1916, and bought a return ticket to Dublin. When he arrived, he knew where to go as he went to Kimmage Mill at Larkfield, Dublin, where about 80 Irish people from England and Scotland took part in military training and munitions manufacture.[8][9] Here he was with another young man from Manchester, Larry Ryan, whose mother lived at 79 Derby Road, Seedley. We do not know when Ryan travelled to Dublin, only that he was at Kimmage by Easter Monday.[10]

Larkfield Mill, Kimmage - Liam Parr and Larry Ryan

Larkfield Mill was situated a few miles west of the centre of Dublin, and consisted of twelve acres of land housing a nineteenth century stone watermill, a manager's house, some cottages, a barn, out buildings, yards and fields and gardens.

The mill in Kimmage was owned by, or leased to, Josephine Plunkett, a wealthy local landowner. She owned and controlled such a wide portfolio of property in the Dublin area, that when her son Joe offered to help the Union during the 1913 lockout, Jim Larkin declined because, he said, the family were slum tenement landlords. According to his sister Geraldine, Joe was mortified to discover this.[11]

Josephine Plunkett had taken on the lease of Larkfield Mill with the object of generating income by subletting, but in 1914 both her daughter Geraldine, and son Joseph, moved from the family home in Fitzwilliam Street to one of the cottages. Joseph was ill with advanced glandular tuberculosis (TB). By the beginning of 1916, Josephine Plunkett had moved to the USA, and the rest of the large Plunkett family had left the family home in Fitzwilliam Street, and moved to Larkfield House.

Geraldine described it as, "a beautiful middle-sized house containing twelve rooms with a garden full of roses and a hen yard".[12]

Josephine's husband (Count) George Plunkett also came from a family whose wealth had come from property, his father having been a wealthy builder. George became a quiet academic, curator of the national museum of Ireland, and international expert on renaissance art. It was in recognition of these services, as well as for his support for the Little Company of Mary, (a Roman Catholic nursing order) that he was created a papal Count. He rarely chose to flaunt his title.

All the family had long been in the Catholic and nationalist tradition but the sons, in particular Joseph, had become significantly more radical. All three sons, Joseph, George and Jack had joined the volunteers, and by late 1915, Joseph was a member of the IRB Military Council and director of military operations of the Irish volunteers.

80

Larkfield Mill was therefore a useful military base for the volunteers, and had been used as such by the Dublin 4th Battalion since 1914. At one time, before the split in the volunteers, 6000 men gathered in the mill to take part in a route march. After the split in the volunteers, Larkfield was only used by the more militant Irish Volunteers.

During 1915 Joseph Plunket travelled around Europe, supposedly for his health, which was certainly very poor because of TB. He grew a beard in Italy and became 'Johann Peter of San Francisco' and travelled to Berlin where he and Roger Casement met the German Chancellor. With difficulty, they arranged the importation of weapons. That year he also travelled to America to raise money carrying secret documents from the German government hidden inside a hollow walking stick. The customs officials examined the stick but failed to discover the hidden compartment.

Joe had also worked on developing his skills with radio transmission, intending to be able to broadcast the news of an uprising to shipping in international waters. He wanted international news media to hear of a rising before the story was censored by the British authorities. This was a hobby he had had since he was young, and he had been able to transmit Morse code messages for short distances, for some years. Now he was working with Con Keating, a ship's radio operator, and together they hoped to be able to tell the world of the progress of the revolt.

Also in Larkfield, Rory O'Connor and Tommy Dillon (who subsequently married Geraldine Plunkett) were trying to set up a chemical works. Tommy Dillon was a chemistry lecturer, and he and O'Connor were trying to procure a phenol still for the manufacture of explosives.

It had only been a couple of months before Liam arrived that IRB organiser Joseph Gleeson had travelled to Dublin to set up Kimmage as a base for English and Scottish volunteers waiting for the rising.

"It was at a January meeting 1916 of the Supreme Council that we decided on Kimmage and I was sent to Eoin MacNeill and Fitzgibbon to make things right to send the men over. Things were not put right until the men in Kimmage put them right, it was like an old mill. We got men there from Liverpool, Manchester, London, Glasgow and Edinburgh".[13]

The mill had been disused for many years and parts had recently been flooded, so the first job of the 'refugees', as they were usually known, was to make it habitable.

Geraldine Plunkett remembered; "Some of the people who helped us to make dams and trenches to direct the flood were the first of the refugees from conscription, christened 'the Liverpool Lambs' by George. Up to the time the Lambs arrived in Larkfield it was a rather desolate place... Some days Volunteers drilled in the barn. Tommy and Rory O'Connor were still trying to get the tar still for their chemical factory erected. The double-sided, three-storey mill was nearly empty. Suddenly one morning about 40 young men descended on us. Many of them were members of the IRB, or their fathers were, and they had come over to avoid conscription and join the Volunteers. The first serious attempt at conscription had just begun in England. George was put in charge of them and they set up living quarters in the barn. When they got an agricultural boiler and tried to boil a stew in it, George came in to the house to ask me, 'How long does it take to boil potatoes?' I told him three quarters of an hour and he said, 'Well, they should be boiled now, it's three hours since they started'. The poor things knew nothing. Some of them found digs at once and their people sent them money, others had to stay on in Larkfleld and they got better at looking after themselves quite quickly. George said they were a handful and that they grumbled all the time, especially at having to sleep on mattresses on the floor. George stopped the grumbling by giving up his bedroom in the house and bringing his mattress out to the barn to sleep there".[14]

Some of the members of the Kimmage Garrison got work outside (it was never called a garrison at the time, being simply known as Kimmage or Larkfield). Most often members who succeeded in finding jobs would work in the De Selby quarries, where they also gained skills in the use of explosives and managed to acquire some quantities of gelignite. Working outside will have brought in an income which would have been helpful because only some of the 'refugees' had money sent for their keep. It is unclear how nearly a hundred people, appearing from nowhere, were fed, but fed they were, and most remember being well fed. At this time there was no clarity about any of the financial arrangement relating to Larkfield Mill and the Plunkett family. Geraldine, in her memoirs, seems to have been near her wits end trying to look after the ailing Joseph, her other-worldly father, assisting in planning an insurrection and all the while avoiding creditors who were threatening prosecution, and threatening to take over the Mill. Geraldine's mother, who owned at least 60 properties, was in America refusing to be contacted, having left no comprehensible written records. It was obvious that Geraldine needed an astute financial expert to sort out the mess, but it would have to be someone who could be trusted with so many secrets. Her brother Joe suggested that one of the London volunteers might be the man for the job.

"That afternoon a very tired young man - I can still see him - arrived from London and asked for me. This man was slim and of medium height and I thought not remarkable until I looked at his eyes. He was completely honest and direct and it was quite obvious that he was the right man. He was twenty five… This was Michael Collins (we knew him as Mick) and no one ever had a better clerk. He had been a boy clerk in the post office in London, followed by work in a bank and then in a stockbroker's as a stock exchange clerk. I quickly realised that he was far too good for the work I had for him to do but he did not despise it. He was shrewd, serious and downright, very quick and clear. I paid him £1 a week and he took pot luck with the family. For about three months he did a couple of hours' work every day making new rent books, answering letters and filing papers. He had never done this kind of work, which was all related to the family house property, but thanks to his help the property was gradually being put in order and it was wonderful to see".[15]

Collins had told his London employers that he was asking for leave to see a very sick relative, a Miss Kathleen Ní Houlihan.

"Joe put Mick on his staff after only a few days; they got on well together and Mick sometimes acted as Joe's bodyguard, becoming deeply attached to him... For his part, Mick was a good actor and could be a silly countryman with a Cork accent and so pass unnoticed through police cordons. Mick had left home when he was very young and his education had been almost entirely commercial. Apart from his knowledge of Irish history, he had read too little and he told me after a week or two that he was only beginning to be able to follow the conversation at lunch or tea. He was unsophisticated, except financially, but he was really intelligent and his business judgment was excellent. His social manner was not so good and he often offended people who did not understand his sincerity".[16]

Neither Liam Parr nor Larry Ryan wrote about their time at Kimmage, but many of their comrades did. Liam arrived at the end of February, when the camp would already have been established and the flooding dealt with. Life at Kimmage must have been busy and spartan.

"Our life in the garrison was only mildly exciting. There were no baths, and few disinfectants. Existence became most uncomfortable; a dry shampoo against a wooden stanchion was not much of a palliative. It did, however turn some back-biters into bosom pals".[17] Joe Good, from London, said, "The food was simple, wholesome and plentiful; the breezes blowing through the mill made us hardy and hungry".[18] The volunteers took it in turns to cook in pairs.[19]

Much of the food was provided by nationalist supporters. "Members of Cumann na mBan were requested to obtain old tweed costumes to be converted into sleeping bags for the men. Friends also contributed such things as baskets of eggs and other articles to help with the catering".[20]

James Connolly's eldest daughter, Nora, was chief officer of the 'Betsy Gray' sluagh of the Fianna in Belfast at this time. The North was the only part of Ireland which had girl's branches (they came down to the annual convention in Dublin and unsuccessfully campaigned for the national acceptance of female members). Nora visited Kimmage.

"...I met the Kimmage garrison- those volunteers who had come from England and Scotland to resist conscription. They had no money, and were short of food and cigarettes. When I went back to Belfast, I called a meeting of the Cumann na mBan. I told them about these lads. I suggested we could get food and cigarettes. We had a tobacco squad, a cigarette squad, a butter squad, and bacon and general groceries squad. We arranged to collect these and send hampers to Kimmage. I was on the tobacco squad". [21]

Many of the Volunteers have recorded their memories of their time in Kimmage. "George Plunkett, who was in charge of us, shared our sleeping quarters in this draughty obsolete mill. His bed, like ours, was a bag of straw on the hard boards. George was our 'skipper' and ranked as captain. He was always in the uniform of the volunteers while in barracks. He was a gentle soul and it seemed inappropriate for him to be in charge of a pretty hard crowd… George kept us busy, taking us nightly on route marches. In the daytime some of us were engaged in making crude pikes, others in filling shotgun cartridges with heavy shot as large as peas".

"Some of us were busiest for most of the time making crude hand grenades out of 2" x 4" cast iron down pipe, with a flange end through which a long bolt passed. A small hole penetrated one of the flanges, through which a fuse was inserted. The fuse was of sulphur or match type- that is to say. One struck it on some abrasive material before it was primed to throw. It was estimated to be a three second bomb. It's doubtful if many of us were able to find out in advance how well they worked - though on one occasion later, I almost did".[22]

"We made buckshot and refilled cartridges with this shot on a large scale. We had some Howth rifles and some Lee Enfields. We also made a large number of pikes…"[23]

"…we even attempted to make a gun. George Plunkett wanted a long range buckshot gun, which simply could not be made out of a piece of malleable iron piping - even though it be called 'gun metal'. The charge was doubled and jammed tightly. The 'gun' was fired. I have heard of Peter Pan losing his shadow and getting it back again. When that gun went off I thought I had lost my zenith that it was trying to fall on my head - something nearly hit me".[24]

Michael Collins was not a member of the 'garrison' but he was often around. "While we were engaged on this work, Michael Collins sometimes visited the place where the munitions were being made to speak to Plunkett. He aggressively tried to hurry us, and even to instruct us, but displayed a lack of the most elementary knowledge of mechanics and made himself unpopular by his aggressiveness. I was impressed by the sense of hurry and earnestness in Michael Collins, although I had little sympathy with his drastic methods for getting the work done, as he was abusive to us".[25]

As Easter approached some of the volunteers were sent to lectures by James Connolly or Pearse. "We had lectures from Pearse on street fighting and barricading of streets, lanes etc. We were told not to man the barricades physically, but to cover them from nearby houses. We also got instructions in boring, in a zig-zag manner. We knew there was going to be a fight but we didn't know when or what it was going to be like".[26]

"I received an invitation to a lecture on street fighting by James Connolly at 25 Parnell Square, and he gave a vivid description of battles fought in city streets in Mexico and how such fighting should be carried on... I little thought that our time was near". [27]

William Daly, who wrote this, was a 'refugee' staying in 28 North Frederick Street which was very close to Parnell Square. North Frederick Street was run in conjunction with Kimmage, so it is likely that some of the Kimmage refugees will also have attended similar lectures.

Gilbert Lynch going to Dublin

Gilbert arrived in Dublin during the week before Easter, when the others from Manchester had already been several months in the city. He said; "1916 was an event that changed the whole course of my life. Some of the members of the Stockport section of the Clarion (a fellowship which organised socialists for propaganda and social activities) had arranged to go to the national meet which was held at Easter. I had arranged to go with them. My mother was not very happy about this as she was afraid that I might leave the straight and narrow path and be led away from my religion, but there was no danger of that".[28]

The Clarion for the week before Easter 1916 advertised five branches around Manchester. There was one in the centre of the city plus others in Gorton, Newton Heath, Levenhulme and Openshaw. All had cycle runs and some ran lantern lectures. In Newton Heath they had a social every Saturday and Wednesday, as well as a fancy dress social on April 15th with tickets for 1s.

Plans were well under way for the national meet in Crewe over Easter. "The Headquarters are to be the Earl of Crewe Arms Hotel". There will be a "conversazione and dance in the town hall. Fred Henderson will explain the position of socialism in the Cooperative Hall and there will be conferences and readings. "Some fine talent is booked for the Easter meet concerts".

The issue of the Clarion newspaper that told of the preparations for the annual meet had on its front page an editorial written by its founder Robert Blatchford. In this he angrily attacked readers who were cancelling their subscriptions because they were opposed to the paper's support for the allied cause in the war. Blatchford's argument was, "It is a good thing to agitate that the servant in a mansion shall have good food and good rooms; but when the mansion is on fire the one interest of all its inhabitants is to put the fire out and save the house. This is no time to talk of the wrong of the poor and the emancipation of the workers. We must save the state. When we have done that, we can go back to our socialism and we shall".[29]

Many of Blatchford's opponents believed that socialism was about more than campaigning for better food and rooms for the 'servants' in the existing 'mansion'. Blatchford described those who didn't support his patriotism as 'traitors'. Gilbert had already made his decision to be a 'traitor'.

Gilbert said he arrived in Dublin on either Thursday or Friday of Easter week. "About a week before Easter week it was decided that somebody would have to go over to Dublin and take some stuff over, and I was deputed to go. The man who was to meet me didn't meet me, and therefore I was at a loss. Going on the boat, I did meet a man from Dublin who lived in Reddish but who had no connection with the movement. I tried to locate the man I was supposed to meet, but I failed to do it and had to find other accommodation that night, but eventually on the Saturday I did find him.[30] I brought arms and arrived on Good Friday morning, prior to the rebellion, and reported to Joe Gleeson, with 500 rounds of .303 and a few pouches of 32".[31]

Joe Good from London arrived at about the same time and talked of the difficulties Gilbert had meeting his contact. "I went into a modest hotel, Neary's of Parnell Square, which was near the tobacco shop of Tom Clarke, though I knew nothing at all of Tom - at that time - or, indeed, of the IRB... We were not long at Neary's when things began to happen. Gilbert Lynch, the trade union organiser, had deposited a case containing arms and ammunition under his bed, and in his absence the police had raided the hotel and captured his stuff. Mick Collins very soon appeared on the scene, looking for Lynch, and asked me 'what the ... hell' I was doing 'in such an obvious place'. He told me to proceed to Larkfield in Kimmage. I did not dispute his orders, though I did not know by what authority he gave them... I was glad to go, however... Mick also ordered me to accompany Lynch to Batt O'Connor's where he was to be quartered. This I did - though there wasn't much left of the cache of 'war-materials' which Lynch had just brought over from Manchester".[32]

Batt O'Connor's was probably the same address as 28 North Frederick Street, the rooms of the Irish American Alliance. Gilbert said he did not go to Kimmage, but to "28 North Frederick Street, which was the same kind of garrison, except that they were men who had actually got jobs".[33] Joseph Gleeson remembered Gilbert arriving there "with a consignment of rifle and revolver ammunition. He took up house duty immediately and was on duty when I left on Easter Monday 24th April 1916. He was to report to Liberty Hall (if no messages came) at 12 noon". [34]

Some records state that Gilbert was at Kimmage but the two addresses were sometimes confused, both being centres for 'refugees' and run largely in parallel. Similarly, some documents suggest that Liam might have been staying at North Frederick Street rather than Kimmage. However lists of Kimmage volunteers often included those at the outpost in North Frederick Street, and references are often vague. For example Brian MacMullan said, "I can verify that Wm Parr was associated with

Kimmage garrison and its auxiliary premises 28 North Frederick Street where I met him in March 1916".[35]

Brian (Bernard) McMullan described how the two garrisons worked together. MacMullan had been staying in Kimmage, but "...our camp was getting rather full. As a matter of fact our men were getting in a bad way as regards clothes and things, the men were even getting verminous. I spoke to a few people around headquarters. The result was Mrs Jifford-Donnolly(?) *(Actually Nellie Gifford Donnelly)* gave me a request, and on her request James Connolly gave us a hall. The outcome was we had a number of men working. We thought it would be more convenient to get a place in town... We approached J.J. Walshe in Frederick Street - he let us have the two top flats for ten shillings". So McMullan was both at Kimmage and North Frederick Street.[36]

The anticipation must have been intense at North Frederick Street. William Daly, a volunteer from London was there.

"It was the following day *(Thursday)* that excitement was intense throughout Dublin, owing to a speech made at the Corporation Council by Alderman Tom Kelly In which he exposed the British Government intention of placing a military cordon around the Archbishop's Palace, Irish Volunteers Offices, The Refugees Camp at Kimmage and 28 North Frederick St. The refugees (about 20 in number) at 28 Nth. Frederick St. were furiously working the whole night barricading the house and preparing for a siege; meanwhile curious sightseers stood in the street to look at the house that had suddenly come into prominence. The next morning, Good Friday, news arrived, that the British military had no such intention, but all the same the excitement continued to grow and we were confined to the house and I was on continual guard. Besides being a haven for Refugees, 28 North Frederick St was also H.Q. of the Hibernian Rifles, Irish American Alliance, to which also was attached the Girl Scouts. There were many comings and goings at 28 on Good Friday and Saturday; men coming in up to 3 a.m. in the morning and during all this time I was the guard on the door, and sleeping in my clothes in the room off the hall".[37]

Sheila O'Hanlon

Sheila O'Hanlon and her sister Mollie were both members of Cumann na mBan, so they would have known that something serious was in the offing. Much of that week they spent moving and preparing weapons, first aid equipment and supplies.

Mollie O Hanlon, Sheila's sister remembered, "My father, sister and brother were all in the movement. Previous to Easter week, a quantity of rifles were stored in my Home".[38]

Margaret Kennedy, who was to be Sheila's commanding officer, remembered the week before Easter. "On the week preceding Easter Week girls were supplied from all the branches to Volunteer Headquarters at No. 2 Dawson Street for the purpose of making first field dressings for the men. On the Thursday of Holy Week we were told that big manoeuvres were being held on the following Sunday, but that is all that was said about it…" [39]

Annie Cooney was a colleague of Sheila and Mollie in the same branch of Cumann na mBan. She wrote: "Our house was a centre of activity for F/Coy. of the 4th Battalion during the weeks preceding the Rising, Con Colbert, Christopher Byrne (who was still living there), Joe McGrath, quartermaster of the 4th,.Phil Cosgrave (assistant quartermaster) were very frequent visitors…

On one occasion a car drove up to the house after midnight. It contained square boxes full of ammunition that, I think, had come off the boat. Christy Byrne was in the car and we helped him to bring the stuff into the house. It remained there till they were ready to take it away for the Rising. We also had a bundle of pikes that were made at Inchicore Railway Works. These, too, were taken away for the Rising. I think they were actually used for breaking in the doors of the various places occupied by the 4th Battalion during the Rising. Nearly every night Con Colbert used to call at our house up to the Monday of Holy Week. On that day he came with all his traps to stay with us. He wanted to be handy for his Company and Battalion because his digs in Ranelagh were rather far away. I remember particularly one night a couple of weeks before that he came after one of his meetings. He had asked me to make some signalling flags. He took two photographs out of his pocket and asked me: 'Would you care to have one of these?' One of the photos was of himself alone and the other of himself and Liam Clarke. I said I would be delighted and he actually gave me both and I have brought in one of them to show you. I was charmed because, to tell the truth, I thought an awful lot of him and, of course, he must have known it. He was not, however, at all interested in girls; he was entirely engrossed in his work for Ireland and devoted all his time to it. He had taken me to a few ceilis and concerts and always brought me home… There would be others in the party. He said, rather significantly: 'Would you mind very much if anything happened to me in this fight that is coming on?' I said I would indeed, why do you ask? - He answered: 'I might just be the one to be killed'.

We all knew a fight was coming on and, when we saw the amount of stuff that was being accumulated in our house, we realised that it was coming very soon. These remarks of Con were as much as telling me about it although no date was mentioned. Things were getting very lively as Holy Week went on. It came up to Wednesday when things began to hum really. On Good Friday they were very active coming and going to our house and I was very busy finishing my uniform coat to have it ready for Easter Sunday. I had cut it on the pattern of Con Colbert's coat. I was not at work that day and was all the time answering the door for the various Volunteers who were coming with the messages and letters and to take stuff away for distribution among the various companies of the battalion. Joe McGrath was handing some of this out. Christy Byrne was connected up with this work all the time. It went on all day and well into the night of Good Friday and again on Saturday, but I was not there in the early part of that day. It was my younger sister who was attending to it then.

I think it was on Thursday or Friday night at a meeting in 6 Harcourt St. that we got our instructions to mobilise on Sunday at that address at 5 o'clock in the afternoon".[40]

Redmond Cox at Martin Conlon's on Good Friday

Redmond Cox, from Moss side, had been staying with Mr and Mrs Conlon, training with F company of the 1st battalion, and awaiting the weekend. On Good Friday, Bulmer Hobson arrived for a meeting at this house at 11 Altinure Terrace (later to be renamed 36 or 72 Cabra Park). Cox was at this house on Monday so it is reasonable to assume that he had been there on Friday and playing his part in the events of the weekend.

Hobson, of course had been a founder of the Fianna. In addition he had been a leading figure in both the IRB and the volunteers but had been excluded from the decisions that led to the insurrection. Éamonn Ceannt said of Hobson that "he is the evil genius of the volunteers and if we could separate John MacNeill from his influence all would be well".[41]

After the rising, Hobson was able to tell posterity his side of the story.

He wrote, "It was towards the end of 1915 that talk of insurrection began to be heard… As far as I can recollect, Connolly, towards the end of 1915, decided to have a little insurrection with the citizen army".

Hobson derided Connolly for this. "His conversation was full of clichés derived from the earlier days of the Socialist movement in Europe. He told me that the working class was always revolutionary, that Ireland was a powder magazine and that what was necessary was for someone to apply the match. I replied that if he must talk in metaphors, Ireland was a wet bog and the match would fall in a puddle".

"Connolly's attitude to the Irish volunteers, and particularly towards some of us on the executive, was one of persistent hostility. The supreme council of the IRB, from which I had resigned, took alarm at Connolly's attitude. Sometime towards the end of 1915, the council, or possibly some members of the council, without acting the knowledge of the others, actually kidnapped Connolly and held him a prisoner for several days. While a prisoner, Connolly had several discussions with his captors, and apparently succeeded in capturing them and committing them to a definite insurrection in 1916…

As I was the officer in charge of the IRB in Dublin, and had to be kept in ignorance of these proceedings, extraordinary precautions and a great deal of duplicity were practiced. It is undeniable that the vast majority of the members would have refused to have been drawn into such a venture if they had known what was taking place.

The policy of the Irish Volunteer executive, for which MacNeill and I were mainly responsible, was to prepare for a defensive struggle using guerrilla tactics, and the military training in the volunteer paper and in the companies was directed to this end. I had suggested to O'Connell and O'Duffy that, in writing for the paper, they should specialise on the development of guerrilla tactics suited to the Irish terrain, and O'Connell's series on hedge fighting developed training in that direction. McDermott and Pearse, and those who thought with them, finding it utterly impossible to persuade the Volunteer executive to abandon this system for their policy of an insurrectionary demonstration, entered into a secret agreement with Connolly to bring the Volunteers out in an insurrection, unprepared and unaware of what they were being let in for".[42]

In March 1916, Hobson said he organised a conference of the volunteer leadership at which he made his accusations against Pearse and McDermott only to have them denied.

"Pearse and McDermott at this meeting specifically disavowed any attention to land the Volunteers in an insurrection, and reproached the rest of us for our suspicious nature".[43]

Hobson described Pearse (who he had originally introduced to the IRB) as "a sentimental egotist, full of curious Old Testament theories about being the scapegoat for the people, and he became convinced of the necessity for a periodic blood sacrifice to keep the national spirit alive. There was a certain strain of abnormality in all this".[44]

Hobson made similarly acid comments about Joseph Plunkett. "Most of us were bending all our energies to outwitting the common enemy, but Plunkett devoted his talents to outwitting his friends. It must, however, be remembered that he was in a very advanced stage of TB and that his condition was far from normal".

In the week before Easter O'Neill (the leader of the Irish volunteers) was given a British document containing secret plans to suppress the Volunteers. O'Neill was convinced it was genuine, but Hobson believed it to be a fake printed for Joseph Plunkett with the intention of persuading O'Neill to back an insurrection which would be doomed to failure. In fact, the document was reasonably accurate, except that it was describing plans that the British authorities would need to implement when conscription was introduced in Ireland.[45] These were not immediate plans, but most people assumed that conscription would come when the government in London thought it was militarily essential, politically popular in London, and when they thought opposition in Ireland would be manageable. None of the main conspirators survived to tell whether they thought the threats were genuine and imminent. However de Valera remembered discussing this with Connolly shortly before Easter Week.

"On this occasion, one of the principal subjects of our conversation was a document which had come into volunteer hands. It was (on the face) the outline of a plan by Dublin Castle for a swoop on the Volunteers and other national organisations. If the document was genuine its bearing on our movement and on our preparations was obvious.

As we talked, he remained, I remember in a squatting position with his hands stretched out, warming them at a small metal stove that stood in the centre of the room. He had been out without an overcoat and the evening was chilly. I cannot recall the details of our conversation, but I have never ceased to believe that he regarded the document as genuine".[46]

Connolly was far from being paranoid in fearing an attack on Liberty Hall; the Castle authorities had discovered that 250lb of gelignite stolen from Tullagh Quarry had been taken to Liberty Hall. In fact on Easter Sunday they had two meetings which decided that "Liberty Hall, together with two other Sinn Féin arsenals - Larkfield Kimmage and the one in Father Mathews Park should be raided tonight".

Plans were delayed after Colonel Cowan, the military commandant, warned that it would need 'a gun' (artillery) which would need bringing from Athlone. "Time was short for adequate preparations to ensure success."

However, the decision that was taken at this time, much to the annoyance of the Viceroy, was only to draw up a list of 'prominent suspects' and not to call for reinforcements for fear that this "would arouse the suspicion of the men we had in view and lead to them absconding".[47]

Hobson was critical, not only of the decision to call for a rising, but also, of its tactics. "There were no plans, and there could not have been plans which could seriously be called military. The tactic of locking a body of men up in two or three buildings to stay there until they were shot or burned out of them was nothing but a demonstration, and one which would have been completely disastrous to this country had it not been saved by the subsequent mishandling of the situation by the English government".

Although Hobson is writing with the benefit of hindsight, he was reflecting some of what had been an accepted policy within the IRB that a rising would need to have a flexible and mobile strategy. Sean Shouldice, an IRB member, had heard early in the year that a rising was being planned around Easter.

"I believe there was a general plan for the whole country and that such a plan did not contemplate immobilisation in buildings as our instructions originally provided for a retiral (sic) to the country, North County Dublin and Meath. These instructions were afterwards cancelled and we were ordered to fall back to the Four Courts".[48]

Late in the evening of Holy Thursday, Hobson was visited by 2 men who told him that the rising was planned for Easter Sunday.

"With them I went immediately to MacNeill's house in Rathfarnham, arriving a considerable time after he had gone to bed. We got MacNeill up and hastened then to St. Endas's to see P.H. Pearse, arriving about 2am knocking Pearse up... Pearse then admitted that an insurrection was to take place, and told us that nothing we could do could prevent it. This was in striking contrast to the assurances which he had so recently and so frequently given, that he was acting loyally with his colleagues on the executive committee".[49]

MacNeill's widow wrote about the rising, saying, "The first he knew about it was when Bulmer Hobson and someone else called on Friday before Easter when we were all in bed to tell him about it. They had a long discussion and then went to Pearse to protest against going on with the rising because the Volunteers were so unprepared and unequipped that they would be simply slaughtered. But Pearse was very much under the influence of Connolly who, with Plunkett and others, had been making secret preparations for a rising".[50]

Hobson said that MacNeill then gave him instructions to do all in his power to avoid the volunteers taking offensive action against the government. However MacNeill did for a period vacillate, having been convinced that the rising was inevitable and that he could do nothing.

"I arrived early on Good Friday at the volunteer office after this night long activity, and immediately my office staff arrived, I set them all to work burning correspondence and lists of names, so that, whatever happened, the authorities should not come into possession of the names of our members throughout the country...

That afternoon I was asked by Seán Tobin... to attend a meeting of the Leinster Executive of the IRB at Martin Conlon's house in Phibsboro. I was reluctant to go, and did not see any purpose to be served, and at the same time I had a suspicion that this was a ruse to get me out of the way.

I was, therefore, not surprised when, as I entered the house, some members, who were armed with revolvers, told me that I was a prisoner, and could not leave the house. I felt I had done all that I could to keep the Volunteers on the course which I believed essential for their success, and there was nothing further I could do".[51]

Martin Conlon also wrote about what happened: "In 1916... I was centre of an IRB Circle - one of the Dublin Circle" (Not on the Supreme Council) "...living at 11 Altinure Terrace, Cabra Park - subsequently changed to 76 Cabra Park" (There is some confusion between documents as to whether this address was number 36 or 72).

He had been given orders to arrest him: "...Mr Hobson was taken into custody on Good Friday 1916 and brought to my house. A volunteer and IRB member John Tobin, accompanied possibly by another volunteer, came with the prisoner... A brother of his, Jim Tobin, was one of those who acted as guards over Mr Hobson during the next few days" (They were not related to Liam Tobin).

"I believe the position was that he was given to understand that he was on his way to attend a meeting. It was on his arrival at my premises that he was actually informed that he was a prisoner. This was done by two or three men, IRB men of course, who were awaiting him there. The names of these men I cannot now recall with certainty, but I do remember that Maurice Collins and Murt O'Connell were the principle men engaged in carrying out the task of keeping Mr Hobson in custody. They may also have been the men who were waiting for him and actually took him into custody, but of this I cannot be certain".[52]

1 Pearce, Cyril. Comrades in Conscience. Francis Boutle, London 2014

2 Heath, Nick, Anarchists against World War I: two little known events- Abertillery and Stockport at libcom.org accessed 8 aug 2015 at

https://libcom.org/history/anarchists-against-world-war-one-two-little-known- events-abertillery-stockport

3 Daly, William, witness statement WS 291

4 Cox, Redmond. Pension application. MSP34REF1983

5 Conlon, Mrs Martin . Witness statement WS 419; Manchester 1911 census; Ireland census 1901 , Tumna South , Roscommon; Lynch, Gilbert; ed O Cathasaigh, Aindrias; The life and times of Gilbert Lynch; Irish Labour History society.

2011;Dublin, (description of Martin Conlon's overcoat)

6 O'Flanagan, Michael. Witness statement. WS 800

7 Cox, Redmond. Pension application. MSP34REF1983

8 Seumas Robinson's witness statement including Liam Parr of Manchester Witness statement WS156,Bureau of Military History.

Matthews, Ann. The Kimmage garrison 1916. Making billy cans at larkfield. Four courts press. Dublin 2010. (includes Kimmage list on pp 60,61)

9 Gilbert Lynch found himself with Liam Parr's return ticket. Lynch, Gilbert; ed O Cathasaigh, Aindrias; The life and times of Gilbert Lynch; Irish Labour History society. 2011; Dublin

10 Heuston, John M. O.P.; Headquarters Battalion: Easter Week 1916.Joannes Carolus. Dublin.1966; also Seumas Robinson witness statement WS 1721 and Kimmage garrison MA/MSPC/RO/607 military archives pension file; Also his own pension files in his name William Parr DP9542 and that of his wife Margaret Parr 11/RB/4077; Also Ryan Laurence; Pension application,DP6862

11 Plunkett Dillon, Geraldine. ed O Brolchain, Honor, All in the Blood. , A and A Farmar. Dublin. 2006.

12 Matthews, Ann. The Kimmage garrison 1916. Four courts press. Dublin 2010.

13 Joseph Gleeson . Witness Statement WS 367

14 Plunkett Dillon, Geraldine. (ed O Brolchain, Honor) All in the Blood. , A and A Farmar. Dubin . 2006.

15 Plunkett Dillon, Geraldine. (ed O Brolchain, Honor) All in the Blood. , A and A Farmar. Dubin . 2006.

16 Plunkett Dillon, Geraldine. (ed O Brolchain, Honor) All in the Blood. , A and A Farmar. Dubin . 2006.

17 Seumas Robinson witness statement WS 1721

18 Good, Joe, Enchanted by Dreams, the Journal of a revolutiony. Brandon.1996. Dingle

19 Arthur Agnew witness statement WS 152

20 Ceannt Aine, witness statement. WS 264

21 O'Brien, Nora, Ne Connolly. Witness statement WS 286

22 Good, Joe, Enchanted by Dreams, the Journal of a revolutionary. Brandon.1996. Dingle

23 Arthur Agnew witness statement WS 152

24 Seumas Robinson witness statement WS 1721

25 Good, Joe, witness statement WS 388

26 Arthur Agnew witness statement WS 152

27 Daly, William. Witness statement WS 291

28 Lynch, Gilbert- The life and times of Gilbert Lynch. Ed Ó Cathasaigh,Aindrias,Dublin Irish Labour History Society. 2011;

29 Clarion March 31 1916

30 Lynch, Gilbert- The life and times of Gilbert Lynch. Ed Ó Cathasaigh, Aindrias, Dublin, Irish Labour History Society.2011;

31 Lynch, Gilbert, Pension application MSP34REF41334

32 Good, Joe. Enchanted by dreams. The journal of a revolutionary, Brandon, Dingle, Co Kerry. 1996

33 Lynch, Gilbert, Pension application MSP34REF41334

34 Letter from Joseph Gleeson in Gilbert Lynch pension application MSP34REF41334

35 Parr, William pension application II/RB/4077

36 McMullan, Bernard (Brian) Pension application. MSP34REF14737

37 Daly, William, witness statement. WS 291

38 O'Hanlon, Mollie, pension application. MSP34REF4351

39 Kennedy, Margaret. witness statement WS 185

40 O'Brien, Annie (neCooney) witness statement WS 805

41 Ceannt, Aine. Witness statement. WS 264

42 Hobson, Bulmer, Witness statement WS 81

43 Hobson, Bulmer, Witness statement WS 81

44 Hobson, Bulmer, Witness statement WS 84

45 Smith, Eugene, witness statement. WS 334

46 Marx memorial library. Connolly papers. Éamon de Valera's recollections of Connolly. 7 Dec 1960

47 UK parliamentary papers quoted in Townshend, Charles Easter 1916.Penguin. London 2005

48 Shouldice, John F. Witness statement WS 162

49 Hobson, Bulmer, Witness statement WS 84

50 MacNeill, Agnes, witness statement WS 213.

51 Hobson, Bulmer, Witness statement WS 84

52 Conlon, Martin. University College Dublin archives. P97/13 (1)

Chapter Seven
Saturday 22nd April 1916

That Saturday evening none of the rank and file volunteers had been told how imminent the rising was, though many had guessed. "Holy Saturday evening came. The air was rather electric; almost all the officers suspected that the Easter manoeuvres arranged for were really 'the day,' but no positive orders had been issued to company commanders".[1]

Everyone must have been very busy this weekend. Even the ceilidhs were partly intended as a cover to disguise the unusual amount of activity. One of the last concert programmes recovered from the ruins of Liberty Hall after the Rising has Andy Dunne singing 'The Memory of the Dead' as the grand finale.[2] But this weekend other activities kept him busy...

"There was a lot of stuff, *(stuff usually meant explosives and weapons)* here, there and yonder. I was in close contact with the Countess and James Connolly, and I had the job of clearing out this stuff to Liberty Hall, gelignite and dynamite. Then on Holy Thursday night James Connolly came to me and said, "Are you doing anything on Saturday?" and I said, "Not unless Madame - the Countess - wants me for something". Then he said, "Because I want you on Saturday to look after Mrs Connolly and the children". I saw Madame and I asked if she wanted me on Saturday, as I said, "Mickser - that's the nickname we had on Connolly, wants me on Saturday." And she said, "Very well," so I brought Mrs Connolly and the children out to the mountains to a house and put up beds, and told them where to get water and things".[3]

The house in the mountains where Andy Dunne helped Mrs Connolly and the younger children set up temporary home was Markievicz's house at Ticknock in the Three Rock Mountains.[4] Markievicz's cocker spaniel, Poppet, also spent the week there.

Gilbert Lynch, Liam Parr and Sheila O'Hanlon

This weekend the Volunteers in both North Frederick Street and Larkfield Mill had all been confined to their bases. Yet it was during this very weekend that Liam took Gilbert out and introduced him to the O'Hanlon family and in particular the older daughters Sheila (21) and Mollie (18).

Gilbert remembered: "Sometime during 1915 I remembered reading in the Evening Herald a report of the ambush of the National Volunteers, the Redmond crowd, by the Irish Volunteers at a place called Dolphin's Barn and being relieved of the Italian rifles, which were mostly wooden ones. Dolphin's Barn had always struck a chord in my mind. I thought it was a terrible name to give any place - what kind of a barn was it? So I asked Liam Power, Billy Power *(otherwise Liam*

Parr) as we used to call him, about Dolphin's Barn and told him what I had read. 'Oh,' he said, 'I am going to take you there. In fact, I am going to take you to the very house in which the rifles were stored'.

So he did, and introduced me to the family. The family's name was O'Hanlon. Billy was a Dublin man, and his parents and Mr and Mrs O'Hanlon were friends, and he very often visited there and had often talked about our house and our family. He wanted me to meet the eldest daughter, but she was upstairs and busy and I couldn't meet her because we were in a hurry. He called up to her that there was a céili on that night, and if she were outside the Rotunda Cinema at 9.30 we would take her to the céili. We went on to the Kimmage (Garrison) to meet some other men over from the other side who were forming a garrison at Kimmage. We then went back to 28 North Frederick Street where the other section of the cross-channel people were staying. It was owned by the Hibernian Irish Alliance, and that was where we were having the céili.

We went at 9.30 to the Rotunda to meet Miss O'Hanlon, but we had to wait until 11.00 before she turned up. I told him there was no girl or no woman worth waiting that long for, but he would wait, and I had to wait with him as I didn't like going back on my own. Eventually she turned up, and had a good alibi. She had been recruiting her section of the IRA for mobilisation for 4.00 on Sunday, so that was a good enough alibi. We had a very good night at the céili, they kept it on all night. Going to the supper, I kissed Miss O'Hanlon and got my face well smacked for it!

We danced until 6.00 the following morning, and then went on to meet the boat at the North Wall as we expected some more to come across that morning".[5]

1 Tannam ,Liam. Witness statement WS 242
2 Bucknill, Rt Hon Sir Alfred; programme attached to Witness statement. WS 1019
3 Dunne Andy, Pension Application MSP34REF18903
4 O'Brien, Nora Connolly. Witness statement WS 286
5 Lynch,Gilbert-ed Ó Cathasaigh,Aindrias, Irish Labour History Society. Dublin, 2011;

Chapter Eight
Sunday 23rd April 1916

Gilbert Lynch and Liam Parr

It was on Sunday morning that Liam and Gilbert saw the coded message in the Sunday papers telling them that the uprising had been cancelled by Eoin MacNeill.[1] The following was printed in the Dublin Sunday Independent.

"Owing to the critical position, all orders given to the Irish Volunteers for tomorrow, Easter Sunday, are hereby rescinded and no parades, marches or other movements of the Irish Volunteers will take place. Each individual Volunteer will obey this order strictly in every particular".[2]

On Saturday, while Hobson was imprisoned, MacNeill had been persuaded to attempt to take action to cancel the rising; he sent out messengers and placed an ad in newspapers.

Gilbert wrote about seeing the order. "It was while going down to the boat that we bought the morning papers and saw the advertisement there signed by Eoin MacNeill, president of the Irish Volunteers, that the Easter manoeuvres had been cancelled. This meant that all the arrangements all over the country for 4.00 that afternoon were off. There was great activity amongst the leaders of the Irish Volunteers all that day, but we did not know about it until later". After reading this announcement, it is likely that Gilbert returned to North Frederick Street to try to discover what was going on. Liam might have gone to Kimmage with the same object but may well have remained with Gilbert.[3]

Liam had spent most of the previous few months at Kimmage, but seems to have been with Gilbert at North Frederick Street for much of this weekend; they went together to meet the O'Hanlons on Saturday, and then to the ceilidh. On Sunday morning they went to the North Wall together and saw the paper.

There is some uncertainty about why Liam was at North Frederick St and Dolphins Barn that weekend when Arthur Agnew remembers that everyone in Kimmage was supposed to be confined to camp from Saturday, because of the imminence of the rising. Liam Parr is on a list of volunteers leaving Kimmage at around midday on Monday, so it seems he had been reunited with his comrades by then. After a hundred years, it is impossible to be certain of the details, but if Liam asked his comrades to cover for him while he took his friend to a ceilidh, where he met his future wife, it is the sort of story that wouldn't appear in many historical records. It would be wonderful human footnote for those serious and often tragic times.[4]

Daly remembered being at North Frederick Street during Sunday. "Sunday was a day of intense excitement at 28 as we were awaiting word and had all our gear and equipment packed ready to go. Word came in that everything had been called off and then came word to carry on; we were on tenterhooks to know the truth. The O'Rahilly had gone to the country to call things off; so we were told, and that Eoin MacNeill was undecided what to do. I had already been since Thursday without removing my boots from my feet and had been practically on continual duty at the door".[5] On Sunday evening, Padraig Pearse was himself at an address in North Frederick Street issuing orders... additional couriers were summoned to meet Pearse that evening at the Keating Branch of the Gaelic League at North Frederick Street. By them went forth the final order for the rising on Easter Monday".[6] Gilbert continued, describing what happened on Sunday night, "Billy Power and myself went across to Dolphin's Barn to O'Hanlon's house and had a very good night there. There was always a crowd there - it was something like our house, there were always people in - and we danced that long until we missed the tram and had to walk back to North Frederick Street. We then learned that the mobilisation was for 12 noon on Monday".[7] Gilbert had previously said that "he didn't like going back on his own", presumably because he didn't know Dublin. This left Liam at North Fredrick Street late on Sunday night when his base was Kimmage.

The tension and uncertainty must have been palpable, even to those who could only guess what was happening. Father Aloysius was an eye witness who observed the emotional build up; he was a priest who was in the Father Mathew Hall where there was a concert on Sunday night. This Hall was in the centre of the 1st battalion area and reasonably close to the Conlon's house so it is likely that Redmond Cox and Martin Conlon would have attended events there. It was a very sympathetic environment for the nationalists so it is quite possible that Redmond Cox was there that night, unless he was needed to guard Bulmer Hobson.

Father Aloysius remembered: "The House was full and I can well remember how Miss Joan Burke sang 'The Minstrel Boy' with a spirit that electrified the large audience - the atmosphere seemed charged, and I rarely saw a gathering so enthusiastic. Of course there had been rumours of all sorts in the city that day. There had been preparations for a parade of volunteers and it had been called off; and that was enough to account for the tense spirit and the pitch of enthusiasm that characterised the meeting. Perhaps some of those present were in the know - perhaps some of the artistes had an inkling or suspicion of something. I do not know..."[8]

Sheila O'Hanlon

Sheila O'Hanlon's weekend must have been even more busy and exciting than Gilbert's and Liam's. Not only was she attending the ceilidh, and meeting and entertaining the boys, but she was also 'standing to' awaiting orders and was responsible for mobilising her squad, and safeguarding the equipment hidden at her home.

Margaret Kennedy, one of Sheila's commanding officers, remembered: "…On Sunday morning… all was confusion and upset due to Eoin MacNeill's order, but we learned that they were 'standing to' awaiting developments. We were told to go home and await further orders, but to keep ourselves in readiness. These orders were given us at Harcourt Street".[9]

Kimmage - Sunday

The countermanding order caused consternation at Kimmage. One of the 'refugees' at Kimmage, Arthur Agnew, remembered, "we knew there was going to be a fight but we did not know when or what it was going to be like. When Holy Week arrived all our stores were cleared out of Kimmage. It was then apparent that something was going to happen and all preparations were made for closing down. On Holy Thursday this was verified by the departure of Denis Daly and Con Keating for Kerry. On Saturday we had an extra special breakfast, everyone got two rashers and two eggs. We were told this was the last we would have in Kimmage. Everyone was confined to camp that day and night. On Easter Sunday we were allowed to go to Mass at Mount Argus. We were getting ready for parade on Sunday when the countermanding order arrived. The Officer Commanding ordered us to be still confined to camp. We were standing to all day Sunday and nothing further happened. Food was scarce as no rations were issued".[10]

The bright spot of the day at Kimmage was that Geraldine Plunkett and Tommy Dillon were getting married, and Geraldine was leaving Larkfield to go to Rathmines Church. It had long been planned as a double wedding with Joe Plunkett and Grace Gifford making up the foursome. However Joe had postponed their ceremony saying that "it would not be fair to Grace as she did not know the smallest thing about the political situation and had no idea whatever of such things". He was hoping they could marry after a rising, in prison if needs be.

Geraldine said, "I got a terrific send off from the Liverpool Lambs at Larkfield and Ma and I went to the church in a taxi… George and Jack were there in volunteer uniform and Rory O'Connor (not in uniform) was best man…" After the wedding service and breakfast, "Tommy and I put our bicycles on top of a cab and went to the Imperial Hotel, which was over Clery's opposite the General Post Office".[11] Geraldine and Tommy heard about the countermanding order after the wedding. Rory O'Connor, who had been working with Tommy to set up a chemical plant at Kimmage, visited them in the Imperial telling them that the rising was cancelled for Sunday, and the new plans were not settled, but told her "to look out from twelve o'clock the next day".[12]

Another 'refugee', Joe Good was specific about the effect that the cancellation order had on morale. "We had learnt that the mobilisation for Sunday had been cancelled; as a result, some of the garrison were inclined to be insubordinate".[13]

All the documents suggest that by Monday morning, Liam Parr was at Kimmage and that Gilbert Lynch was at North Frederick Street.[14] If Liam had been with Gilbert on Sunday, he had returned to Kimmage by Monday morning.

1 Agnew, Arthur witness statement WS152
2 Published Dublin Sunday Independent 23 April by Mac Neill, Chief of Staff of the Irish Volunteer Force.
3 Lynch,Gilbert- Ed Ó Cathasaigh,Aindrias, ,Dublin, Irish Labour History Society.2011;
4 Heuston, John M. O.P.; Headquarters Battalion: Easter Week 1916.Joannes Carolus. Dublin.1966; also Seumas Robinson witness statement WS1721
5 Daly, William, witness statement. WS 291
6 Henderson, R, witness statement WS 1686.
7 Lynch,Gilbert-Ed Ó Cathasaigh,Aindrias, Dublin, Irish Labour History Society.2011;
8 Aloysius,Father OFM. Witness statement WS 200
9 Kennedy, Margaret. witness statement WS 185
10 Agnew, Arthur, witness statement. WS 152.
11 Plunkett Dillon, Geraldine. All in the Blood, ed O'Bronchain, Honor. A and A Farmer. Dublin 2006
12 Plunkett Dillon, Geraldine. All in the Blood, ed O'Bronchain, Honor. A and A Farmer. Dublin 2006
13 Good, Joe. Witness statement WS 388
14 Lynch,Gilbert-Ed Ó Cathasaigh,Aindrias, Dublin, Irish Labour History Society.2011; MA/MSPC/RO/607 Kimmage garrison 1916,military service pensions collection; Robinson, Seumas. Witness statement WS 156; Parr pension file DP 9542; Heuston,John.M,OP, Headquarters Battalion Easter week 1916. Dublin1966

Chapter Nine
Easter Monday 24th April 1916 - The Rising Begins

Kimmage to Liberty Hall and GPO - Liam Parr and Larry Ryan

At Kimmage, Liam, Larry Ryan and the other Volunteers were waking up believing the rising to be cancelled.

"Normally we rose early in Kimmage, but on Easter Monday most of us were dilatory and were lounging about. There was talk of going to Liberty Hall where, apparently, they meant business".[1]

Meanwhile Liberty Hall "was humming... Joseph Plunkett was there looking very ill with his throat bandaged and his fiancée (Grace Gifford), Madame (in great spirits), members of the Dublin and Glasgow Cumann na mBan, Mrs Connolly and her son, Roddy. Thomas MacDonagh came in, looking very gay and debonair in his spick and span uniform, and very much different from the much perturbed man we had met on Sunday morning. James Connolly came from another part of the building and said smilingly, 'Well girls, we start operations at noon today. This is the proclamation of the republic'. It was still wet from the press and we read it with wildly beating hearts".[2]

Sean McLoughlin was waiting outside for a message from James Connolly. "After about half an hour Connolly came out bare-headed and said to me, 'Can you get a bicycle?'" I said. "Well. I can borrow one". He then handed me a despatch and said, "You will give this to the officer in charge at Kimmage. When you deliver this you will report back to your unit". Then he told me to tell him that everything in the way of food and arms that could be carried were to be carried and that nothing of any use was to be left behind. I set off for Kimmage on the bicycle and when I got there the Kimmage men were having breakfast. I saw, I believe it was, George Plunkett, and handed him the despatch... I had a cup of tea with him and recognised some of the 'refugees' as they are called. After spending about twenty minutes I then left. This was about seven o'clock".[3]

It was nearly noon before the 'refugees' got to hear the news. George Plunkett "...read a despatch saying we were to parade to Liberty Hall. The Company broke ranks cheering and ran for kits and arms without being formally dismissed. We reformed and marched off as instructed. On arriving at the tramline, the 64 or 84 of us, I cannot remember which, boarded one tram, George Plunkett paying our fares".[4]

"Honest George Plunkett paid the fares, giving the conductor about ten shillings and saying 'fifty-nine two penny fares and please don't stop until we reach O'Connell Bridge'. (Some of our number had been detached for action elsewhere.) It had been raining for a fortnight, but that day, I remember, it was bright warm and sunny, with high clouds in the sky. We were as cheerful as excursionists off to the seaside. The civilian passengers protested, and demanded we be put off the tram. Each of us was carrying bulky equipment, including a rifle or shotgun and a spare pike. I carried a woodsman's axe as an extra. As 'Blimey' played on his flute, we sang on the top of the open tram. We were jeered at, and cheered back at travellers on the trams passing in the opposite direction. We arrived at O'Connell Bridge and then marched down along the Eden Quay by the River Liffey to Liberty Hall, headquarters of the Irish Citizen Army, by Butt Bridge".[5]

"I was standing at ease in the rank by the path and an old man, tall and stout, black soft hat and flowing beard, looked at me and spoke. I immediately summed him up as a Fenian. He wished us luck and God's help in our terrible task. He gripped my hand and I noticed his palm was terribly calloused and dry. Its feel was peculiar when he gripped my hand, and tears ran down his face as he walked away. I often think of that old man whoever he was. He knew all that was to be known and I suppose he had been through it before I was born".[6]

Among those at Liberty Hall were Liam Parr and Larry Ryan who had come from Kimmage. Brian MacMullan remembered "On Easter Monday he *(Parr)* formed up at Liberty Hall eventually going to the GPO on Monday afternoon".[7]

"I remember seeing Joe Plunkett standing with plans in his hands outside Liberty Hall. He was beautifully dressed, having high tan leather boots, spurs, pince-nez and looked like any British brass hat staff officer. Connolly looked drab beside him in a bottle green thin serge uniform. The form of dress of the two men impressed me as representing two different ideas of freedom. Some packages or boxes were taken from Liberty Hall and loaded on a hired four wheeler, which was the total amount of our transport going to the GPO. Then the whole party, including some Citizen Army men, I think, proceeded to the GPO; Pearse, Connolly and Plunkett marching in front followed by the four wheeler. The Kimmage Coy were in the rear. We went via Abbey Street".[8]

"On arrival at the GPO, George Plunkett gave the order 'Into line. Left turn' This brought us into two lines facing the main entrance to the GPO. I heard him say 'A section right turn', and A section went to Henry Street. Then he said 'D' Section left turn'. This brought the section I was in facing in the direction of O'Connell Bridge. I heard George say; 'B and C Sections charge'. He had nearly lost his voice by this time".[9]

"…an officer immediately in front of the section of men in which I was placed gave us an order 'about turn' and leading us into Lower Abbey Street, pointing out shops and houses into which we were to make entrance and to barricade. About 20 yards down Lower Abbey Street was a bicycle shop and about 30 yards further was a paper store of a newspaper; in any case we were soon rolling out huge rolls of paper and placing them across the street soon had an effective barricade made comprising of this paper, a new motor cycle out of the window of the cycle shop, and numerous bicycles and furniture out of houses adjoining".[10]

Larry Ryan from Manchester must have been in either B or C section to take part in that first charge into the GPO because he is described as being the first into the building with Sean Nunan and M. O'Shea.[11]

Sean Nunan remembered this; "I, with others in the leading files, entered the Post Office by the Henry Street door - the main body entering through the main door in O'Connell Street. All civilians and Post Office staff were evacuated, and we proceeded to barricade all windows. I, with most of the Kimmage Company, was stationed on the first floor". Joe Good had been sent off to defend O'Connell Bridge from where he reported hearing a great deal of noise from the direction of the GPO. He said, "The orders to smash all glass, as per lectures in street fighting, to avoid flying splinters, were being carried out and there was a considerable amount of smashing".[12]

Liam Tannam remembered, "...we reinforced the barricades at the windows with all kinds of heavy books etc. Later we built up a second line of barricades on top of the counters with bags of coal in case we were beaten back from the windows. After that the O'Rahilly got me to assist him in collecting postal orders, money, stamps and everything that might be of value from the drawers. They were emptied into sacks from the drawers and, with the assistance of a couple of men were carried upstairs and placed in a room overlooking Princes Street. The room next to that was used for prisoners and I think that the guard on the prisoners was also keeping an eye on the valuables... I raided the Metropole Hotel for food and bedding. Our transport was one of those Post Office basket cars...[13]

"Glass clashes, locks are being blown in, all hitherto undefended windows are being barricaded with sacks, sandbags, boards, books, typewriters. We meet a priest in biretta and cassock. He wears a worried expression hastily adjusts his stole. A florid and dazed DMP *(Dublin Metropolitan Police)* man sits upon a barrel, his head buried in his hands (later on, he plucks up courage to ask the 'rebels' for beer as he has five children and one wife, he gets nothing but kindness.)... Men are constantly rushed to different positions. Noise and excitement, desolation without, disorder within - these are the prevalent impressions. The interior grows more orderly every minute. Reinforcements come and go. The rough and courtly heroes of the republican forces make a gallant show. Some are splendidly accoutred in the trim green Volunteer uniform, modern rifle, and automatic pistol, neatly rolled puttees and martial sabre, soldierly cap or dashing turned up hat. Some - the majority - are attired merely in Sunday or everyday clothes, crossed and intercrossed with shoulder straps, water bottle and haversack, shotgun, and in some cases, twenty two miniature rifle".[14]

"Inside the central postal hall, round the three sides of which run the newly -built letter counters, all is hustle. Every inch of space between the counters and windows is occupied with uniformed men, boxes of ammunition, pikes, blankets, mess-tins, bandoliers, knapsacks, and all the paraphernalia of warfare. The central portion of the hall is set apart for headquarters use, and at a table P. Pearse, W. Pearse and T. Clarke are conversing together. Farther over J. Connolly is dictating something from a piece of paper. He looks very stern and care-worn. Behind him a lady typist is calmly click-clacking away, as though accustomed to working in this martial atmosphere all her life. Ammunition of every description overflows counters, tables and chairs, while revolvers and automatic pistols of all shapes and sizes are scattered among them. The O'Rahilly and Joe Plunkett come in from tour of the defences. The former, as usual, is relating some joke at which they both laugh heartily".[15]

Amid the slowly increasing order in the main Hall sits Winifred Carney at a high desk near the Henry Street end of the room, typing messages and orders from Connolly. She is a member of the Citizen Army who takes Connolly's messages with a revolver beside her on the desk. "She acted as his secretary all through. She was a good shorthand typist".[16]

After attempting to make the building secure, their highest priorities were to tell the world of the existence of the Irish Republic. Hence the importance they placed on raising the Irish flag, and attempting to establish a radio transmitter. That afternoon Pearse read the proclamation of the Irish Republic.[17]

"POBLACHT NA h-EIREANN
THE PROVISIONAL GOVERNMENT OF THE IRISH REPUBLIC

TO THE PEOPLE OF IRELAND

Irishmen and Irishwomen:
In the name of God and of the dead generations from which she receives her old tradition of nationhood, Ireland, through us, summons her children to her flag and strikes for her freedom.

Having organized and trained her manhood through her secret revolutionary organization, the Irish Republican Brotherhood, and through her open military organizations, the Irish Volunteers and the Irish Citizen Army, having patiently perfected her discipline, having resolutely waited for the right moment to reveal itself, she now seizes that moment, and, supported by her exiled children in America and by gallant allies in Europe, but relying in the first on her own strength, she strikes in full confidence of victory.

We declare the right of the people of Ireland to the ownership of Ireland, and to the unfettered control of Irish destinies, to be sovereign and indefeasible. The long usurpation of that right by a foreign people and

government has not extinguished the right, nor can it ever be extinguished except by the destruction of the Irish people. In every generation the Irish people have asserted their right to national freedom and sovereignty; six times during the past three hundred years they have asserted it in arms. Standing on that fundamental right and again asserting it in arms in the face of the world, we hereby proclaim the Irish Republic as a Sovereign Independent State. And we pledge our lives and the lives of our comrades-in-arms to the cause of its freedom, of its welfare, and of its exaltation among the nations.

The Irish Republic is entitled to, and hereby claims, the allegiance of every Irishman and Irish woman. The Republic guarantees religious and civil liberty, equal rights and equal opportunities of all its citizens, and declares its resolve to pursue the happiness and prosperity of the whole nation and of all its parts, cherishing all the children of the nation equally, and oblivious of the differences carefully fostered by an alien government, which have divided a minority in the past.

Until our arms have brought the opportune moment for the establishment of a permanent National Government, representative of the whole people of Ireland and elected by the suffrages of all her men and women, the Provisional Government, hereby constituted, will administer the civil and military affairs of the Republic in trust for the people.

We place the cause of the Irish Republic under the protection of the Most High God, Whose blessing we invoke upon our arms, and we pray that no one who serves that cause will dishonour it by cowardice, inhumanity, or rapine. In this supreme hour the Irish nation must, by its valour and discipline and by the readiness of its children to sacrifice themselves for the common good, prove itself worthy of the august destiny to which it is called.

Signed on behalf of the Provisional Government,

THOMAS J. CLARKE
SEAN MAC DIERMADA
THOMAS MACDONAGH
P. H. PEARSE
EAMONN CEANNT
JAMES CONNOLLY
JOSEPH PLUNKETT"

The proclamation was also distributed around Dublin.

"On Easter Monday evening 1916, while on a window barricade in the GPO, Commandant General P. H. Pearse instructed me to hand bundles of the proclamation to the newsboy for distribution through the city. I called a newsboy of about 18 years of age whom I asked to have the proclamation distributed. He took a large bundle of same, and in less than an hour, he came back holding his cap by the peak and the back, full of silver coins, mostly 2/- and 2/6d pieces. I refused the money, telling him he was told to give them out free. He said we wanted the money to buy food for the garrison. I asked him who he had at home and he informed me he had a widowed mother and small brothers and sisters, so I told him to go and give the money, which he had got for the proclamation to his mother. (This I believe he did.) He came back again and collected the balance of the proclamations, stating he would give them away without charge (which I believe he did.) This boy came to the barricade on Easter Tuesday and asked to be allowed into the GPO so he could fight for Ireland…"[18]

Inside the building, most of the Kimmage Garrison were stationed on the first floor defending the building through barricaded windows.[19]

Across O'Connell Street Geraldine Plunkett was a perfectly positioned eye witness because she was looking out of the window of the front sitting room of the Imperial Hotel. The previous day she had married Tommy Dillon, and they had spent their wedding night overlooking the GPO.

"We had a complete view of everything. At 12.20 a company of volunteers, about 100, wheeled round from Eden Quay, walked up the street, halted in front of the GPO, and turned left into the PO. We recognised Pearse, Connolly, McDermott, Willie Pearse, and my brother Joe - George was with the Liverpool Lambs, and I think they came later. Liam Clark dropped a bomb accidentally on the new tessellated pavement in the centre, and immediately he was carried away on a stretcher. We watched the volunteers stopping milk carts, and food carts, and bringing the food into the GPO. At the same time, the staff of the GPO began to run out, hysterical girls screaming, clutching coats etc. The tricolour was run up at the south front corner of the building and the recruiting posters ripped off the pillars with the bayonets to the cheers of the crowd at the pillar. I saw a man driving up, and getting out of a car, and Tom said it was McBride…

They started to make a barricade in Princes Street with motor cars commandeered from people going to Fairy House Races. When Rory *(O'Connor)* came over afterwards he told us stories about some of the owners - army officers saying they would complain to the military authorities etc. They then started to make a barricade in Earl Street by driving a tram into it. The tram driver could not get up enough speed around the corner to turn it over, though he tried several times. It was at that time that some cavalry men appeared up near the rotunda and the crowd in the street who were getting rather excited, started running about. A number of priests suddenly appeared from Marlborough Street and started to shoo the people off the streets. Most of them went, but a few refused to go. Then the cavalry charged down the street".[20]

Inside the GPO, Liam Tannam was in command of the volunteers in some of the windows. "…it was reported that the British were moving into action against us. The Nelson pillar partly obscured my view of the oncoming lancers but orders were issued, I think by Joseph Plunkett, to hold fire until a general order was given. We all crowded to the windows and thrust our weapons through the barricade and just as the first two lancers came into view of my window, someone let off a shot, and I immediately gave the order to fire. Some lancers and several horses were shot and the remainder of them galloped away".[21]

"The GPO men had orders to hold their fire - Rory told me this - until they were opposite the building. But the volunteers could not hold their fire, some of them fired before the Cavalry got level. One man fell off his horse, killed by a bullet. We could see others being held on their horses by their comrades. Among the civilians was a tall man, dressed in black at the foot of the Father Mathew Statue. He stood for what seemed a few minutes, and then he dropped dead. A horse dropped dead too, and the rider ran off down the street with the rest of the cavalry, towards the quays. I think it was then Pearse came out of the GPO and read the proclamation right in the middle of the street.

The tram I mentioned, was still in Earl Street and they put a bomb into it, but it did not go off. They put another one inside it, and Joe came out of the GPO and shot at it with his Mauser from about 30 yards. The shot exploded the bomb and smashed the chassis which could now could not be moved, and served the purpose intended…

The bomb that exploded in the tram smashed Noblett's window, and the crowd started to take out the sweets. They then started to break the other windows and general looting started. George came out of the GPO and asked for civilians to volunteer help to stop the looting. Some did volunteer and George handed them white sticks. It was no use. The separation allowance women began to gather in the street. They crowded round the post office, and abused the volunteers inside, throwing the broken glass from the broken windows at them. They knelt down in the street to curse them. I remember one woman kneeling with her scapular in her hand, screaming curses at them. George came out again, and waved a big knife at them, which produced some effect.

Rory came over to us with a message from Joe, that I was not allowed to go into the post Office, there were enough women there, and that Tom and Rory were to go back to Larkfield to try to get the big tar still running, so that if it should happen that things turned better than was now anticipated, the phenol could be used for munitions".[22]

Within the GPO there was no source of news from beyond the rebel areas of Dublin. "Rumours of Ireland ablaze are as common as rosary beads round the necks of the watchers in the front window. Cork and Kerry and Limerick are up and the

Curragh line is held on both sides. Soldiers are attacking the Archbishop's Palace in Drumconda. Forces are marching to our relief. Jim Larkin is fighting his way across from Sligo with 50,000 men. Submarines have sunk a transport in the Irish Sea.

'Holy Ge!' cries John A Kilgannon, in his American accent, to two bewildered postal officials; 'this ain't no half-arsed revolution! This is the business. Thousands of troops and siege guns outside. The whole country is ablaze. Twenty transports are coming in when the submarines have sunk the rest of the warships. We have our own mint. Light your pipes with treasury bills and fling all but gold away. When we do things, we do things.'" [23]

Shortly after they entered the GPO, the volunteers and members of the Citizen Army were joined by the first members of Cumann Na mBan. Catherine Rooney (Byrne) claimed to have been their first in the building.

"I was the only woman in the Post office for a considerable time because I had not waited at home for any mobilisation order... When the Cumann na mBan representative... came to mobilise me, my mother told her that Alice and I had been gone for some time but she did not know where... Some of the other volunteers who had climbed in through the windows had received cuts from the broken glass and while I was dressing them my sister arrived...

I first advised her to go home, but some of the volunteers were shouting for food, so I agreed she might as well stay and help me out. Some of the men brought us to the kitchen which was upstairs and we started right away to prepare food of which there was a plentiful supply. My sister made sandwiches and I prepared tea. I went down with some of the men and the food leaving my sister above. I told the men to help themselves and I went back upstairs as I was starving too. It was then I saw three British officers in the dining room having some food. I asked my sister why she had given them food before the volunteers and she replied that she was told to do it.

Before I had time to have any food myself I was told by a volunteer that one of the guards in the storey above had been wounded and required first aid... I applied a large bandage, really a belly band, and tied it at the side in an attempt to stop the bleeding. There was not much blood as the bleeding was internal. The soldier was taken immediately to hospital where I heard afterwards, he died.

There were other volunteers wounded in the legs and arms as they were entering the GPO, mainly by broken glass and some had been sent upstairs to take up their positions. They were mostly belonging to the Kimmage Company".[24]

Another job that Catherine Rooney was given, this time on the express and specific instructions of Tom Clarke was to pour all the beer in the bar down the drain. He said he didn't want any of the men to be tempted".[25]

Liam Parr under the command of Tom Weafer

Liam's pension files say that he was commanded by Thomas Weafer. It is most likely that he was one of the party of, so called, 'London Irish' led by Thomas Weafer to occupy buildings across Sackville Street from the GPO. This was the block bounded by Eden Quay, Lower Sackville Street and Lower Abbey Street. Most importantly it included Reis's the jewellers where they were planning to install the radio transmitter. The plan was to use the block to protect the GPO and construct a barricade across Lower Abbey Street and to expand the area of occupation into adjacent buildings, particularly the Hibernian Bank across Abbey Street.[26]

The English participants in the rising are often described as 'London Irish' even though most were from other parts of England, particularly Liverpool.[27]

"Captain Tom Weafer was a tall, energetic man, a small moustache, and certainly a popular man with his company; his enthusiasm was unbounding and he infused it into his company".[28]

The area they were taking over included a bar which was still serving customers. "…at about 12.30 Frank Drinán (*Frank Thornton)* lead a party of us into the Ship Hotel and ordered, at the point of a gun, everyone out of the place, and going through the public bar into Sackville Lane, began to disperse the crowds that had gathered, which was a difficult thing for us to do and it was only by firing shots over their heads and taking up threatening attitudes that people realised that we were serious.

In passing, I wish to record with pride that a few of the men I was in company with, although hardened drinkers, were stationed in the Ship Tavern, and had the taking of anything that was there, did not touch anything and refused the offerings of the barmen…"[29]

The people trying to set up the radio seemed to include a number of members of the Kimmage garrison, including some 'London Irish' such as William Daly. He said, "In answer to our knock a fierce-looking man opened the door. I told him my instructions and he would not believe me, (My strong Cockney accent put me in a bad position and Blimey's accent was even worse), and his red moustache bristled up and he dragged me in, presumably to make a prisoner of me, when suddenly a voice was heard saying 'Hallo, Peter'; coming down the stairs was my own Coy. Capt. Tom Weafer, saying to the man at the door, 'It's all right, Paddy, that lad is one of us'. He brought us upstairs and I explained my mission to him. He introduced us to Captain Breen who was not ready for us as our job was to be done during the night. Tom Weafer said he would borrow me for a few hours. Having brought me to the ground floor he showed me an iron door leading to the jewellery shop which was left intact both by the Volunteers and the looters (looting was wholesale at this time and was unchecked, we having our hands full in fighting and barricading, although care was taken to prevent looting at Reis's as it was an important post). Weafer gave me a pick and two crow bars, hammers and chisels and told me to break down that iron door as quickly as possible. Working in a confined space, I managed single-handed to break down the door by about 11 o'clock and, leaving one of the guards over it, reported to Weafer, who came down with Sean McGarry to inspect my work. Weafer, McGarry and myself went into the shop. I was asked if there was anything I liked, so I selected a cheap luminous watch which I considered of military value and had no qualms about taking it. Weafer did likewise and I suggested that there may be field glasses which could also be taken and used. 3 pairs were found of which Weafer kept 1 pair, the others I presume were given for use to other officers. I was at this time absolutely fagged out and being brought to the top of the house, although very hungry I was too tired to eat, and lying down on a mattress I fell asleep immediately".[30]

"...the group that I was with broke into the Hibernian Bank with Captain Weafer in charge. This building would have been occupied between five and six pm. Orders were immediately issued to have the windows barricaded and have vessels filled with fresh water. For barricading the windows we used the caretakers bedding and other articles of furniture that were lying around. We were only in possession of the building about an hour when we saw women going down O'Connell Street with goods looted from shops in the surrounding streets there. We were ordered by Tom Weafer to shout at these women from our windows and order them to drop their loot. The majority of them obeyed our instructions and piled up the loot in the middle of O'Connell Street, or Sackville Street, as it was then known and Abbey Street junction. One rather amusing incident that comes to mind is that I saw a very stout lady crossing O'Connell Street into Abbey Street, she appeared to be very heavily burdened with loot, under her shawl. When I shouted at her to drop what she was carrying she opened her shawl to reveal an almost naked infant. Despite the seriousness of the situation at the time it offered my colleagues and myself a good laugh.[31]

"Looting begins. The plate-glass of Noblett's is shivered. The crowd breaks in. A gay shower of sweet-stuffs, chocolate boxes, huge slabs of toffee tosses over amongst the crazy mass. Tyler's suffers in its turn. The old women from the slums literally walk through the plate-glass panes. Heavy fragments of glass crash into their midst inflicting deep gashes and bloody hurts, but their greedy frenzy is unchecked. Purcell's tobacco shop and the Capel Shoe Co.'s store are also attacked. Lawrence's next falls a victim. Volunteers emerge and remonstrate, baton and revolver in hand. They deal sturdy blows with rifle butts and threaten with the bayonet's point when all else fails. Rifles are levelled threateningly and once or twice are discharged over the looters' heads. Water is thrown from above the chemist's shop on Henry St. corner. McDermott limps across the street and protests vehemently, his hands raised passionately above his head. A looter rushes madly past flinging away a valise in terror, the smack of a baton synchronising with the thud of the valise upon the cobbles. The looters would never have dared to come into O'Connell St. had a full mobilisation taken place. Batons had been manufactured for the especial benefit of the turbulent element and could not be employed effectively for want of veterans to wield them. Even in commandeering, the Volunteers exercised discretion and paid their well-wishers for value received. Thus one baker was given £20 for bread. P. H. Pearse gave out money for butter and other foodstuffs to the Cumann na mBan. Wilful damage was as severely eschewed as indiscriminate shooting. Orders were given that prisoners were to be treated courteously. No firing was to take place except under orders or to repel attack".[32]

During that evening three members of Cumann na mBan were requested by Tom Weafer to join the contingent in the Hibernian Bank building, but had to cross O'Connell Street under fire to get there. These were Leslie Price, Christina O'Gorman and Catherine Rooney (Byrne) who remembered:

"The men with Captain Weafer in command were upstairs in the Hibernian Bank barricading windows when we arrived. We prepared food for them. We rested during the night, the three of us lying dressed on the manager's bed".[33]

By the end of that evening Weafer had outposts in Reis's , Tylers, on the north west corner of Earl Street and at Nobletts, according to Henderson.[34] [35]

Gilbert Lynch

Gilbert was at North Frederick Street on Monday morning having been told to report to Liberty Hall (if no messages came) at 12 noon.[36] He remembered: "On Easter Monday we had instructions to report outside Liberty Hall... I was at the door for a while and then I went with the men. I stayed in Liberty Hall until it was evacuated [*at*] approximately about 3 o'clock as near as I can say the same day".[37]

"Our crowd was mobilised at Beresford Place. I turned up with them, and we marched along into O'Connell Street and into the GPO. We had not been in the GPO long until one of the Liverpool men came to me - I am not certain now who it was - and asked me would I go back to 28 North Frederick Street, as a good number of their men had gone out after word had come about mobilisation, and send them down to Liberty Hall. I was to wait there until 1.00. I waited, and whoever came, I told them to go to Liberty Hall, and then at 1.00 I myself left and went to Liberty Hall.

Liberty Hall was like an armed camp. The tune that was very popular in England at that time was 'Keep the Home Fires Burning' and I remember going round whistling this, and suddenly a big man came along to me and told me to cut that out – 'They've cut the painter now, and no more of those tunes to be whistled!' Orders were given to break a way through the buildings upstairs from Liberty Hall to Marlborough Street. Only one hole had been partially broken through when orders came to evacuate Liberty Hall".[38]

"Somebody got hold of a horse and cab which was brought into the yard at Liberty Hall, and stuff that could not be carried was brought in the cab to the yard at the GPO where all the stuff was taken out".[39]

"…A few minutes later a number of men came along - three of them, in fact, got into the cab. An officer seemed to be in charge, and asked if anybody there had a revolver. I had a .32 revolver, and he said, 'Get into the cab with them'. I got in, but didn't know where they were going to. It transpired that they were going to raid a place to get wire to set up a wireless station. We crossed over O'Connell Bridge and turned right I am not even now certain where it was, but from looking round the area afterwards, I believe it was at the back of the GEC. Anyway, we broke the door in and got the wire that was required, and we came back. One thing that struck me when we did go into the yard was to see a policeman half sitting and half lying on some bags. He looked very ill, and I believe he had had a seizure".[40]

"We got the wire alright, *(but)* I do not know *(where)* because I was a stranger to the city and nearly all our chaps had gone to different parts of the GPO, or in Jacobs Biscuit factory".[41]

"At about 7.00 that evening a crowd was called together and told we were being sent out as reinforcements for the Church Street area. We came out of the GPO, went down O'Connell Street and via Middle Abbey Street to Church Street, and from that time I was in the Church Street area. They had barricades at Nicholas Avenue, and also had barricades at North King Street".[42]

When asked if he was on a barricade, Gilbert said, "Yes, in North King Street area". He remained there until Thursday or Friday.[43]

"The clearest thing I remember that night was a visit from the inspecting officer who was inspecting the outpost, Piaras Béaslai. I had never met Piaras Béaslai before, but I did know his uncle who was editor of the Catholic Times".[44]

During Monday, F company, under Captain Fionan Lynch had built three barricades across Church Street. One was at the bottom of the street at its junction with the Quays, and facing Church Street Bridge. Another was built near the top of Church Street where it crossed North King Street. The third barricade was constructed half way up the street outside the Father Mathew Hall. This incorporated bedsteads which were linked together to block the street. In addition cobbles were prised up from the road, and combined with bricks and other materials from a building site across the road from the Hall (probably from the site where the tenements collapsed in 1913) to make an improvised wall. Glass and broken bottles was strewn in front of the barricade to hinder any attack by cavalry. There were also barricades blocking some of the side roads off Church Street.[45]

"By the evening barricades had been erected on the bridge and at the mouth of Church Street where two houses overlooking them had been fortified to cover them. On Monday evening a British military convoy travelling along the South Quay were engaged by volunteers based in around the Four Courts. This action brought them 5 rifles and 1000 rounds of ammunition. Further north, on Church Street, barricades were constructed on its corner with North Brunswick Street and at the Red Cow Lane/ North Brunswick Street Corner.[46]

Redmond Cox - Church Street

Gilbert was not the only 'refugee' from the Manchester area who was in Church Street that night.

'Standing to' at the house of Martin Conlon and his wife was Redmond Cox from Manchester. Still in the sitting room under guard was Bulmer Hobson.

Mrs Conlon said, "…some of the lads told me that Hobson had been giving them trouble. He was getting fainting fits and wanted to get away… Hobson was still in the sitting room, there was no bed there and he must have been lying on the couch… I took two men from England who came to our house and wanted to take part in the fight, down to Church Street. One of them was Redmond Cox. I can't remember who the other one was".[47]

Cox said that he "…mobilised in Blackhall Place with the company and after the mobilisation we took up our station in North King Street in the Convent".[48]

The first battalion had mobilised at 11 am at the Colmcille Hall in Blackhall Place but with only about 130 men and women from the volunteers, Fianna Éireann and Cumann na mBan instead of the 400 who would have been there without the countermanding order. One of the volunteers remembered seeing his commanding officer rushing out of the room as he entered, "I saluted him but got the impression he did not see me… I learned afterwards that Alright had lost his nerve and ran away when he discovered what was to take place".[49]

According to another witness, "This officer said the whole thing was lunacy, and he left the hall and went home".[50]

Despite the shortage of numbers, Commandant Edward Daly warned that each of those present would be required to defend the Republic with his life, and that any who withdrew would not be thought the worse of for it. In fact only two left, and the rest cheered loudly. The volunteers left the Hall at about 11.45, were given extra ammunition, and marched in ranks towards the four Courts.[51]

The battalion split into sections and occupied the Four Courts and the streets to the north and west as far as the North Dublin Union beyond North Brunswick Street. Daly set up staff headquarters in the Convent of St John between North King Street and North Brunswick Street, and first aid posts in Father Mathew Hall and the Four Courts.

It is likely that Redmond was in the convent, as he said this himself. He also said he was in F company of the 1st Dublin Brigade and his commanding officer was Captain Fionan Lynch. Although Seán Prendergast includes Cox in a list as being in A

113

company, all the other evidence suggests he was in F company and commanded by Captain Fionan Lynch as he states himself.[52] Gilbert Lynch was based further south near the Father Mathew Hall so was never commanded by Fionan Lynch (who was unrelated).

On Good Friday, Fionan Lynch and two of his lieutenants, Sean Shouldice and Liam Hegarty had walked around the area they were planning to occupy.

"We laid all our plans for barricades, for the occupation of certain houses within the area, for food supply, and for every other eventuality that could be foreseen by us. Hence we had no difficulty when we got the order to move on Easter Monday. Each of us took up the position we had already decided upon; we set up our barricades and occupied houses and vantage points as we had already decided".[53]

The area that F company occupied stretched along Church Street from North King Street as far as May Lane, where their patch adjoined that of C company who were holding the Four Courts. They controlled their territory by building three barricades across Church Street and occupying buildings commanding the street.[54] [55]

Cox himself was stationed at the north end of Church Street, near North King Street".[56] His commanding officer, Sean Shouldice goes into more detail about the activities of F Company during Monday.

"The duty allocated to me by vice commandant Beasley and Captain F Lynch was to hold and fortify the crossing at North King Street and Church Street and to occupy and fortify the adjoining houses and erect barricades. On our way to the crossing we attacked the balance of a small party of British Lancers apparently on their way to their depot at Marlborough Barracks. I later learnt that the main party had been held up earlier in O'Connell Street. After a few shots from our men the Lancers surrendered and were put under guard in the Father Mathew Hall in Church Street which had been taken over as a hospital. We put the horses, about four, in Sammons horse repository in North King Street.

The plan was to defend the crossing from enemy attacks from British Barracks, e.g. Royal and Marlborough on the West or Smithfield side or from military posts such as Broadstone Railway Station and the North Dublin Union on the north and east sides, and to keep the crossing open for our own forces from the Four Courts, and to maintain a line of communication with the GPO garrison.

The barricades were built with a variety of articles taken from adjoining houses, stores, yards etc. (excepting necessary articles of furniture) such as barrels, full and empty, boxes, carts, cabs, old furniture, planks, sacks filled with sand and rubble. One of the corner houses was unoccupied; it bore the name Reilly on the sign board. We removed three windows and fortified the place with sacks of flour and meal taken from the Blanchardstown Mills shop on the opposite corner. During the week it became known as Reilly's Fort and served as a good shelter and place of rest for the first two or three days and nights while it was possible for the men on the barricades to get relieved. Communications were made through Reilly's and an adjoining house by boring through the walls with crowbars obtained locally, to the back of Lenihans public licenced premises and so on to North Brunswick Street. Part of a house on the opposite corner, diagonally from Reillys, was occupied and put in charge of Frank McCabe assisted by Maurice Collins. This house commanded the North King Street/ Smithfield side from which sniping took place and later machine gun fire from armoured cars. The main attack, however, did not come from this side but from the Capel Street side. New cottages were in the course of erection between Church Street and Beresford Street, backing on Jamieson's malt house granary. These cottages were manned by a group of men under Sean Byrne, and the malthouse by a small group under Frank Shouldice. The malthouse was used as a sniping post and as company headquarters by Captain Lynch".

"Monks Bakery, part in Church Street and part in North King Street, was held by G Coy under G Laffan. Commandant Daly put some volunteers in charge and compelled the bakers to continue at their work as long as the supply of flour lasted. A small tricolour flag was mounted on a lance captured from the Lancers at the centre of the crossing, Kings Street/Church St".[57]

"The total garrison of my post in Reilly's and at the crossing was about 20 men, about 10 in uniform. They were practically all members of F Coy, with a few from other companies of the 1st battalion. We had about ten or twelve service and carbine rifles suitable for .303 ammunition, about six Howth Rifles for which the supply of ammunition was limited, and about six bayonets. There were about three or four revolvers. We had no explosives or grenades.

In addition to the rations brought by some of the men, we obtained our supplies of bread, meat etc. by requisitioning them in the name of the Republic from local grocery and provision shops. We were able to cook for the first few days in the fireplace at Reilly's, but the cooking ceased on the last few days we were there. Two members of the unit did the cooking. The meals generally consisted of rashers and eggs and tea and stew.

Father Mathew Hall was a first aid station but it was also used to detain prisoners and suspected spies. Some of our first activities were to regulate the hundreds of people who came clamouring for bread to Monk's Bakery in North King Street in the early part of the week. Most of the city bakeries had been closed down by Tuesday and a number of people from outside areas came to Monk's. On Monday and Tuesday a number of the local residents especially those who had relatives fighting for England in the European war, were very antagonistic and their womenfolk especially made our fight none the easier. However we gradually got the sympathy, or if not, the respect of the great majority of the people when they saw for themselves that we were conducting the rising in a fair and clean manner and with such small numbers against the might of England. On Monday evening and night we had quite a busy time with returning race goers and holiday makers who were unable to get along by the main route by the Quay to O'Connell Bridge etc. They were mostly in a state of panic and anxious to get through our barricades at the crossing as speedily as possible - a few were inclined to be obstreperous at being held up and wanted to know what it was all about".[58]

Although the volunteers were occupying the area, and were controlling who went through the barricades, this does not mean that they were perfectly safe in their territory. Snipers from outside the area could still take pot shots at anyone showing themselves in the open, and the first volunteer casualty, Edward Costello, was shot in the head in Church Street by a sniper on Monday evening. He was carried by stretcher bearers to Jervis Street Hospital where he died. He was 19 and married.

That evening the streetlights were extinguished, perhaps to hinder sniping, which continued sporadically all week. The threat of sniping made carrying despatches between the Four Courts and the GPO more hazardous for the garrison's three couriers, who had unsuccessfully asked the GPO headquarters to send more forces. One of the couriers was a volunteer, one a member of Fianna Éireann and one from Cumman na mBan. As night arrived, numbers of additional men who had missed the mobilisation joined the garrison. The chaos of the mobilisation and the countermanding order meant that many men who had earlier failed to join the units arrived and joined their own, or other, garrisons during the week.[59]

Redmond Cox remembered spending the day near the Convent until "that night and there were some British military prisoners taken".[60]

By Easter Monday evening, it now seems clear that the men we know about from Manchester were all positioned for a not very restful night, either in the vicinities of either the Four Courts or the GPO.

Larry Ryan was probably with most of the rest of his Kimmage comrades on the first floor of the GPO taking turns behind the barricaded windows keeping watch. Liam Parr had probably been sent out from the GPO with the contingent under Thomas Weafer, so was in the block containing Reis's where they were trying to set up a radio transmitter. Gilbert Lynch had been out searching for copper wire for the wireless, but was now defending the street barricades in Church Street, close to the Four Courts. Redmond Cox was somewhere near the junction of North King Street and Church Street.

Sheila O'Hanlon - Marrowbone Lane

In a time of excitement and chaos like this, it is hard to imagine how much Gilbert or Liam had time to wonder what Sheila O'Hanlon and her comrades were doing, but she had been equally busy. Sheila O'Hanlon and her sister Mollie had been active members of the Inghinidhe branch of Cumann na mBan for several years, so would have been involved in a wide range of preparations getting ready for this day.

116

On the Sunday, both had received the mobilisation order though, like everyone else would have had to deal with the confusion caused by the countermanding order. Sheila also, of course, had spent Sunday evening entertaining Gilbert and Liam at her parents' house in Dolphin's Barn until they both missed the last tram home.

The confusion was dispelled when, on Monday, she received orders from Margaret Kennedy, her commanding officer. Kennedy had a written order from Éamonn Ceannt to mobilise the Cumann members for Cleaver Hall, and bring supplies which had been stored there, and at Sheila's home, to Emerald Square.

Kennedy said; "On Easter Monday morning I had a mobilisation order. I was in the 4th Battalion group, and we were mobilised for Cleaver Hall, Donore Avenue at 10 o'clock a.m. Six or eight of us were sent to O'Hanlon's, 7 Camac Place, Dolphin's Barn, to collect stretchers, lanterns and other goods stored there. Two girls of this family were with us" (these were Sheila and her sister Molly).[61]

It is likely that these were the preparations that made Sheila late for her meeting with Liam and Gilbert on Saturday prior to the ceilidh. Eye witnesses seem to describe a ceilidh both on Saturday and on Sunday, which Sheila, Gilbert and Liam could all have attended. It is unfortunate that Sheila, like most of our other participants, has not recorded her memories of Easter Week. What does remain is a sworn statement made in 1936, before the pensions advisory committee. It is in question-and-answer form.

> "Q. On Monday what did you do?
> A. On the Monday I mobilised my squad. Éamonn Ceannt sent me word to mobilise my own squad. I have a reference here, but I would like to keep it.
> Q. Did you go to Marrowbone lane on Monday?
> A. Yes. I went to Cleaver Hall and I brought stuff from my own home. I had them for the 4th battalion, stretchers and things.
> Q. You went into Marrowbone Lane eventually on Monday?
> A. Yes and remained there for the week. We were kept busy of course.
> Q. You were there up to the surrender?
> A. Up to the surrender and went from there to Richmond Barracks".[62]

The phrase, "we were kept busy of course", is tantalisingly vague to read after a hundred years, but it is fortunate that a number of those who mobilised with Sheila wrote witness statements, so we have a good idea what they were busy doing.

Margaret Kennedy was part of the Cumann na mBan group that collected stores from the O'Hanlon house and came with Sheila and Mollie to Cleaver Hall on Monday morning.

"Two girls of this family were with us. When we returned to Cleaver Hall, we were ordered to proceed to Emerald Square to link up with the 4th battalion. We moved off in the rear of A company in the battalion: all the girls on parade went together to Marrowbone Lane Distillery with A company..."[63]

Annie Cooney tells her story, after she had said goodbye to Con Colbert. "When we arrived at the Cleaver's Hall most of the section were there - 21 or 25 of us in all. We had to wait there for the word to tell us where we were to go. While waiting we did a bit of Irish dancing and amused ourselves generally. Word came for us to march down to Donore Avenue. We halted head on Cork St. and fell in behind Seamus Murphy's Company A, which was about to take over Marrowbone Lane Distillery. Con Colbert and Christy had led their Company F to Watkins' Distillery in Ardee St. We marched into Marrowbone Lane Distillery after the Volunteers just as the Angelus was ringing. Rose McNamara led us in".[64]

"...We marched to Emerald Square for orders from Commandeant E Ceannnt; got orders to follow company of volunteers just forming up. We marched behind until we reached the distillery in Marrowbone Lane (used as forage stores for the British government) at 12 o'clock. I next saw Captain Murphy, who was in charge of volunteers 4th battalion, knock at small gate and demand same to be opened in the name of the Irish Republic. As soon as we got in prisoners were made of the lodge keepers, also a soldier in khaki. We remained in the cellar all day, waiting for work to do. We heard heavy firing from both sides all day. There were four workmen on the premises who were also made prisoners but were later blindfolded and were let out at dark".[65]

"We were told off - one squad of us - in which I was - to the front of the building and the rest to the rear of the building. We had a full view of the front gate and could see everything that was going on. When our rations were exhausted we had to provide food for ourselves and the Volunteers. Food that was passing by was commandeered and brought in. There was a butcher among the Volunteers who killed and prepared a beast that was brought in. This gave us food for a few days.

We were not long in the building when we heard the firing from the direction of the Union. Our captain was busy placing his men in position. I cannot remember whether our men had started any shooting that day. We had our quarters up in a barley loft and there was a sniping post just beside us, and the firing from there went on the whole week and our business was to look after the men who were there. There were other sniping posts in other parts of the building".[66]

Robert Holland was one of the volunteers who described his experiences there. "The rooms were like dormitories about 80 feet long by about 40 feet wide. These rooms had been used as stores for kiln drying wheat. The building lay between

Marrowbone Lane at one end, Forbes Lane on one side and the canal in front. At the right hand side was the 'back of the pipes'… There were a lot of air ventilators in each wall about 12 inches from the floor level and these had small wooden shutters which could be pulled to one side. The walls of the building were about 2 feet thick, and we used the ventilators as port-holes to fire through.

There seemed to be more women than men in the garrison, In fact all the girls who were there were members of the Cleaver Branch of the Gaelic League and had been at the ceilidhe the night before. All there were also members of the Cumann na mBan… At this time the garrison had not occupied the other portion of the Distillery the far side of Marrowbone Lane. We were brought into what could be called the main hall. It was a large round room with a distiller's vat in the middle of the floor. This vat had just been cleaned out and when we got there they were filling this vat with water using hose pipes and buckets from all available taps. Both men and women were working at top speed…

Murray also gave me some brush handles and some long sticks with about half a dozen caps and hats. I put the caps and hats on the long sticks and put them at the edge of the of the windows so that they could be seen from outside and with the intension of drawing fire from any British military outside…"[67]

Some of the Cumann na mBan girls had a role which extended beyond cooking and first aid. Robert Holland said, "…I would teach (*Josie O'Keefe of Cumann na mBan how to*) load them (*rifles*) and leave them on the floor at my hand, as I might have to fire from either side of the building. I opened up all the ventilators and she went away and brought back with her a Lee Enfield and a Mauser and a haversack full of ammunition… I showed Josie how to load the two rifles and she remarked how heavy the Mauser or 'Howth' rifle was. She learned her job of loading them very quickly. As a matter of interest each cartridge for the 'Howth' rifle was about 6 inches long and weighed about a quarter of a pound. It had a lead top about an ounce and a half in weight and made a large entrance and exit hole.

The time was now about 5 p.m. At this time I got my first sight of khaki in the cabbages in Fairbrothers Field. There was a rise in the middle of the field like a place where manure had been stored and it ran along for about a hundred yards parallel to the distillery and about 200 yards from it… The soldiers appeared to delay and one of them seemed to walk up and down giving them some orders as to what to do. I sighted this particular individual on my rifle but before I had time to press the trigger of my rifle I was taken by surprise myself. A volley of shots rang out both from over and under me and then I fired. The soldiers went down and returned the fire. This fire kept on until dark. Josie O'Keefe kept loading up the rifles for me and then Josie McGowan came along with another rifle. The two of them stayed with me until it was almost dark and they brought up a can of tea and some bread and a can of fresh water. I was completely blackened at the time from the powder of the 'Howth' rifle.

When the girls had gone I took of my shirt and left it off and put back my coat and waistcoat. In using the 'Howth' it was a bad weapon for street fighting. Flame about three feet long came out through the top of the barrel when it was fired and a shower of soot and smoke came back in one's face. After three shots were fired from it, it would have to be thrown away to let it cool and the concussion of it was so severe that it drove me back along the floor several feet.

The girls told me that they had to report in the main hall to Miss Cumiskey and Mrs Murphy as all Cumann na mBan girls must stay in the Main Hall through the hours of darkness".[68]

According to Sheila's commanding officer, Rose McNamara, the women were mainly responsible for providing first aid and food for the volunteers as she describes. "One slight casualty - P. McGrath - which we dressed with success. Firing continues till dark; reinforcements of 60 man arrive in the evening; towards evening two women bring us in some food, tea etc., which we needed badly. We divided up into squads and posted ourselves in close touch with the different firing lines, and lay on sacks of oats or grains, which was very uncomfortable".[69]

According to Ruaidri Henderson, there were initially about 25 to 30 at Marrowbone Lane which increased to about 40-50 as stragglers joined during the week. It was commanded by Captain Séamus Murphy. Its role was to provide covering fire to protect the South Dublin Union Garrison from attack.[70]

Mollie O'Hanlon, like her sister, spent most of the week in the distillery. When asked what she was doing each day, replied, "Cooking was the principal work".[71]

The Plan
We don't know how much individual participants knew about the plans for the uprising. They were only rank and file volunteers, but many did remark that they felt no inhibitions about talking to their leaders. Perhaps all had a reasonable understanding of the strategy of the uprising.

The rebel's plan had been to muster all their forces in Dublin, set up their HQ in the GPO building and post battalions in four main positions outside of the city centre to command the routes that British troops would take to attack the GPO. In addition, there were to be risings around the rest of the country. However, because of the countermanding instructions, the insurgents only had a small fraction of the volunteers they had expected, so when they mustered at Liberty Hall, they only had at most about 1,000 people. They decided to carry on with the plans in the hope of inspiring support, even though they may have suspected that this might only come if they were defeated and became martyrs.

Battalions were sent out to secure the Four Courts to protect from attack from the NW. One battalion, under de Valera, was sent to Bolands Bakery in the South East - to guard the route from the sea. The Citizen Army, under Michael Mallin with Constance Markievicz as second in command, went to St Stephen's Green, south of the centre. The 4th battalion, under Éamonn Ceannt, occupied the South Dublin Union (Workhouse) to control any attack from the west. Marrowbone Lane Distillery was chosen as a vantage point to command the approaches to the Union. The Second Battalion occupied Jacob's factory between the 4th battalion and the Citizen Army.

1 Good, Joe. Witness statement WS 388

2 Corr, Elizabeth witness statement WS 179

3 Sean Mc Loughlin Witness statement WS 290

4 Good, Joe. Witness statement WS 388.

5 Good, Joe. Enchanted by Dreams, the journal of a revolutionary. Brandon . 1996. Dingle.

6 O'Shea , James. Witness statement. WS 733

7 Parr, William, pension application II/RB/4077

8 Good, Joe. Witness statement, WS 388.

9 Good, Joe. Witness statement, WS 388.

10 Daly, William Witness statement WS 291

11 Ryan ,Laurence, pension application DP6862

12 Good, Joe. Witness statement, WS 388.

13 Tannam, Liam witness statement ,WS 242

14 Ryan, Desmond, witness statement. WS 724

15 Humphreys, Dick. Easter week in the GPO. Nat lib Ireland MS18829 in Jeffery, Keith, The GPO and the Easter Rising. Irish Academic Press, Dublin. 2006

16 Molony, Helena, witness statement. WS 391

17 Various witness statement describe journey from Kimmage to Liberty hall, and to GPO. Particularly Mcgallogly WS 244; Seumas Robinson, WS 156; Gleeson WS 367; Sean Nunan WS 1744 ; and William/Liam Daly WS 291. Also R Henderson provides chronology of Easter week WS 1686

18 Donnelly, Charles ,Witness statement WS 824

19 Sean Nunan WS 1744 describes Kimmage going to GPO first floor

20 Dillon (Plunkett), Geraldine, witness statement WS 358

21 Tannam, Liam. Witness statement. WS 242

22 Dillon (Plunkett), Geraldine, witness statement WS 358

23 Ryan, Desmond, witness statement WS 724

24 Rooney,(Byrne), Catherine, Witness statement WS 648

25 Nunan Sean, witness statement WS 1744

26 Weafer's activities described by William Daly WS 291, R Henderson WS 1686.

27 Confusion between Manchester, Liverpool and London in Robinson's Kimmage list.

28 Daly, William Witness statement WS 291

29 Daly, William Witness statement WS 291

30 Daly, William .witness statement WS 291

31 Carrigan, James. Witness statement WS 613

32 Ryan, Desmond. Witness statement WS 724

33 Rooney,(Byrne), Catherine, Witness statement WS 648

34 Henderson R. witness statement WS 1686 It is worth noting that Henderson's witness statements are intended to be a distillation of other first-hand evidence.

35 McCabe, witness statement WS 926

36 Lynch, Gilbert. Pension application.MSP34REF41334

37 Gilbert Lynch pension application MSP34REF41334

38 Lynch, Gilbert; ed O Cathasaigh, Aindrias; The life and times of Gilbert Lynch; Irish Labour History

society. 2011;Dublin

39 Lynch, Gilbert; ed O Cathasaigh, Aindrias; The life and times of Gilbert Lynch; Irish Labour History society. 2011;Dublin

40 Lynch, Gilbert; ed O Cathasaigh, Aindrias; The life and times of Gilbert Lynch; Irish Labour History society. 2011;Dublin

41 Gilbert Lynch pension application MSP34REF41334

42 Lynch, Gilbert; ed O Cathasaigh, Aindrias; The life and times of Gilbert Lynch; Irish Labour History society. 2011;Dublin

43 Lynch, Gilbert. Pension application. MSP34REF41334

44 Lynch, Gilbert; ed O Cathasaigh, Aindrias; The life and times of Gilbert Lynch; Irish Labour History society. 2011;Dublin

45 O'Brien, Paul. Crossfire - the battle of the four courts 1916. New Island, Dublin, 1912.

46 Henderson Ruaidhri. Witness statement WS 1686. This was written in 1945 for the purposes of distilling existing evidence for a military tattoo so is essentially secondary evidence.

47 Conlon, Mrs Martin. Witness statement WS 419

48 Cox, Redmond. Pension application. MSP34REF1983

49 Kelly, Patrick. Witness statement WS 781

50 Lynch, Fionan. Witness statement. WS 192

51 O'Brien, Paul. Crossfire- the battle of the four courts 1916. New Island Dublin , 1912.

52 Prendergast , Seán. Witness statement . WS 755.

53 Lynch, Fionan , witness statement WS 192

54 Lynch, Fionan , witness statement   WS 192

55 Prendergast, Sean witness statement WS 755

56 Cox, Redmond. Pension application. MSP34REF1983

57 Shouldice, John, Witness statement. WS 0162

58 Shouldice, John, Witness statement. WS 0162

59 O'Brien, Paul. Crossfire- the battle of the four courts 1916. New Island Dublin , 1912

60 Cox, Redmond. Pension application. MSP34REF1983

61 Kennedy, Margaret witness statement WS 185

62 Lynch , Sheila Pension application MSP34REF2399

63 Kennedy, Margaret witness statement WS 185

64 O' Brien, Annie. (Cooney) witness statement WS 805

65 Mc Namara, Rose . witness statement WS 482

66 O' Brien, Annie. (Cooney) witness statement WS 805

67 Holland, Robert, Witness statement WS 280

68 Holland, Robert, Witness statement WS 280

69 Mc Namara, Rose . witness statement WS 482

70 Henderson Ruaidhri. Witness statement 1686. This was written in 1945 for the purposes of distilling existing evidence for a military tattoo so is essentially secondary evidence.

71 O'Hanlon, Mollie, pension application. MSO34 REF4351

Chapter Ten
Tuesday 25th April

Larry Ryan - GPO

"The sun rises about 4am. It is a beautiful summer-like morning. Firing has ceased and everything is silent save for the soughing of a slight breeze through the glassless sashes of countless windows. O'Connell Street presents a strange aspect. The cobbles as far down as the Monument are snow-white with sheets of paper and cardboard boxes. Not a living thing is in sight. Even the birds shun the district. On a house-top near the D.B.C. (Dublin Bread Company) two slender poles rise up high above the chimneys. Silver-like aerials stretch between them. It is the wireless station, our only method of communication with the outside world.

Some distant clock booms five times. The sound seems terribly pregnant in this unnerving silence. Scarcely have the last vibrations died away in tiny pulsations when a volley of shots rings out with startling distinctness away up in 'The Green' direction. For some minutes an irregular fusillade goes on. One can clearly distinguish the heavy boom of the 'Howth' rifle (these were some of the 1,500 'elderly but serviceable Mauser rifles' - landed at Howth by Erskine and Molly Childers' yacht Asgard in July 1914) from the sharper crack of the Lee-Enfield. Eye-weary men rise up anxiously from their sleepless couches. Then it stops as suddenly, and the stillness becomes more intensified".[1]

Larry Ryan woke up in the GPO on the first morning of occupation. No records have been discovered telling us exactly what Ryan was doing day by day in the GPO but his role is most likely to have been the same as that of the other Kimmage Volunteers which was to guard the GPO and its environs from any attack from the British military. Most believed that the British would not use artillery in Dublin, partly because they wouldn't want to cause such damage to property, and partly because this level of military force would demonstrate to the world that they had lost control of one of their capital cities. The rebels were therefore awaiting an infantry attack, and were posted in the sandbagged windows and on the roof. When they entered the GPO, some of the Kimmage contingent were sent to the first floor, but there is no knowledge whether any remained there all week. It is likely that Ryan would have been posted to guard one of the windows when he arrived, but at times would have joined volunteers when ordered to other parts of the building. Volunteers who recorded their memories seemed to have moved around in the building. They would have noticed the leaders working on the ground floor, visited 'the canteen' and rested anywhere they could find.

"We strengthen the position with boards and sand-bags and wait for those gentlemen who never come. But in rumour they arrive every half-hour from Tuesday onwards. Talbot Street is blocked up by a tram-car and a barricade. Children dance and ring the bell inside the car... I pay a few visits to the food room below. The knight of the pen (Desmond Fitzgerald) sternly refuses brandy to his prisoners. New country contingents stream into meals. As one sees familiar faces arriving one realises what a terrific night, Easter Monday must have been throughout Ireland. Everyone is in good spirits. Tom Clarke sits benignly upon a chair pensively surveying the scene. In the officers mess the tale is the same. Some even read the 'Irish Times', and the rumour is current that conscription has been applied to Ireland".[2]

"By this time everyone has been allotted to his different station, and the building no longer presents the appearance of an overturned anthill, as was the case the evening before. All street-facing windows have been barricaded and manned by single, double or treble guards of Volunteers, as the case may demand. An ambulance department and hospital have been prepared. Armourers have collected all the loose and spare ammunition, rifles, revolvers, pikes, etc., into one central depot. Another room has been set apart for hand and fuse grenades. Chemical fire extinguishers are distributed at the different danger points, while in the yard outside other parties are busy filling sandbags".[3]

A group of volunteers are sent out in the O'Rahilly's car to commandeer supplies. One of these included his nephew, Dick Humphries. "The O'Rahilly gets in touch with me on Tuesday morning, and tells me to see Desmond FitzGerald who is in charge of the commissariat department and find out what supplies he may require. My uncle has driven his De Dion car into the G.P.O. on Monday, and it now rests down in the yard after being emptied of its initial load of rifles, revolvers, and ammunition. Desmond FitzGerald gives me a long list of items which he considers he needs and I set off with two volunteers through the Princes Street gate. We call at various addresses in the vicinity of O'Connell Street, Pearse Street and Ringsend, and encounter mixed receptions from the amazing number of citizens who still throng the streets in this area. As the majority of shops are either closed up completely, or pretty empty when broken into by looters, we become expert house-breakers in our efforts to fill the car with the required foodstuffs. I become quite proud of one particular exploit where my assistants lift me up to a trap door high in the wall. I experience a most exciting moment where I more or less dive head-first, and in compete darkness, into a stack of cardboard and wooden boxes. This place proves to be Anne Lynch's depot in Westland Row. We remove sufficient supplies in our two trips to this address to withstand a year's siege.

My greatest difficulty, indeed, is to prevent my good bodyguards from utterly overloading the poor car. Our first trip proves to be very nearly our last one as the sadly overloaded vehicle creeps along on completely flat springs, and with both rear mudguards scrapping the tyres".[4]

Bridghid Fhoghudha arrived at the GPO on Tuesday morning after travelling as a secret courier carrying urgent messages around Ireland telling volunteers of the forthcoming rising. On her mission she had never been more than half a step ahead of the 'G' men, who were following her. She had arrived at the GPO late the previous night, and found Pearse and the rest 'in great form'. They had told her to get some sleep and to return in the morning.

"There was an atmosphere of great elation and excitement. I made a tour of the PO visiting the restaurant and all the other places. The faces of many of the volunteers were black from making the munitions. They had lead from the Freeman's journal offices. I can still see the vision of the big sides of beef going into the ovens for their lunches".[5]

Several people remembered meeting the same characters. Fergus de Burca met Jack White on Tuesday.

"Each night we said the Rosary and indeed at frequent intervals during the day. It was not an unusual sight to see a volunteer with his rifle grasped firmly in his hands and his rosary beads hanging from his fingers. Eoghan ÓBriain 'gave out' the Rosary in our corner. He was much older than either Brian or I and was a married man with more responsibilities on his shoulder than we had. He couldn't stand any cursing or swearing or strong language. In this connection there was a famous character by the name of Jack White whose language was of the lurid style. He belonged to the Citizen army and had been engaged by Commandant J Connolly for special work and had afterwards re-joined him at the GPO. One would have to see Jack to appreciate the stories about him. He was a seafaring man and, according to his own yarns, had seen the seamy side of life in many lands. A small sallow man, with ear rings, you'd take him for a foreigner, certainly. The story of how he succeeded in cutting the head of a Greek in one of his 'foreign encounters' thrilled us, but his mode of expressing himself had poor Eoghan in a state of collapse almost".[6]

This was a different Jack White from Captain Jack White, the anarchist son of a British general, who had been the first commander of the Citizen Army.

Around midnight on Tuesday there was a message that British troops had been seen advancing from Phoenix Park direction towards Parnell Square. This caused the volunteers, who had succeeded in getting some asleep, having to be woken as a result of fears of an impending attack, but nothing happened.[7]

Gilbert Lynch - Church Street

Tuesday dawned for Gilbert on the barricades in Church Street. "Early on Tuesday morning a young lady came down and wanted to cross a barricade. I asked her where she was going, and she said, 'To Mass at the Franciscans'. I went to help her over the barricade, but she told me she did not need any help from any ruffian blackguards like us, so I did not let her get over the barricade, and I'm afraid she missed mass that morning. I'm sure she said some prayers for me!"[8]

The houses on Church Street, extending from the four courts northwards, were occupied and the walls between the houses were burrowed through so the volunteers could safely go up and down the street without having to go out the front and risk enemy fire. Father Aloysius was in the Father Mathew Hall all week.

"On Tuesday …the volunteers took over the Father Mathew Hall as a hospital for first aid, and Cumann na mBan girls attended to emergency cases. Some of our Fathers were also constantly in attendance. Serious cases were removed to the Richmond… The volunteers took possession of the newly built (but unfinished) corporation houses in Church Street. The windows were protected with sandbags".[9]

Father Mathew Hall had been built in 1891 as a temperance hall to commemorate Father Theobald Mathew, an important figure in the movement for Catholic total abstinence. The building adjoined St Mary's in Church Street and continued round the corner into Nicholas Avenue. It was extended in 1909 and included a stage, dressing rooms, gallery, refreshment rooms and facilities for 'lantern and cinematograph operating'. It was   run by the Capuchin friars who allowed it to be used for feiseanna or music and drama competitions organised by the Gaelic League. The musicians must have felt at home there as it was decorated with elaborate panels of Celtic interlace, harps, seated figures of Ceol (music) and drama, landscape panels and Celtic Crosses. The proscenium arch has been described as ranking among the 'most evocative examples of Celtic revival ornament in Ireland'.[10]

Across the road from the Father Mathew Hall was the site of two, four- storey tenement houses which had collapsed in September 1913, killing 7 tenants. This had shown up the national housing scandal, happening as it did to a building that had been just been repaired to the satisfaction of Dublin Corporation inspectors. It had occurred in the middle of the Dublin lockout, killing one of the strikers, while he was trying to rescue trapped children.

Redmond Cox - Church Street

Redmond had been stationed overnight in the area of North King Street and the Convent. This was only a couple of hundred yards north of where Gilbert was based. The Convent had been Commandant Daly's headquarters overnight, but in the morning he decided to move his HQ to the Father Mathew Hall, which was nearer the centre of the area occupied by his battalion.

Moving the HQ also meant that volunteers had to carry boxes of ammunition and explosives to the Hall. Cox probably spent the day helping to move the munitions and guarding the barricades.

"The fighting in the early part of the week mostly consisted of sniping from elevated positions like the top of the Malthouse, the roofs of Reilly's and adjoining houses at the crossing where our men had some narrow escapes from enemy snipers. Bullets spattered around the chimneys of Reilly's fort where some of our snipers including Tom Sheerin, William Murphy, Michael O'Kelly etc. were busy sniping enemy posts. The roof tops soon got too hot for our men who were forced to come down".[11]

In the evening Redmond was sent to the North Dublin Union to guard some prisoners who had been captured on Monday. He said: "About four o'clock we got an order to take the prisoners to the Four Courts and when we got to the Four Courts we were again ordered to take the prisoners back and let them into Richmond barracks. After that I took up my station in the Temperance Hall *(Father Mathew Hall)* in Church Street and we remained in Church Street attending to the hospital that night".[12]

Liam Parr - Sackville Street

The volunteers under Weafer's command continued to extend the area they controlled within the block bounded by Sackville Street, Lower Abbey Street and Eden Quay. This block included the wireless school above Reis's and DBC (Dublin Bread Company). They expanded into the block across Lower Abbey Street, which occupied the Hibernian Bank. It seems that Gilbert's efforts to requisition wire had not produced sufficient as Denis Daly remembered being sent in the O'Rahilly's open topped touring car to get more from Dame Street on Tuesday. Daly described driving in the O'Rahilly's car on raids for electrical supplies, and to Findlaters for food. "...we were sent out a few times by Pearse to disperse looters from business houses in the Henry street area. Enormous damage had been done. Men, women and even children seemed to have gone mad. In the cellars of one house in Henry Street I saw them wading in wine more than a foot deep".[13]

Weafer's men occupied the blocks including Reis's and the Hibernian Bank, while some also went to Nobletts and also made a connection to Hoyt's (on the corner of Sackville Place) where a hospital was set up. The particular importance of Reis's is that above the shop, men were working to set up the wireless transmitting apparatus using the wire which Gilbert had requisitioned the day before.[14]

The radio transmitter in the building required an external aerial to be fitted on the roof which was in full sight of the snipers on Amiens Street railway station. The plan was for the electricians and their helpers to do this very early on Tuesday morning hidden by the darkness. William Daly was asleep in Reis's.

"I was awakened at 2.30 a.m. on Tuesday morning and found that someone had put a pillow under my head and covered me over with a blanket, and taken off my collar and tie while I was sleeping. A pint jug of steaming hot tea was handed to me while sitting upon the mattress and in another minute a plate with three fried eggs and sausages with plenty of bread and butter was placed before me. I had only two packages of biscuits since 9.30 a.m. the previous day. That early morning breakfast was one of the most glorious meals I have ever had, the memory of it lingered with me for many a day as I was young and healthy and had not a care in the world even in the midst of the events taking place around me. I made short work of that grub, both because I was ravenous and had to report to Capt. Breen at 2.45. On reporting he asked me of my knowledge of wireless, which was limited, and explained then the reason of the importance of the building in which we were. There was a wireless school there which had been sealed up by the British Government owing to the war, but all the instruments had been left intact. My job was to re-erect the aerials and poles on the roof in preparation for sending messages by wireless to the outside world and thus break down the wall of silence built by the enemy. On the roof there was [sic] about 4 men waiting to push the poles in position when the aerials were fixed to the pulleys. Blimey fixed one pole in the Abbey St side of the roof which was an easy matter. I had to fix the other on the O'Connell St end of the roof which was a difficult proposition as there was only a shallow valley to the roof at that point and necessitated clamping the poles to the wall of a higher building adjoining and for which a clamp was already in position. To reach the clamp I had to climb a narrow ledge which exposed me above the ridge tiles and gave me about 10 minutes work unbolting the clamp, fixing the pole into position and bolting up the clamp again. Dawn was breaking at this time and the roof of Dublin made a lovely silhouette for anyone interested in that type of beauty, but I was interested in my work and wanted to get it done. I had been working for about five minutes when something struck the wall at the side of me. I did not take any notice; then two or three more pebbles struck the wall. I then shouted to the fellows about 8 feet below to stop throwing things. I'll not state the words I used as they were spoken in a strong cockney dialect and I was assured that they were not doing anything. When I had just completed the clamping of the pole a corner brick of the wall was shattered. I then realised, that I had been a target for at least half a minute and the pebbles I thought were bullets fired apparently from the tower of Amiens St. Station. I was thankful that it was the last bullet and not the first that made me know the actual conditions of affairs, otherwise I doubt whether I would have carried out my job. I dropped from the ledge into the valley all of a heap and remained there for a while in a faint as the reaction set in and the fear of being under fire passed away. Some of the lads thought I had been hit. After that incident I went and had another feed and slept until about midday. I then took up post at a window facing Mid Abbey St. and, with the exception of taking an interest in a fire which occurred at Lawrence's toy shop, and in the goings and comings of looters with whom Sheehy Skeffington was remonstrating and appealing to go to their homes, there was nothing of importance occurred at Reis's on Tuesday until about 5.30 p.m.

At this time a buzz of excitement and bustle took place. The wireless apparatus was ready for transmitting. Patrick O'Donoghue a wireless operator, was given instructions to send out the Proclamation of the Irish Republic on the ether (*this was probably Thomas O'Donoghue*). This was done twice on Tuesday and three times on Wednesday morning. I was relieved at 6 o'clock, but remained at the window and had a sleep on the floor until 9.30 p.m. When I took up duty again, there was an arc lamp alight in front of us which was a nuisance; we were told to put it out. I fired five shots before I could break the carbon to extinguish it. The firing throughout the city was very heavy at this time. When the light was extinguished Leo Henderson came in and got 12 men to go with him to establish or strengthen another post on the opposite side of O'Connell St. Nothing more of interest took place in my immediate vicinity that night".[15]

The transmission went ahead successfully but the electrical activity of the transmitter was visible from outside the building. Fintan Murphy remembered seeing "the wireless on the D.B.C. with its flashes in the dark. Apparently the attempt to broadcast succeeded since we afterwards got a U.S. paper of Tuesday's date with a huge Streamer: 'Ireland declares Republic' on front page".[16]

"The Hibernian Bank came under fire sometime late on Tuesday evening. By that time the British had succeeded in getting machine gun posts established at Frewen and Ryan's outfitters close to Lemon's. Machine gun fire from that post continued to play from that post throughout Tuesday evening and all day Wednesday. As far as I can recollect, it was on Tuesday evening that our officer, Tom Weafer, was killed, at around 8 pm. When Tom Weafer, was killed, a man, I think, by the name of Fitzgerald took charge. He was I think, a company lieutenant".[17]

In fact it seems more likely that Weafer was only injured on Tuesday, as he was taken to a first aid station from which he returned the following day. However, there is considerable confusion and contradiction between the witness statements of those who were stationed in Reis's.

When Connolly heard, on Tuesday, that Weafer was injured, he dictated to Winifred Carney an order which he gave to Liam Tannam... It was addressed to the Officer in Charge, Reis's and DBC (Dublin Bread Company)

Liam Tannan recorded it in his statement. 'The main purpose of your post is to protect the wireless station. Its secondary purpose is to observe Lower Abbey Street and Lower O'Connell Street. Commandeer in the DBC whatever food and utensils you need. Make sure of a plentiful supply of water wherever your men are. Break all glass in the windows of the rooms occupied for fighting purposes. Establish a connection between your forces in the DBC and Reis's building. Be sure that the stairways leading immediately to your rooms are well barricaded. We have a post in the house on the corner of Bachelors Walk, in the Metropole Hotel, in the Imperial Hotel, in the GPO. The directions from which you are likely to be attacked are from the Customs House, and from the far side of the river, D'Olier Street and Westmorland Street. We believe there is a sniper in McBirneys on the far side of the river. Signed James Connolly'

Tannam continued, "I went over to Reis's and had to introduce myself as I knew nobody there. Paddy McGrath and his son who got his eye out, and a man called

Mulvey from Bray were there; the rest were black strangers… Blimey *(O'Connor, one of the Kimmage refugees)* was engaged on the job of climbing up the wireless mast to fix some wires, and he was being sniped at all the time, but he fixed it. How he had the pluck to carry on, and how he was not riddled, beats me… I learnt from Fergus Kelly that he could send out messages but that the instrument was not able to receive. He could not send them very far but perhaps ships could pick them up and relay them".[18]

Sheila O'Hanlon - Marrowbone Lane

At Marrowbone Lane on Tuesday, sniping continued.[19]

Sheila and her comrades' role of providing food and first aid continued throughout the week, but they were also posted to keep watch from the high windows of the building.

Margaret Kennedy, one of Sheila's comrades listed the activities of the day, "No one was seriously or fatally seriously wounded, D.G. but none got much sleep or rest, as attack on a big scale was always expected and prepared for. We were an outpost of the South Dublin Union. There was intermittent sniping at us from the Canal Bank and from Guinness's Brewery, but the sniping from the canal side was not so persistent as that from the Brewery. Six of us were detailed for duty on a loft near a gangway that was held by the Volunteers, to prevent any possible surprise attack that might be launched by the military on the front gate of the Distillery".[20]

"Quinn's bakery cart was held up and some bread captured, also two cans of milk from a passing cart. Some visitors called. Two enemy snipers taken down by our men; light firing all day".[21]

Annie Cooney said: "On Tuesday night a small band of C/Coy., who had vacated Roe's Distillery after their Captain had left, joined our garrison. Among them were the three O'Brien brothers, Larry, Paddy and Denis (whom I afterwards married). I only knew their names at that time. They were brought up to our loft to rest. They had spent the night (Monday) trying to reach our post, having failed to get into the Union. We had been told that Con Colbert and his company were coming to join us as soon as they could and when I heard the footsteps on the stairs I thought it was they. I was quite disappointed when I saw the C/Coy, boys. They were all very young, most of them under 18".[22]

"My father visited us on Tuesday to see how we were getting on and to see if we wanted anything and to bring us a change of clothing. Someone had told him we were seen going into the Distillery".[23]

"About 11 pm two clergymen from Mount Argus came to hear confessions, all the girls - 22 in all (3 having gone away) - went to confession and I believe most of the men. Priest brought up to the firing line on top and blessed the camp".[24]

1 Humphreys, Dick. Easter week in the GPO. Nat lib Ireland MS18829 in Jeffery, Keith, The GPO and the Easter Rising. Irish Academic Press, Dublin. 2006

2 Ryan, Desmond, witness statement WS 724

3 Humphreys, Dick. Easter week in the GPO. Nat lib Ireland MS18829 in Jeffery, Keith, The GPO and the Easter Rising. Irish Academic Press, Dublin. 2006

4 Humphreys, Dick. Easter week in the GPO. Nat lib Ireland MS18829 in Jeffery, Keith, The GPO and the Easter Rising. Irish Academic Press, Dublin. 2006

5 Martin, Bridghid witness statement WS 398

6 De Burka, Feargus, witness statement WS 694

7 Henderson R. witness statement WS 1686 It is worth noting that Henderson's witness statements are intended to be a distillation of other first-hand evidence.

8 Lynch, Gilbert;e d O Cathasaigh, Aindrias; The life and times of Gilbert Lynch; Irish Labour History society. 2011;Dublin

9 Aloysius,Father OFM. Witness statement WIT 200

10 Casey,Christine, Dublin: the city within the Grand and Royal canals and the Circular Road. Yale University Press 2005

11 Shouldice, John Witness statement WS 162

12 Cox, Redmond. Pension application. MSP34REF1983

13 Daly, Denis. Witness statement WS 110

14 Henderson,Ruaidhri, witness statement WS 1686

15 Daly, William .witness statement WS 291

16 Murphy , Fintan witness statement WS 370

17 Carrigam, James witness statement WS 613

18 Tannam, Liam, witness statement WS 242

19 Henderson Ruaidhri. Witness statement 1686. This was written in 1945 for the purposes of distilling existing evidence for a military tattoo so is essentially secondary evidence.

20 Kennedy Margaret. Witness statement WS 185

21 Mc Namara, Rose witness statement. WS 482

22 O, Brien, Annie (Cooney) witness statement WS 805

23 O'Brien, Annie (Cooney) Witness statement WS 805

24 Mc Namara, Rose witness statement. WS 482

23. Irish Citizen army outside Liberty Hall.

24. Winnie Carney.

25. Tram as barricade near GPO.

26. Father Mathew Hall from Church Street in 2015.

27. Marrowbone Lane distillery.

28. One of the few photos taken inside the GPO during Easter week.

29. HMS Helga .

30. Armoured personnel carrier.

31. Detail of William Paget's watercolour, 'The Birth of the Republic'.

32. Father Aloysius.

33. The Moore Street area. The GPO is the large building on the lower right edge.

34. After the rising looking up Sackville Street towards Dublin Bread Company.

35. GPO after the rising.

36. Prisoners in Stafford Jail. X marks Michael Collins.

37. Inside the huts at Frongoch.

38. Release from Frongoch. probably Christmas Eve 1916.

39. Gilbert Lynch and Sheila in Blackpool, 1931.

40. Wedding of Liam Parr and Margaret Madden.

41. Liam on left and Margaret, 2nd right. Church performance.

42. Margaret Parr.

43. Liam Parr's Kilt pin.

44. Liam Parr in the uniform of the James Connolly Pipe Band.

Chapter Eleven
Wednesday 26 April

Liam Parr under the command of Weafer - Sackville Street

Liam Parr awoke in buildings that were under intense fire. He had been under the command of Tom Weafer, who was having first aid, so now his commanding officer this morning was Liam Tannam.

That Wednesday morning, Tannam was exploring the area he had responsibility for. He investigated the tower of the Dublin Bread Company. "We could see the Helga down the river, we could also see an enemy group in the top of Trinity College. They must have observed us. Machine gun fire was opened on the tower of the DBC, (which I think was mostly constructed of copper) and the bullets went clean through it, luckily without striking either of us.

We dived down through the opening into the room below in which were stored boxes of raisins, currents and all things used in confectionary. We lifted one of these into the opening of the tower, pushed another beside it and so on until we had a barricade on the Trinity College side of the tower. We then got into position and replied to the fire from Trinity College, and to our amazement they cleared off the roof... The Helga bombarded Liberty Hall".[1] After this, they only used the DBC as an observation post.[2]

About noon on Wednesday, Tannam saw that Weafer had returned to the Hibernian Bank from the first aid station. "I shouted to Weafer, 'Welcome back. I am now returning to the GPO'. He waved his hand and shouted, 'Right Oh'. I had great difficulty getting down the stairs at Reis's as we had it barricaded with chairs from the door up. I emerged on the street and suddenly there was a burst of machine gun fire hitting the Hibernian Bank. The firing was so intense that clouds of dust were falling down on the path from the impact of the bullets... As I started to sprint I heard something flop on the first floor of the Hibernian and thought I heard, 'My Jesus, Mercy' but do not know whether I had heard it right or not, I was wearing hob nailed boots. When in the middle of O'Connell Street I wanted to change direction suddenly as the machine gunner was on to me and bullets were striking the roadway at my feet, the nails on the boots then slid on the paving stones and I came a cropper..." [3]

Firing on the buildings where Liam was posted became more intense from about noon onwards, until it became impossible to continue radio transmissions. The memories of those who were stationed in those buildings are very confused and contradictory and perhaps this shows the fierceness of the attack they were facing. This makes it difficult to be certain of the order of events.

Throughout the day, Cumann na mBan women were kept busy looking after casualties. "...a civilian was brought in terribly wounded on a stretcher... Dr Touhy came in… He asked me to hold a bowl of water while he was washing the wounded man. He was an awful sight as he was frightfully badly wounded in the stomach. I stuck it out as long as the doctor was doing his part, but when I took away the bowl of water I got well and truly sick. I think he died soon after…"[4]

Tannam heard that Weafer had been hit when he had returned to the GPO. "When I returned to the GPO, I returned to my window, saw George Plunkett who suggested I take a rest. I lay down under a counter. I was about to settle myself when Joseph Plunkett looked at me and said, 'Aren't you supposed to be in charge of Reis's and the DBC?' I told him that Captain Weafer was again on duty and I was glad to see him out of hospital. I asked Plunkett was there anything wrong and while I was talking to him word came along that Captain Weafer had been killed in the Hibernian bank and possibly this was the thud and flop I had heard…"[5]

During that morning, preparations had been made to transport food from the DBC to the GPO, but it is unclear whether this was part of a plan to evacuate the block on the east of Sackville Street. William Daly wrote:

"Early on Wednesday morning a party of us were told off to collect all foodstuffs in the Dublin Bread Coy's building next door, our method being to walk across planks from one window to another at rear. Huge quantities of roast beef, cooked meat and hams, bread, confectionery, pastries, sides of bacon, eggs; in fact anything that was edible was transferred to a horse- drawn lorry waiting in Lr. Abbey St. for removal to the Commissariat's Dept. in the GPO."[6]

"In the meanwhile the receiving apparatus of the wireless was dismantled in readiness for removal also to the GPO. The driver of the lorry started off to HQ with all the grub under an intense fire from the British stationed in McBirney's and Carlisle Building, so there was no hope of his returning to bring over the apparatus. We therefore, got a large table and, having upturned it, placed in the wireless gear and covered it over with a white table cloth and six of us, of which I was of the number, started off to cross O'Connell St. with our burden. Immediately we came into the line of fire, the firing ceased and not a shot was fired as we went on our journey. We were amazed and for the time being could not understand why we were respected in this manner. The only reason that could be attributed was that it was thought we were carrying a badly-wounded or dead man across to the GPO. Having left our burden in the PO we started off under heavy fire to get back to our post and got across safely. I did not mind this in the least as I had passed through my baptism the previous morning".[7]

Some people stayed in Reis's, but then crossed Abbey Street and retired to the Hibernian Bank, where Weafer was lying injured. According to Henderson the order from GHQ had been to cease sniping from the cupola of Dublin Bread Company DBC, but in the confusion this was misinterpreted as an instruction to evacuate Reis's.[8]

"At this time a message was signalled to us to get ready to evacuate the post and to retire to the Hibernian Bank of which Capt. Tom Weafer was O/C. At about 1 p.m. I saw Paddy Mitchell with a Red Cross armlet on the run round the corner from O'Connell St into the Bank and he came out a few minutes later shouting to us that Weafer was badly hit and he's returned to the temporary hospital (which had been a mock auctioneer's shop) to get a stretcher and bearers to bring Weafer out, but owing to the intense firing, was unable to get back to the bank. We could hear Weafer yelling with pain and groaning in agony. The bullet struck through the liver and kidneys and the pain must have been terrible. It was at this time we left Reis's and went into the Bank to bring picks and sledges to break through to the adjoining house, which-proved to be the hospital. Orders were signalled to evacuate the hospital and bring over the wounded to the GPO but before this could be done, we had to break through the walls into the hospital. A half hour's hard work sufficed to make a hole through the wall, but the hole on the Bank side of wall was about 3 feet from the floor and 2 feet from the Ceiling in the next house. Having made the hole large enough I got feet first through it and completed the attack on the wall from the either side and by means of boxes arranged a rough flight of steps down in the room. Two wounded men were first assisted through (one of them was Ignatius Flynn a member of E/Coy)".[9]

The contingent of volunteers in the Hibernian Bank, probably including Liam Parr, remained there under heavy fire until late afternoon. Although most witness statements suggest that the volunteers evacuated the block of buildings which included the Hibernian Bank on Wednesday afternoon, there is some ambiguity and some suggest that this finally happened on Thursday.

"Word was brought down to us at this time, 3 p.m. that Poor Tom Weafer was dead, (the Hibernian Bank was his crematorium). Capt Liam Breen was the next in command and ordered the vacating of the bank and was the last to come into the hospital building. We brought along with us the crude grenades as we left each post. The firing eased down considerably while the nurses and wounded made their way to HQ. We who remained behind in the hospital gathered together all the mattresses and other material of value in preparation for a rush across the road. There were nineteen of us left. Six of us took the grenades and the remainder took a mattress apiece. First of all a couple would rush out for about 3 yards and then run back and immediately we heard the burst of firing, seven or eight would rush across the road and, running in a zigzag fashion, made us difficult targets. The whole lot of us got across in this manner with only one wounded as he got into Prince's St. I had hobnailed boots on and half-way across I slipped and fell directly behind the Statue of Sir John Grey with a mattress I was carrying on my shoulder. I got to my feet instantly and continued my rush while a cheer went up from the Post Office, but in my haste the rifle had slipped from the mattress and was lying in the centre of

O'Connell St. Another man running behind me picked it up and continued on with it. Having left the mattresses down we were ordered off to different posts; so, until the evacuation of the PO I was placed at Henry St end of the building on the 1st floor under the command of Liam Cullen. I was delighted, as at this time I was with other London-Irish lads among whom was Joe Reilly, who was always ready to liven up things with a rousing songs or crack a few jokes".[10]

Daly was with some of the Kimmage volunteers guarding first floor windows facing Henry Street. This suggests that Liam might have been there also. "By this time we were very fatigued as we had had practically no sleep since we occupied the Hibernian Bank. I remember one of the Cumann na mBan girls, Miss Bridie Walsh, suggesting to me I should lie down and have a sleep".[11]

"I was not in my new abode long when I felt the pangs of hunger and decided to look for grub and found the kitchen in the upper portion of the GPO, but found it hard to get food as it was rationed in very small quantities by Desmond Fitzgerald, who was commissariat. Joe Reilly then went through the various openings broken in the walls of the GPO and other buildings along Henry St until he came to a provision shop and came back with a flitch of bacon and we started a cooking class of our men in Liam Cullen's post. On one sortie we came into the Waxworks Exhibition and after killing a dog which had gone mad in the basement of the house we had an inspection of the wax figures and came away with the effigies of King Edward and Wolfe Tone and brought them to our post. Some genius put the figures at the windows and immediately a fusillade of bullets came through and we had to duck for a few minutes until the firing died down. The idea of the wax figures of Wolfe Tone and King Edward being riddled by bullets amused us a great deal. The room in which we were stationed was the 'dead' parcels office and in the cupboards was [sic] a large number of parcels that for some reason or other could not be delivered and were held in safe custody. Among them was a small parcel of spectacles and Thomas O'Donoghue was testing them to replace his own when he must have exposed himself - through the window a couple of bullets came whizzing in and scattered the parcel off the table and he was quite indignant thinking that one of the men in the room had thrown a missile at his prize, and it was fully a minute before he realised that he was under fire. He was careful after that.

Wednesday night was rather uneventful in our quarter, except of course the heavy firing throughout the city and the terrific reports of the Howth Mausers whenever fired".[12]

Larry Ryan - GPO

Most people in the GPO who wrote witness statements seem to have spent some of the time guarding the windows, and some on the roof, as well as attempting to rest wherever they could. It is likely that Ryan was on the roof for part of the week. Desmond Ryan (no relation) was on the roof of the GPO on Tuesday night and Wednesday morning.

"Above rain falls with the evening and drenches us to the skins. We procure oilskins and await a threatened attack. We notice the nervous movement of the crowds in the streets. Dark descends and still we do not sleep. I see queer faces in the sky while I lie on the slates and the rain drizzles gently down. A drunken man below yells in the porchway: 'Yiz are Irishmen and if yizrere bet tomorrow, yiz are Irishmen!' Exposed to English bullets, a stray shot puts an end to his life. The fires proceed, gaining in intensity and flickering low by turns. Dawn finds us sleepless but happy…"[13]

"Wednesday morning finds things beginning to get lively. Bullets are pattering on the walls and windows of the Imperial, Reis's, the D.B.C., Hopkins, etc., all of which are held by us. An ever inquisitive crowd is standing in D'Olier Street and O'Connell Bridge, right between the two firing parties. They appear quite unconcerned. Indeed, one would think from their appearance that the whole thing was merely a sham battle got up for their amusement. Towards ten o'clock, however, they gradually disappear, and half an hour later the streets shine bare in the sunlight".[14]

"On Wednesday morning, shells began to fly a bit. We heard them. That was when Father O'Flanagan came up onto the roof to us in the early hours of Wednesday morning".[15]

It was on Wednesday that British troops succeeded in getting their artillery in place to launch explosive and incendiary shells at the GPO and the buildings around it.[16]

Also that morning at 8am the gunboat Helga came up the Liffey and began shelling Liberty Hall.[17]

"For the next few hours we work hard, rendering our section of the defences (the east room) as bullet-proof as possible. Stationery presses are raided, and a wall of notebooks six or seven feet deep is built inside the window. Then follows a line of sacks full of coal, all the sand having been utilised in the lower storeys. To prevent these rather inflammable materials catching fire the whole place is drenched by means of one of the large fire hoses. Four loopholes have been left in the barricade, through which we place our rifles. There follows an unexciting vigil during which we watch the empty streets unceasingly. Our window commands O'Connell Street from the Imperial Hotel to Carlisle Building and the fire station on the opposite side of the Liffey. Intermittent fire is going on on all sides, but, save for the occasional spent bullet, our building is not touched as yet!"[18]

"About 2 o'clock p.m. a gigantic boom shakes the edifice to its foundations and everyone looks up with startled eye. From all sides come questioning words. Some say that a bomb has exploded in the lower room. Others that it is a dynamite explosion, but a second and third in quick succession prove the correctness of

137

those who proclaimed it heavy artillery. The detonations are truly tremendous, and were we not absolutely certain that the gun was situated on the opposite side of the river, one could have sworn that it was at least in Abbey Street. For a time the men are uneasy at this their first experience of heavy gun-fire, but soon they become quite accustomed to the sound, and take no more notice of it than of the ordinary rifle fire".[19]

As the week progressed, with few of the volunteers sleeping, their memories seem to become more confused. Desmond Ryan remembered,

On the Tuesday morning *(or possibly Wednesday?)*, they were all seated together on boxes and barrels, pale and tired. But they were very calm and humorous. Connolly startled them with the announcement that the Citizen Army had captured the King and Kitchener "…in the wax-works", he added with a twinkle in his eye. When asked his opinion on Monday night, he replied scornfully "They are beaten". He never expected artillery would be used against the city until things had gone to the last extremity. He gave two reasons for this opinion: the admission such a use implies of the occupation of the capital by formidable hostile forces, the destruction of property such a use would cause.[20]

Within the GPO, defenders on the roof had to lie almost prone because the parapet was very low.[21]

One of the defenders on the roof was Desmond Ryan. "We remain upon the roof with an odd visit below. Tap-tap-tap. Tap! Tap! Tap. Machine guns and artillery are destroying Liberty Hall. The air quivers and the machine guns play down O'Connell Street. Bullets whizz over our heads and strike the pillars of the porch way and cut grooves in the cobble stones, Duels are waged across the roofs between our snipers and the machine guns on Trinity and Westmorland Street. Tap. Tap Tap. Then the zip-zip-zip-zip-zip of our automatic Mausers. We have just got used to this sensation and learnt the news of the death of Captain Weafer's death when we are visited by a priest who gives us conditional absolution. He wants a kid of 14 years to go below but the blood thirsty young kid is offended and obdurate. The priest passes on and a member of the Citizen Army, (Jack White, not to be confused with Captain White) who has travelled in foreign parts, proud possessor of the most fluent vocabulary of 'cuss words' ever moulded by the sins of man arrives. He teaches us how to throw bombs".[22]

Jack White also gave grenade instruction to Fintan Murphy. "About eight o'clock the late Father O'Flanagan, formerly of Marlboro Street came bravely clambering over the roof. He wore his stole and told us he was going to give us General Absolution in view of what appeared to be the beginning of a serious attack and then proceeded to do so. Shortly after a very different figure scrambled across and with a very different mission. He was a squat, thickset figure, with the ruddy face of a sailor, with a red muffler around his neck and a large black sombrero-like hat. His side pockets were bulging with something or other, and he had a large knife thrust in his belt. There was no nervousness or agitation about this one - in fact he had somewhat of an air of jubilation and was clearly enjoying himself. He was none other than Jack White of the Citizen Army. Jack was a rough diamond but certainly a cheery companion in a tight corner. He had seen a bit of the world; in fact, according to himself, he had seen all the world from China to Peru and regaled us with gory yarns of some or his amazing adventures, in 'furrin parts'. He could relate these stories with a wealth of descriptive power which was nothing short of miraculous but I haven't time to tell you any of them much as I'd like to. Jack's visit to us, however, was for the purpose of telling us how to use the home-made grenades; so, pulling one from his jacket pocket he began to tell us in the most lurid language imaginable not only how he suggested we should use them but also how they came to be made. My companion beside me did not relish the fluency of his speech and mildly asked him to restrain it. This, I think, pained Jack because be left us soon after and I did not see him for some days - in fact not until just before the surrender in Moore Street when, I gathered, he was packing up to move on to another revolution, ours having apparently failed to come up to his expectations".[23]

"PHP *(Padraig Pearse)* and Willie *(his brother)* inspect our positions. PHP receives a genial and languid warning to keep under cover. 'A curious business', says Willie to me as he passes, 'I wonder how it will end. Of course a lot of good work has been done but there is more to do'. We are promised relief and shortly afterwards a company takes our place. We go downstairs through the holes now broken in the slates, and see many of our friends. I return to the centre room where we are to sleep behind the counters on mattresses. All is dark within. Outside the fires glare from Tyler's corner. We have already commandeered the Imperial. Willie Pearse gazes at the fires. 'Nothing will stop that fire from spreading down the whole block' he says. I later have a conversation with PHP. I stood beside him as he sat on a barrel looking intently at the flames, his slightly flushed face crowned with his turned-up hat. He suddenly turned to me with the question: 'It was the right thing to do, wasn't it?' 'Yes', I replied in astonishment. He looked at me again more keenly. 'If we fail, it means the end of everything, Volunteers and all'. 'Yes', I answered. He looked back, at that fantastic and leaping blaze. He spoke again: 'When we are all wiped out, people will blame us for everything, but for this the war would have ended and nothing would have been done. After a few years, they will see the meaning of what we tried to do'. He rose and we walked a few paces ahead. 'Dublin's name will be glorious forever', he said with deep passion and enthusiasm. 'Men will speak of her as one of the splendid cities, as they speak now of Paris! Dublin!'

'Ireland is a splendid nation', I answered. – 'They can never despise us again, and the women' - 'Yes', he broke in, 'the women, hundreds of them - carrying gelignite along the quays in spite of every danger'.

I slept for ten hours and was then sent to a corner room where the rest of us were. We sat behind our loopholes. Time dragged. We even wrote letters. We watched the bleak and deserted street tumble into ashes. We watched the smouldering ruins rise. We watched for the soldiers who never came. A cheerful sniper from the roof returns now and then from the roof. He has the happy knack of laying out untold fellows. He tosses his hair and cries 'Do you mind that now?' as his 'bag' mounts. Time and space vanish to a sniper, he tells us. One feels only the heated rifle and the desire to reach the target".[24]

"Sleeping accommodation, as far as the rank and file are concerned, is pretty non-existent. When our 'off-duty' turn arrives we hunt around for a reasonably quiet spot where we might snatch a short sleep. But despite its huge size the GPO seems to possess no amenities of this kind and the best most of us can do is to bed down under a table, or desk, with a top cover thrown over us in lieu of the normal sheet or blanket. Needless to say no- one gets much sleep. The short intervals of silence outside are even more ominous in their eerie intensity than the shots, explosions, strange whistling and odd bursts of patriotic song which punctuate the night".[25]

Gilbert Lynch - Church Street

Gilbert was still stationed in the Church Street area, probably near the Father Mathew Hall. He would have been in the houses and out buildings overlooking the barricades where holes had been broken through the dividing walls. He spent at least some of the time in the middle of the week on the roof of a shed, from which he was to injure himself.

That day, members of A and G companies attacked and captured Linenhall Barracks which was at the back of Monk's Bakery off Coleraine Street. This was several hundred yards north of where Gilbert was positioned. The garrison of about 20 'non-combatant soldiers' surrendered and were imprisoned in the Father Mathew Hall. The volunteers decided to set fire to the barracks as they felt they lacked the manpower to occupy and defend it. However the fire soon got out of control.

"Dinny O'Callaghan and myself spilled the oils and paints we had brought from a druggists shop in North King Street in a large room on the first floor and then piled up the bed boards. We then lighted the fire. The fire spread with amazing rapidity and Dinny suggested it might be better if we opened the windows. I crossed the room to open the windows and I will never forget the heat. It took me all my time to get back and the soles were burnt off my boots in a few moments. The fire continued throughout the day and Wednesday night, and we had to use hoses on it to keep it from burning the dwelling houses in the vicinity".[26]

"To the front of the barracks was a block of tenement houses. They were in danger of becoming alight and that, had it occurred, would have rendered our positions untenable. We procured a hose and standpipe from the North Dublin Union. We played water on the front of the houses and prevented the fire spreading in our direction".[27]

"…we proceeded to save the adjoining houses and protect our fire fighters from possible attack by enemy forces. The fire was eventually got under control or burned itself out. The barracks were completely burnt to the ground".[28]

"During the night the fire had spread in an easterly direction and involved Hugh Moore and Alexander's wholesale druggists premises, where large stores of oils and inflammable goods became ignited. Barrels of oil and spirits burst occasionally and sent flames, with a loud explosion, hundreds of feet into the air. The entire neighbourhood was as bright as day".[29] The fire continued burning for days.

On Wednesday night Commandant Daly discussed with his officers whether to attack British snipers in Capel Street, but decided against it because light from the fires made it too bright for them to have any chance of surprise.[30]

During the night the sound of sporadic sniping and machine gun fire continued as well as the whistling of signal flares.

Redmond Cox - Church Street

Redmond Cox spent Tuesday night 'attending to the hospital in Church Street'. This was the Father Mathew Hall and he would have been helping Martin Conlon who had been "appointed Red Cross Officer and was in charge of the sanitary arrangements there. At this time Conlon was a Corporation employee either in the sanitary Office or in the Rates office".[31] Mrs Conlon joined him there and "stayed there till the end of the rising, giving assistance all round, nursing the sick and preparing food for them".[32]

Redmond said, "On the following day we were taken out on the barricades first in May Lane. That was Wednesday. That's the morning portion. In the evening and night we were put on the barricade at the Temperance Hall (*Father Mathew Hall*) again, and after that about 8 o'clock that night, after refreshments, I and 2 other men were put in a window in a side street at the Temperance Hall".[33]

That morning British troops had opened fire on the battalion's posts from the other side of the River. Artillery had been fired at the Four Courts building but it had little effect on the thick stone walls. Some of the Royal Dublin fusiliers occupied buildings just south of the Liffey on the corner of Bridge Street and Usher's Quay and opened fire on the barricade at the bottom of Church Street. This put the volunteers there at extreme risk until two volunteers ran across the bridge with 4 cans of petrol and set fire to the buildings, returning unscathed.[34]

Mairead Ni Cheallaigh (O'Kelly) was a member of Cumann na mBan who was attached to F company. One of her brothers was serving in this company with

Redmond. "I think it was on Wednesday the Volunteers started to burrow through the houses and after that they did not let us go on the street at all. Some of the men, of course, had to man the barricades. There was a boy called Reynolds killed in the Church Street area but we did not see it happen. We saw various civilians being killed. They would not stay indoors. We had instructions from the Volunteers to see that all civilians got food. This we gave them - mostly uncooked. They were always coming for tea, and we made cans of it for them until the Volunteers stopped that as the civilians took unnecessary risks coming for it. Also the tea was getting scarce... That sort of thing went on with the fighting getting hotter. All of the fighting was done with the Howth guns. None of the boys I knew had revolvers".[35]

On Wednesday night Maurice Collins, another member of F company arrived to join his comrades in Church Street. Until then, he had been at Martin Conlon's house guarding Bulmer Hobson. "We found Hobson in a rather distressed state of mind and had to warn him several times to remain calm and quiet. He did not discuss the situation with us; neither did he show any animosity to us personally. While he was a prisoner with us, his fiancé called, inquiring if Bulmer Hobson was there, but we considered it better to deny his presence. We held him prisoner until Wednesday night when an order came from either Pearse of Connolly, that Hobson could be released... I had to endorse this order to the effect that I would comply with the order. There and then we released him and Michael Lynch and I proceeded to Church Street to re-join our company..."[36] This contradicts Martin Conlon's statement that Hobson had been released on Monday.

Sheila O'Hanlon - Marrowbone Lane

Wednesday was a fairly quiet day at Marrowbone Lane. "At Dawn on Wednesday the garrison, which had been at Watkins brewery, arrived to join their colleagues at Marrowbone Lane. They had decided that they were serving no purpose there. There were about two dozen of them. Sniping continued all day".[37]

"Nineteen chickens captured from messenger boy. Quiet day. We cooked the chickens for dinner, having to take them out of the pots with bayonets, not having any forks or utensils for cooking. Dinner very successful. Captain's wife (Mrs Murphy) came to stay with us. We emptied out the oats from the sacks and made the beds(?) more comfortable, very cold. Miss Cosgrave and myself did not sleep and we envied the other girls, some of whom were snoring. We both keep watch while the guard gets a well deserved sleep. Captain calls the men together and addresses them with good news. Very slight firing today".[38]

Another visitor was Annie Cooney's father, who had also been the day before. "He came again on Wednesday. On that day he took messages from the Inchicore men of the company to their people who were probably worrying about them".[39]

Although Wednesday was described as fairly quiet at Marrowbone Lane, both sides continued sniping. "The next event was a sniper in a tree about two hundred yards on the Dolphins Barn side of the canal. He was sitting on a branch half way up with the trunk of the tree between him and us. We all saw him and Mick Liston potted him out of it and this soldier remained hanging out of the tree all day. As darkness came on the firing eased off but usual odd shots and thuds hit the building from time to time. Then we began to see the glow from the city. As night fell the light of this glow spread over the whole city. Shots and heavy explosions could be heard frequently. We got word that the city was on fire but that we had only few casualties whilst the British were suffering heavy losses. We certainly believed this as this was our own case. We had no one killed and only two wounded and these were back in the fight again. If all the garrisons were like ours, and we had no reason to doubt that they were, we were doing very well indeed. We had only to bide our time. We must win and none of us thought otherwise. Failure was the last thing that I or the rest of us thought of… A trickle of reinforcements kept coming in and we were in high spirits, all young men determined to win and this was our only object. I and the rest of us had made our Easter duty and God would see us on the winning side.

At about 11 o'clock on the Wednesday night, I got word that a priest was in the main hall and that I was to go down for confession. I went down and told him I had been at Holy Communion on Easter Sunday. He gave me his blessing and I went back to let another man down to him…"[40]

1 Tannam. Liam witness statement 242
2 Tannam. Liam witness statement 242
3 Tannam. Liam witness statement 242
4 Martin, Bridgid (Ni Floghludha) witness statement. WS 398
5 Tannam. Liam witness statement 242
6 Daly, William .witness statement WS 291
7 Daly, William .witness statement WS 291
8 Henderson R. witness statement WS 1686 It is worth noting that Henderson's witness statements are intended to be a distillation of other first-hand evidence.
9 Daly, William .witness statement WS 291
10 Daly, William .witness statement WS 291
11 Carrigan, James witness statement WS 613
12 Daly, William .witness statement WS 291
13 Ryan, Desmond . witness statement WS 724
14 Humphreys, Dick.Easter week in the GPO. Nat lib Ireland MS18829 in Jeffery, Keith, The GPO and the Easter Rising. Irish Academic Press, Dublin. 2006
15 Murphy, Fintan, witness statement WS 370
16 The 1916 Rising- personalities and perspectives. Nat library of Ireland. Website. www.nli.ie/1916/1916_main.html
17 Henderson R. witness statement WS 1686 It is worth noting that Henderson's witness statements are intended to be a distillation of other first-hand evidence.

18 Humphreys, Dick. Easter week in the GPO. Nat lib Ireland MS18829 in Jeffery, Keith, The GPO and the Easter Rising. Irish Academic Press, Dublin. 2006

19 Humphreys, Dick. Easter week in the GPO. Nat lib Ireland MS18829 in Jeffery, Keith, The GPO and the Easter Rising. Irish Academic Press, Dublin. 2006

20 Ryan, Desmond . witness statement WS 724

21 Henderson R. witness statement WS1686 It is worth noting that Henderson's witness statements are intended to be a distillation of other first-hand evidence.

22 Ryan, Desmond, witness statement WS 724

23 Murphy, Fintan. Witness statement. WS 370

24 Ryan, Desmond, witness statement WS 724

25 Humphreys, Dick. Easter week in the GPO. Nat lib Ireland MS18829 in Jeffery, Keith, The GPO and the Easter Rising. Irish Academic Press, Dublin. 2006

26 Holohan, Gary, witness statement. WS 328

27 Kelly, Patrick, witness statement. WS 781

28 Shouldice, John, witness statement. WS 162

29 Kelly, Patrick, witness statement. WS 781

30 Shouldice , John, witness statement. WS 162

31 Conlon, Mrs Martin. Witness statement. WS 419

32 Conlon, Mrs Martin. Witness statement, WS 419

33 Cox, Redmond. Pension application. MSP34REF1983

34 O'Brien, Paul. Crossfire- the battle of the four courts 1916. New Island, Dublin 2012

35 O'Kelly, Mairead, witness statement WS 925

36 Collins, Maurice J. witness statement WS 550

37 Henderson Ruaidhri. Witness statement WS 1686. This was written in 1945 for the purposes of distilling existing evidence for a military tattoo so is essentially secondary evidence.

38 McNamara, Rose. Witness statement. WS 482

39 O'Brien, Annie (Cooney) Witness statement WS 805

40 Holland, Robert witness statement WS 280

Chapter Twelve
Thursday 27 April

Liam Parr - GPO

Liam had been among the contingent of volunteers who had rushed across Sackville Street into the GPO the previous day protected with mattresses, so he might have hoped to catch up some rest on Thursday, despite the noise of the shooting. (However it must be remembered that some such as James Carrigan said that the last seven only evacuated the Hibernian Bank on Thursday at 4 pm. It is therefore quite possible that this seven included Liam. Unless new information comes to light, it will probably remain impossible to be absolutely sure of the details. The level of ambiguity in the memories of the participants seems to increase as the week progressed, presumably as a result of the stress and lack of sleep, yet the differences are usually in matters of detail and timing. Generally speaking the record is remarkably consistent.)

The weather remained beautiful. In later years some older Dubliners with long memories would describe sunny late spring days as 'rebellion weather'.

"It is a glorious day again with a burning sun glowing in a cloudless blue sky. A sullen rumble of heavy shooting from Jacob's direction vibrates on the cool breeze like the rattle of a deadly snake. At the O'Rahilly's orders we spend the morning constructing imitation barricades in every window which opens outwards. This work necessitates the breaking in of numerous locked doors. The building seems immense. The number of separate rooms in the place is unbelievable. Meantime the bombardment has recommenced. Hopkins', the D.B.C., and the Imperial being under continuous fire, while the GPO is subject to much sniping. The everlasting wait for the unexpected is terribly nerve-racking. Machine-guns stutter irregularly from all sides and add to the growing uproar".[1]

That day, Peter Ennis, the caretaker of Liberty Hall, arrived having fled the shelling of his building. Frank Robbins reported hearing him tell his story. "Peter Ennis reported daily to Connolly in the GPO as to the developments, if any, around Liberty Hall. Ennis used the side entrance at 29 Eden Quay instead of the front entrance in Beresford Place. He had the terrible experience of seeing Ernest Kavanagh shot dead by the British forces on Tuesday morning. Ernest Kavanagh was employed as a clerk in the National Health Insurance section of the Union, that portion of the Custom House facing the main entrance of Liberty Hall, which was occupied by British forces, and it was from there the shots were fired that blasted his life from this earth. He was responsible for many very fine cartoons in 'the Irish Worker', signed E.K., and was a brother of Maeve Kavanagh. Peter Ennis had nothing extraordinary to report until Wednesday, when he informed Connolly of an attempt on the part of the S.S. Helga to shell Liberty Hall, and of her failure to do so because of the obstruction of the railway bridge running across Beresford Place to Tara St. station. The first effort on the part of the Helga was to fire a direct shot at Liberty Hall from the river, but it struck the lower portion of the steel framework of the bridge. The Helga then moved down the river in order to get an angle to allow her to clear the bridge and lob the shells over the bridge on to the roof of Liberty Hall, but this also proved a failure.

Next day Peter Ennis saw the preparations to shell Liberty Hall from the Liffey wall near Tara Street. The officer in charge found that the muzzle of the gun was not clear of the wall to give him a direct shot at Liberty Hall, and a number of soldiers then prized the coping-stones, with the aid of crowbars, into the river. Ennis told me that when the first shell hit the building he thought that the whole place was collapsing around him, and he made his way to the top landing of Liberty Hall to try to escape through the hole, already broken since the previous Monday, into the Colonial Bar. Ennis related how this hole in the wall, being near the ceiling of the next house and not on the floor level of where he was in Liberty Hall, caused him grave misgivings, but he was eventually forced to make the decision to throw himself from the floor space of Liberty Hall on to the bed below in the next house. During all this the shelling of Liberty Hall continued. He then went to the GPO and reported the matter to Connolly, who advised him not to go back to Liberty Hall but to find some other place of abode".[2]

Larry Ryan - GPO

Larry Ryan, of course, was also in the GPO where he had probably been all week. The rebels feared an infantry attack and had been trying to make barricades on Lower Abbey Street but the shelling was so intense that they abandoned these and thereafter carried out all the defence from in the GPO. It was while Connolly was inspecting defences outside the GPO building that his foot was shattered by shrapnel.

"Towards 3 o'clock we learn that there is going to be an attack from the north-west side. All the available men, therefore, are withdrawn from the eastern posts, and take up positions at the western windows. The excitement grows intense. Everyone is waiting. Suddenly rumour has it that an armoured car is approaching up Henry Street. Men show themselves insanely at the window to obtain a view. Then comes a tremendous explosion rising high above the raffle of rifle and machine-gun fire. The shooting dies down all at once, and there is a lull".[3]

"Pearse takes this opportunity of speaking to the men. His words consist of a short resume of events since the Monday morning. He commences by saying that K has succeeded in overturning the armoured car with a bomb. 'All our principal positions', he continues, 'are still intact; Commandant Daly has captured the Linenhall Barracks, taken two officers and twenty-three men prisoners, and set fire to the building. The country is steadily rising, and a large band of Volunteers is marching from Dundalk on Dublin. A successful engagement between a large body of police and an inferior number of Volunteers has taken place near Lusk, between thirty or forty police being captured. Barracks have been raided throughout the country, and especially in the Counties Dublin and Meath. Wexford has risen and a relief column, to be marched on Dublin, is being formed. A large store of food supplies has been discovered in the building which will enable us to hold out till reinforcements from the country arrive and release us'.

He concludes by saying that we have now successfully held out as a Republic against the might of England for three full days. Wherefore, according to International law, we are legally entitled to the status of Republicanists and the presence of a delegate in that Peace Conference which must inevitably follow the war.

His words are answered by a deafening outburst of cheering which spreads throughout the whole building. Needless to say, this account puts new vitality into the men which three days' uncertainty and suspense had rather dispersed".[4]

"3.45 p.m. The military commence shelling us in real earnest, and shrapnel shells begin to drop on the roof in quick succession. Two howitzers have been mounted near Findlater's Church, *(in Parnell Square)*. For ten or fifteen minutes our roof-snipers stand the fire, but begin to suffer heavily, three being wounded severely. Word to evacuate this position is accordingly given, and a minute later they come tumbling down through the safety man- holes into the telegraph room. These man-holes are just rough spaces torn in the slates and mortar through which a rope stretches down to the floor. Some of the men in their hurry fail to catch the rope altogether, and take the eighteen foot drop as though it were an everyday occurrence. The wounded are lowered safely by means of two ropes. This cannonade continues for about two and a half hours, but the shells, the majority of which seem to be shrapnel, fail to do any serious damage to our position. Snipers on the Gresham [Hotel], however, are sending a fusillade of bullets in through the western windows, and we are ordered to keep under cover as much as possible. We allow them to continue firing till, mystified at our silence, they grow bolder, and incautiously show themselves over the top of the parapet. Immediately a single volley rings out. There is no more sniping that evening from the Gresham.

The continuous 'boom' of the Howth guns echoing from all sides of the building show that the military are at length beginning to show themselves, but towards seven o'clock the cannonade slackens, and finally subsides to an occasional report now and again. The GPO, Imperial, Reis's, and all our minor posts are still intact".[5] The 'Howth' guns were fired so incessantly that they overheated and defenders needed to cool them using the oil from tins of sardines.[6]

By the evening barricades had caught fire as well as the buildings on East side of O'Connell St. Several eye witnesses reported seeing molten glass flowing across the pavement.[7]

"7.30 p.m. The surplus men return to their former positions in the eastern rooms, where the single guards have spent a most uninteresting and nerve- shattering evening listening to the firing all round them, but seeing nothing tangible. Hopkins is just beginning to blaze, while somewhere down in Abbey Street a thin column of smoke is rising into the still evening air. Not realising that this is the commencement of that huge conflagration which is to devastate O'Connell Street we watch the leaping flame while gradually night darkens over the city.

On returning to our posts after tea we are appalled at the stupendous increase the fire has made. The interior of our room is as bright as day with the lurid glow of the flames. Reis's jewellery shop is a mass of leaping scarlet tongues of light. Behind it huge mountains of billowing jet black smoke are rolling up into the heavens. A roaring as of a gigantic waterfall re-echoes from the walls. Hopkins is completely hidden from view by a curtain of shimmering, hissings sparks. Up through the ever-changing haze of smoke and flame, lifting itself proudly like one who scorns to notice the taunts of an enemy, rises the tower of the D.B.C. Ringed round with fire it stands undaunted while overhead the very sky quivers with the simmering heat. It seems symbolical of Ireland. Suddenly some oil works near Abbey Street is singed by the conflagration, and immediately a solid sheet of blinding, death-white flame rushes hundreds of feet into the air with a thunderous explosion that shakes the walls. It is followed by a heavy bombardment as hundreds of drums of oil explode. The intense light compels one to close the eyes. Even here the light is so terrible that it strikes one like a solid thing as blasts of scorching air come in through the glassless windows.

Millions of sparks are floating in impenetrable masses for hundreds of yards around O'Connell Street, and as a precaution we are ordered to drench the barricades with water again. The whole thing seems too terrible to be real. Crimson-tinged men moved around dazedly. Above it all the sharp crackle of rifle fire predominates, while the deadly rattle of the machine-gun sounds like the coughing laughter of jeering spirits.

Gradually the fire spreads along O'Connell Street, and from a hissing murmur the sound grows to a thunderous booming, like the song of a great dynamo. Awe-stricken, the men gather together at the different posts and discuss the outbreak in hoarse whispers. 'How will it end?' 'Will it reach the Imperial?' 'Will the Post Office catch fire?' 'Is the whole city doomed?' Such are some of the questions that pass from lip to lip.

Suddenly an armoured car appears in Westmoreland Street. It moves towards us, and seems about to advance, but reverses instead, and disappears in the direction of Dame St. A shout rings out from the Imperial Hotel, and we see a figure standing at one of the windows. He makes a trumpet of his hands, and in clear tones informs us that the building has caught fire at the rear. He asks for further orders, and is told to get his men across to the GPO if possible. Five minutes later four Volunteers are seen at the door of the Hotel. They signal to open the main door downstairs, and rush across the street in turns. From their windows we watch their passage breathlessly.

Ten minutes later the Imperial, together with the buildings on either side, is well ablaze, while over in the Henry Street direction another fire has broken out. We seem to be situated in the midst of a circle of flame. Inside the central telegraph room, which runs along the whole length of the GPO, the men standing silently at their posts, black and bronze statues against the terrible glare of the sky. Unawed and undaunted, their gaze ever fixed on the glistening cobbles and shadowed lanes whence all attacks must be directed, they wait expectantly. Now and again the flames beat upwards in a flash of light that reveals every detail behind the barriers, then they subside as suddenly, and lines of black shadows, rays of darkness, as it were, creep over us. Fortunately the wind is blowing seawards, and the myriads of blazing fragments are carried away from the GPO. Glowing sparks, however, now begin to shower down with a pattering like soft rain, and threaten to set everything on fire. All bombs and hand grenades are taken to the centre of the building, and again we drench barricades, walls and floors. Even in the midst of this inferno we are sniped at by the enemy, and occasional bullets come in through the windows. Clouds of dirty grey smoke prevent us from replying".[8]

"The blaze creeps steadily towards the Imperial. Every quarter of an hour we are called to arms. The telephone breaks down. We signal with difficulty to the Imperial. Boom! Boom! Boom!, The place shakes. Boom! Well, let them waste their ammunition. We spare ours – Boom! Gets stale with repetition. Transferred to gate in the evening. The entire block, nay the entire street opposite is one huge leaping flame which makes every cobble stone distinct and murmurs horribly and laps the very clouds. I think over the events of the past few hours as I and my companion Fintan Murphy pace up and down the darkened archway: Connolly wounded, P.H.P.'s address to us, the news we have heard from a visitor of the despondency in the city as well as the news that the country has not risen. We are in the middle of a circle of fire. It is the fire which is stealing in and around us which eventually drives us out. A Volunteer Officer (Gearoid O'Sullivan) looks out of the gate beside me. 'This will have a terrible effect upon the country', he remarks. 'Are we done?' I ask him. He tells me we are. The Metropole men evacuate their position through a misapprehension but return again. I leave my companion occasionally to see my friends kneeling rifle in hand behind lurid barricades. Suddenly the song rings out from all quarters of the building: 'Soldiers all are we'. Fire and death and the beginning of the end but we have lost all fears and cares. The noble side of war appeared. The great strength and goodness of Ireland shone vividly before me. And a deep respect and admiration surged up in me for the men and women in this doomed building. Like the little girl who died after eating ices and hot pudding I felt we were in for a jolly death. Dawn came after this most terrible night".[9]

Gilbert Lynch - Church Street

Gilbert said that he injured his ankle when a roof collapsed and was laid up in Father Mathew Hall on 27th or 28th of April. He said he was on the barricades around North King Street.

"I could not say definitely whether it was on Thursday or Friday, I was at Nicholas Avenue, in a shed, and the shed broke down, and I sprained my ankle, which I did not attend to..."[10] Martin Conlon remembered being "in constant touch with him throughout the whole week. Towards the end of the week, on Thursday or Friday, his ankle was badly sprained in descending from a roof in a yard at the corner of Nicholas Avenue and Church Street".[11]

Gilbert also said that, "During the week I met with an accident getting over the barricade and badly twisted my ankle".[12]

"I did not say anything to anyone, and the result was that the following day the ankle was so bad I couldn't get my shoe on at all".[13]

"He continued on duty until I discovered him with his foot much swollen in a vacant house with other volunteers in Church Street, and insisted on his removal to the auxiliary hospital at Father Mathew Hall".[14]

"The Father Mathew Hall had been taken over as a Red Cross hospital, and I was taken in there to get treatment and I was kept in there. We could hear the firing, especially at night time, and heard all the rumours about the Germans being on the Naas Road coming in to Dublin and things like that".[15]

John Henratty told the pensions board that it was on Thursday that Gilbert Lynch was injured.[16]

Father Aloysius was in the Father Mathew Hall. "On Thursday very extensive fires could be seen and as far as we could locate them they were principally in O'Connell street, and GPO and Clery's seemed to be involved. The rifle and machine gun volleys were almost continuous. The volunteers had taken prisoners; soldiers from Linenhall barracks and a Dublin Metropolitan Policeman DMP, and had them working at filling sandbags in the Father Mathew Hall."[17]

Redmond Cox - Church Street

Redmond had spent Wednesday night in Father Mathew Temperance Hall in a window facing Nicholas Avenue. He would have been facing the buildings on the other side of Nicholas Avenue where Gilbert was guarding the same barricades. He said he spent much of the week there. In addition, "On Thursday evening and Friday morning I was guarding a laneway in Church Street".[18] Also inside the Father Mathew Hall were both Martin Conlon and his wife.

150

At 5 o'clock in the afternoon British troops from 2/6 battalion the Sherwood foresters began to take over and occupy the whole stretch of Capel Street from the river up to Bolton Street. They did this using two newly constructed armoured personnel carriers that had been built at the Inchicore railway workshops. These were constructed from flatbed Daimler lorries, on which were fitted boilers supplied by the Guinness brewery. The cab was then armoured with steel plates. The work was undertaken by some of the workers in the Great Southern and Western railway works in Inchicore. This was the workplace of many of the Volunteers, particularly those of the 4th battalion occupying the South Dublin Union. The boiler held 20 soldiers who could fire with rifles and a machine gun through apertures cut in the steel. The lorries drove up Capel Street, disgorging the soldiers at intervals where they kicked in the doors of houses and tenements and occupied them. They also built barricades with sacks filled with soil which they got by digging up the ground floors of the houses. A courier from the Four Courts on his way between there and the GPO witnessed the arrival of the soldiers so had to report back to Daly that British troops now controlled the area. The courier was a 16 year old Fianna boy called Joseph Reynolds who succeeded in getting his messages past the British soldiers but it took him, he said between 1½ and 2 hours to cover the distance between the GPO and the Four Courts.[19]

"On Thursday the British military were being strongly increased in numbers and severe attacks with rifles and machine guns were directed at our barricades which were strongly defended. Thursday night and Friday, the British military adopted breaking through tactics from house to house to reach our position".[20]

Sheila O'Hanlon – Marrowbone Lane

Sheila spent the day in the distillery with her Cumann na mBan comrades providing food and medical care to the Volunteers. As sniping intensified, some of the men needed more than one rifle to avoid them overheating, so some of the 'girls' continued with their role of loading them. Rose McNamara, made notes about the activities of Thursday... "Three live calves captured; one was killed by a volunteer who was also a butcher (Bob Holland) for dinner on Friday (God forgive us). One of our snipers, Mick Liston) slightly grazed on the forehead which we dressed. Heavy sounds of machine guns (or cannons) in the distance all night. We keep on praying".[21]

Bob Holland was not best pleased when he didn't get any of the meat. "At dawn on Thursday morning we saw that British troops had taken up positions all around us. Trenches had been dug on both sides of the canal, also in Fairbrothers field and we settled down to a 'battle royal'. All rifles were brought into play... At the usual time the girls brought along our breakfast, tea and bread. I did not know what had happened to the beast I had killed the day before as we got no meat. The girls kept loading the rifles and we were allocated three each. I occasionally used

151

one of the Howth rifles and I was driven 12 feet across the floor every time I fired it... Four others and myself were brought down to the yard and given hand grenades. There were about thirty other men and all the women were put in the main hall. There were about 20 men in the Hall at the yard entrance and Con Colbert instructed us in the use of these grenades and in the use of very crude pikes... Jack Saul heard some talking outside the canal gate where he was at the time and he and someone else threw one of the hand grenades over the wall. We heard some screeching and shouting outside and a lot of moaning. As a result the soldiers on the outside of the wall ran away and were fired upon by a volley from the distillery... When I got on top again, the soldiers had become scarce but I could see a lot of bodies all around outside the wall... I could just see a pit and red cross men working at it and putting bodies into it at the bridge..." [22]

"...as night approached again the firing eased off but we could see the bright red glow over the city... All during the night the firing and the banging continued and still our dogged spirit is 100% with us all. We are winning and nothing else matters. We will surely get that help. The Germans could not be far from Dublin now and the country volunteers are showing the way... All this we were told by the odd stragglers that came in and we readily believed it all... We knew that Germany was beating England in France and so a few more days wouldn't matter. We carry on with our spirits getting higher". He also heard that "the men in the Great Southern and Western railway are putting engine boilers on lorries got from Guinness's to act as armoured cars, that these have camouflaged holes painted on them and that they are being brought out with British troops to fight against. The men supposed to be doing this work were fitters on the railway". [23]

On Thursday, Sheila's sister Mollie was sent out of the distillery as a courier. [24] Mollie said, "I had to leave on Thursday. About 1pm I was sent out by Captain Con Colbert to Éamonn Ceannt's house and to some house in Ruben Street. I delivered the letter and went to Ceannt's but failed to get back." [25]

"...I was sent by the late Con Colbert to the house of the late Éamonn Ceannt for supplies and told to call at my own home also. When I arrived there the British military had possession of the bridges. They also had possession of our house where they remained for just four weeks. I found it impossible to return... On Thursday evening... I couldn't get back in." [26]

1 Humphreys, Dick. Easter week in the GPO. Nat lib Ireland MS18829 in Jeffery, Keith, The GPO and the Easter Rising. Irish Academic Press, Dublin. 2006
2 Robbins, Frank. Witness statement WS 585
3 Humphreys, Dick. Easter week in the GPO. Nat lib Ireland MS18829 in Jeffery, Keith, The GPO and the Easter Rising. Irish Academic Press, Dublin. 2006
4 Humphreys, Dick. Easter week in the GPO. Nat lib Ireland MS18829 in Jeffery, Keith, The GPO and the Easter Rising. Irish Academic Press, Dublin. 2006
5 Humphreys, Dick. Easter week in the GPO. Nat lib Ireland MS18829 in Jeffery, Keith, The GPO and

the Easter Rising. Irish Academic Press, Dublin. 2006

6 Henderson R. witness statement WS1686 It is worth noting that Henderson's witness statements are intended to be a distillation of other first-hand evidence.

7 Henderson R. witness statement WS1686 It is worth noting that Henderson's witness statements are intended to be a distillation of other first-hand evidence.

8 Humphreys, Dick. Easter week in the GPO. Nat lib Ireland MS18829 in Jeffery, Keith, The GPO and the Easter Rising. Irish Academic Press, Dublin. 2006

9 Ryan, Desmond Witness statement WS 724

10 Lynch, Gilbert. Pension application. MSP34REF41334

11 Conlon, Martin in Lynch, Gilbert. Pension application. MSP34REF41334

12 Lynch, Gilbert; ed O Cathasaigh, Aindrias; The life and times of Gilbert Lynch; Irish Labour History society. 2011; Dublin

13 Lynch, Gilbert; ed O Cathasaigh, Aindrias; The life and times of Gilbert Lynch; Irish Labour History society. 2011; Dublin

14 Conlon , Martin in Lynch, Gilbert. Pension application. MSP34REF41334

15 Lynch, Gilbert; ed O Cathasaigh, Aindrias; The life and times of Gilbert Lynch; Irish Labour History society. 2011; Dublin

16 Lynch, Gilbert. Pension application. MSP34REF41334

17 Aloysius, Father OFM. Witness statement WIT 200

18 Cox, Redmond. Pension application. MSP34REF1983

19 Reynolds, Joseph , witness statement. WS 191

20 Shouldice, John , witness statement. WS 162

21 Mc Namara, Rose. Witness statement. WS 482

22 Holland, Robert witness statement WS 280

23 Holland, Robert witness statement WS 280

24 Kennedy, Margaret Loo. In O'Hanlon. Mollie, pension application. MSP34 REF 4351

25 O'Hanlon. Mollie, pension application. MSP34 REF 4351

26 O'Hanlon. Mollie, pension application. MSP34 REF 4351

Chapter Thirteen
Friday 28 April

Liam Parr and Larry Ryan in the GPO

In the early hours of the morning, lookouts heard what they thought was the sound of a cavalry charge. All were put on alert to discover that outside the GPO there was a stampede of terrified horses from the direction of Princes Street. These were horses that had broken out of, or been released from, a stables that was threatened by the approaching fires.[1]

At about the same time, the garrison in Nobletts was evacuated to the GPO as it had caught fire.[2]

"The weather is sunny and fine as usual. On the opposite side of O'Connell Street nothing is left of the buildings save the bare walls. Clouds of grey smoke are wreathing around everywhere, and it is difficult to see as far as the Bridge. Occasionally some side wall or roof falls in with a terrific crash. The heat is stupefying, and a heavy odour of burning cloth permeates the air. All the barbaric splendour that night had lent the scene has now faded away, and the pitiless sun illuminates the squalidness and horror of the destruction. The morning is fairly quiet, but occasional shots ring out from the direction of the Four Courts".[3]

"After breakfast we again take up our positions at the windows. The morning passes uneventfully in our area. We hear that Maxwell has arrived in Dublin. Towards twelve o'clock the smoke clears away from Hopkin's corner, and a machine-gun opens fire on our windows. From then on till 3 o'clock the shooting increases on all sides, the report of the Howth guns sounding more like artillery than rifles. About 3.30 p.m. a differently-noted fusillade rings out from the Gresham Hotel direction, and, to our astonishment, the side of the walls where the bullets lodge seem to flash into flame. Finding no hold, however, they became immediately extinguished. A minute or so later someone discovers that the roof is on fire, and immediately commences a perfect babble of shouting, order-giving and talking. The two main lines of hose are quickly brought to the spot, and two streams of water are thrown against the lower part of the roof. Lines of buckets are also organised, and after a quarter of an hour's hard work the outbreak seems to be practically under control. Suddenly, another part of the roof is set on fire by the incendiary bullets, and half the available water supply has to be turned upon it. Heavy firing is meantime going on in all directions, and adds to the confusion. Pearse and J. Plunkett hold a short conversation at the doorway. They both appear very excited. Finally a large number of men are selected for extinguishing work, and the remainder are ordered to the windows. Everyone seems to consider it his duty to give orders at the top of his voice. The noise is terrific. The fire is gaining ground like lightning".[4]

"In the morning, incendiaries had set light to the corner of the roof nearest O'Connell Bridge".[5]

Liam Tannam was one of those on the roof, with Lieutenant Boland. "He, (Boland) preceded me up a ladder which led out onto the roof through a trap door. There was a young man there about eighteen years of age. He was a very thin young fellow and half his body was inside the building and half his body was exposed. He had the job of holding a heavy hose pipe in such a manner as to bend it round a chimney breast on the roof. The roof was then under artillery fire. As Boland and I approached I could hear his teeth chatter. I saw him hold up the hose with one hand and take a handkerchief from his pocket and insert it into his mouth and he bit on that while Boland and I passed so as not to let two officers hear his teeth chatter. I thought that fellow was the bravest man I ever saw. I don't know his name. Boland and I had only just emerged onto the roof when a shell burst beside us. The spot seemed to be suddenly deprived of air and we were left gasping."[6]

"As I rested in the corner room, Éamonn Bulfin, our leader received a message to hold his men in readiness to retire and send two men upstairs as the roof had taken fire. I and another went up. A petrol bomb had struck the glasswork in the topmost room while snipers made the spot more dangerous. We helped to drag hose-pipes to the numerous ladders leading to the roof. Axes were plied. The snipers got as good as they gave. We saw the general clearance of explosives when we went downstairs".[7]

"A lull succeeded in the morning. The report went round that it was arbitration".[8] "But, shortly after that, word went round that all the girls were to be gathered in the main hall. I was very surprised that there were so many; between twenty and thirty young women were assembled before Patrick Pearse, who spoke briefly to them. I watched as they were told that the time had come when they must go. Some of the girls burst into tears, but the majority of them were very angry, and shouted back at him, refusing to leave.... 'No!-No!-We'll stay with the men...! You told us we were all equal...! What about women's rights?' Pearse was very obviously shaken, and did not know how to handle the situation, which was very clearly now getting out of hand.

Pearse, it seems, must have insisted on the departure of the women for shortly afterwards, still protesting, they very reluctantly moved towards a door. A Red Cross flag was raised before them and, after a further delay, they were finally ushered out into Henry Street. Mercifully, there was a short lull in the firing".[9]

Although most of the Cumann na mBan women left (under protest) around midday, some such as Winifred Carney refused and remained to the end. "The street lay in ruins. We strengthened the front defences with three rows of coal bags which we filled and dragged up from the cellars and drenched with buckets full of water, a very tiring labour".[10]

By noon, they were losing the struggle to keep on top of fires in the roof.[11]

At around one pm the sharp shooters on first the roof, and then the upper floors were forced to evacuate by the fire.[12]

"The O'Rahilly comes into the room. He is as cool as ever, one of the very few officers at this moment who really keeps his head. We are ordered to bring all bombs, spare rifles and loose ammunition down to the yard of the GPO. This done, we return to the windows again.

From our posts we can see right down along the telegraph room. It presents a most extraordinary spectacle. In one part the fire has eaten right through the roof, and slates and mortar are commencing to fall on the floor. The two hoses are brought to bear on this spot. They are held six feet above the ground (to enable a better head of water to be obtained) by lines of men. Here and there the water spurts out through small holes in the rubber, drenching the men completely. In one place a huge leak from a faulty connection runs down the uniform of an officer. In a few seconds he is wet to the skin, but stands as unconcernedly as though on parade. Further over a line of buckets extending down to the second floor is working with incredible rapidity. After a few minutes, however, we see that all is useless. The fire is gaining ground in all directions. Huge masses of the roof commence to fall inwards with terrific noise. The floor on which the men are working threatens to give way with each blow. Clouds of smoke from the burning debris writhe around the corridors and passages. It gets into our eyes and noses, and compels fits of coughing. The floors are covered to a depth of three inches with grimy water.

From the yard below comes a noise of shouting, pulling about of bales and packages, and the thunderous report of the Howth rifles. We are warned to be ready for an attack at any moment. A thick pall of smoke has come down over O'Connell Street again, and we are unable to see beyond the corners of the Imperial Hotel. Ten or twelve minutes pass anxiously. The noise below increases in intensity".[13]

"By 3pm the upper stories of the GPO and the front of ground floor had become untenable, so all retired to the sorting room. The badly-injured Connolly was directing operations from a couch in the sorting room.

6pm - All the injured, except Connolly, were evacuated.

7pm - The ammunition needed to be moved again to avoid sparks- now to under Princes Street".[14]

"It was now a race against time of which I had lost all count. As it was getting dark the Post Office was still alight. Connolly was moved towards the other entrance on a stretcher accompanied by some wounded prisoners and volunteers. I went below stairs with the O'Rahilly and the original squad to complete the task we had been interrupted in carrying out, that is the moving of the bombs. The O'Rahilly turned on the water and the first jet from the hose was directed at the bomb savers. We shifted the bombs very hurriedly and rather recklessly. Smoke was now pouring down the lift shaft when we got to the main floor".[15]

"The desperate fight against the flames was abandoned as hopeless. The floors began to give way. Debris crashed in. Thick columns of smoke and flame rose steadily and increased in volume with the minutes. Men on the roof were called down. Some remained an hour and a half after orders to descend struggling vainly to check the fire's progress. The O'Rahilly had to order one obstinate sniper down at the point of the revolver. We hear troops are advancing through the ruins of the Imperial. We have one constant stand to arms and tension. The fire roars through the building. Walls of flame seem to surround the yard. Sheets of flame seem to cover the top of the ground floor and the floor above. Cracks begin to show in the outer walls. Plunkett and Pearse march round and call the various companies to attention before they are marched into the yard. Explosives are carried to and from the cellars. Flames sweep down the shafts. The water supply fails. Plunkett's voice rings sharply out, his eyes have a strange laughing expression, his head and figure have a peculiarly proud and gallant tenseness.

As we watch from the yard, the front floors collapse. We secure rations in what was the hospital. Pearse stands in the midst of the men in the darkened and roaring house of fire. He directs the distribution of food and gives orders that as much as possible is to be packed into haversacks and knapsacks. Cheese and bread are served out. 'Bang!' A tall, dark, handsome man falls in front of me, his face pallid, his eyes closed A moan escapes from his lips. A shot-gun has been discharged by accident. 'Bang.' Within two minutes a similar accident occurs. 'Unload, and hold the muzzles of your guns up'. We can see the street through the crevices in the walls".[16]

"Before the fire reached the ceiling of the ground floor the garrison was assembled and ordered to take provisions in preparation for evacuation. There were piles of cooked rashers, some ham, I think, cases of eggs and bread which were hastily divided I remember one man named Gallagher who was assisting to slice some meat, got his hand in the slicer and sliced a piece off his thumb and he immediately passed it on between two pieces of bread as a sandwich".[17]

"Finally, pieces of burning timber started to fall from the ceiling over us. I remember seeing men carrying bread boards full of bombs, i.e. tin cans with a piece of fuse sticking out the top, the end of which had been dipped in match composition, and damp sacks had to be placed across these for fear they would light and explode.

Although there was no sign of panic, I felt that panic might set in. I had a supply of cigars which I had taken from the Metropole. I lit one of these and walked up and down trying to appear as nonchalant as possible. I did this because I was an officer and felt that the eyes of the men were on me as they would be on all officers, but inwardly I was far from feeling as nonchalant as I assumed to be… At this point I thought a song would be a good thing and I sang 'The soldiers song' accompanied by a Cumman na mBan girl named Madge Fagan.[18]

"It seemed as if the intention might be to delay our departure until daylight had faded. It was dusk by now, but I thought our departure would be as dangerously obvious in the glare of the burning building as it would be in broad daylight. Someone had burst into 'The Soldier's Song', and soon every voice, it seemed was raised in chorus – 'So-ol-diers are we…' - among shards of falling, burning timbers. It was time - high time, I thought - for us to go".[19]

"The fire has practically demolished the whole telegraphic room, and is threatening every moment to cut off our retreat. O'Rahilly again appears, comes over, and tells me to join Desmond FitzGerald down in the restaurant. The GPO is about to be evacuated. With a cheerful wave of his hand, and a smile, he steps quickly down the smoke-filled stairs. Little did I know that this would be the last time I would ever see him alive. Suddenly we hear a great cheer from somewhere beneath, followed by the quick beat of doubling footsteps. A sudden fusillade seems to burst out on all sides. Two or three machine- guns cough threateningly. The first party has left the GPO".[20]

Shortly after 8pm an advance party of about 40 men, led by the O'Rahilly were addressed by Pearse in Henry Street. Their mission was to clear a way up Moore Street and set up a new HQ at Williams and Woods in Parnell Street. Neither Liam nor Larry has been mentioned as being in this party. Denis Daly was one of this advance guard. He said, "We were in two files, each file to take a side of Moore Street, up which we were to go at the double. My position was about the centre of the left file. No sooner had we entered Moore Street than we came under heavy fire. The O'Rahilly was shot and everybody who was in front of me was shot down. A man named McGrath and I got into a doorway about a hundred yards from the British Barricade in Parnell Street. It was impossible to go forward, so we tried to go back towards the GPO. We heard shouts of, 'Come this way' and, following their directions, we entered Coles Lane and got into the rear of Williams grocery shop in Henry Street. It was occupied by about ten men… We decided there that we would attempt to reach Williams and Woods. We moved out into Coles Lane. A fusillade came from the houses covering it. Two were slightly wounded and I fell but found I was not hit. We had to move back into Williams again". [21]

"Practically every member of the little band is hit, the O'Rahilly and two others being wounded mortally".[22]

Sean McLoughlin wrote; "I encountered Sean McDermott who said 'I have been looking for you; we are evacuating the Post Office and I want you to stay with us'. I said 'Where do we evacuate to?' and as I spoke someone said 'Williams and Woods'. I replied 'That is just mad; Williams and Woods is in the hands of the

British'. I believe Pearse said 'Well, O'Rahilly has just gone there'. I said 'My God, he'll be killed: it is certain death'. I then asked 'What way have they gone?' Henry Place was indicated. I drew my revolver and dashed across the road into Henry Place. I ran dawn Henry Place towards Moore Lane. A handful of men were there who had evidently accompanied O'Rahilly. They said 'He's gone' - which I took literally and did not investigate further. We were opposite to Moore Lane when there was a terrific blaze of fire from the far end and we realised the British were in possession of the barricades. I turned back towards the Post Office and saw the whole garrison coming towards me at the run. There was terrible confusion -almost panic. No one seemed to have any idea what to do. Somebody shouted that we were being fired on from the roof of a mineral water factory. I detailed a number of men to break the door down. Another party entered from the opposite door and they opened fire on each other - one man was killed and several wounded. I was incensed with rage calling 'Have you all gone mad - what the hell is wrong?' and I drove them towards the wall threatening them".[23]

The garrison had left the GPO, and retreated across Henry Street and into Henry Place which is opposite where the side door of the GPO was situated. Henry Street led north then west. As it passed Moore Lane they came under heavy machine gun fire from the Rotunda.

Tannam was in command of an advance party. "We rushed across the road into Henry Place, and at the end of Henry Place turned the corner left and when we showed up opposite Moore Lane we came under fire from troops apparently in Parnell Street or some little way up Moore Lane. We stopped and ran across. The only damage done was one man's belt was cut through by a bullet".[24]

The corner house of Moore Street… seemed the best place that could be got especially as my mind was then running on the imminent danger of the collapse of the ceiling in the GPO. I instructed the men to enter and dashed back myself to the angle of Henry Place… and then dashed in the direction of the GPO. The side door seemed rather crowded and I shouted at once, 'Come on', and the garrison poured out into Henry Place with no semblance of order".[25]

The panic must have abated when Connolly and the wounded were brought out. Sean McLoughlin remembered; "A temporary calm seemed to come over them and then Pearse with Connolly being carried on a stretcher and a little cavalcade of wounded followed, with a few women - Julie Grennan, Winnie Carney. Sean MacDermott came up to me saying 'My God. We are not going to be caught like rats and killed without a chance to fight.'

I said. 'There is no need to get into a panic. I can get you out of here but there will be only one man giving orders and I will give them'. He spoke to Connolly and Connolly agreed. He said 'We have no chance now: this is the end'. I then went around to the top of the column and spoke to some of the men in the front, saying 'We must get out of here at all costs…'

I then moved them across Moore Lane. The British were now alive to what was taking place and were opening up with all they had. Beyond us the Post Office was a blazing inferno and the only light in the lane was the terrible glare in the skies. The wounded were groaning but we could not attend to them. I realised we had got to get past Henry Place. We smashed open the door of a mineral water place and found a motor van. I got a number of men to pull this out and we pushed it across the end of Moore Lane to screen us from view…

I then came back down and gave orders that the men were to be moved across in small groups and they were to move into the houses in Moore Street at the top of Moore Lane and that they were to break their way through from house to house as far as they could go. Then the wounded with Connolly were moved across into the place between Henry Place and Moore Street, still leaving them in the open. A woman came to the door to see what was happening and was shot dead by one of our men. They thought we were being attacked. I disarmed him and struck him and Sean MacDermott went to console the mother and as far as I know I believe later in the night he gave her some of the money which he had been carrying for Headquarters purposes. We now managed to get all the men into the buildings and I decided to move Connolly with the stretcher into the first house which was a grocer's shop at the corner of the lane. He was taken into the kitchen and in the meantime I went into Moore Street to carry out reconnaissance but the British were at the other end in force and opened up with machine guns. I could see then we were in an even worse plight than I had realised".[26]

Desmond Ryan: "We move down a passage towards a door opening upon Henry St. We dash across the flame lit and bullet swept street, up Henry Place, into stables, down sombre alleys lighted by machine gun fire. The bullets patter upon the walls. Men fall. Plunkett rallies the men past a bullet swept barricade. Connolly has been borne on a stretcher to Moore Street beneath a red-cross flag.

Pearse, last to leave, charges gallant in green, revolver in hand, his head high, his eyes flashing. Tom Clarke heads another contingent and fires his revolver… We reach Moore St. and enter a grocery store. We soon bore the walls of the adjoining house. Half a dozen houses are bored with pick and crow-bar. While Nelson's Pillar looks down on the blazing GPO we snatch a few hours' sleep".[27]

"The garrison was engaged in breaking through the walls of the houses of this block in the direction of Parnell Street….Plunkett *(Joe)* then said, 'You can now take turns with the squad of men in breaking through the walls with the others.' I was rather exhausted and hungry and the only thing I could get to eat was a raw egg and a square of Chivers jelly. I ate this and made my way through several holes until I came to where men were working. I got some fresh men and proceeded with the work allotted to me".[28]

"Sniping continues all through the night. Though the men are scattered between the various buildings between Parnell Street and Henry Street, the military are still afraid to advance in force. All night long the fire gains ground. The GPO is now nothing but an empty shell. The Coliseum Theatre and the Metropole are rapidly being reduced to ruins. Arnott's [shop] is already licked by the devouring flames. Overhead the quivering sky reflects the angry crimson of this furnace. It looks like a pall of blood. The ever- changing roaring sounds like the shrieks of a thousand demons. So our last night of freedom passes. Everyone seems to realise that our chances at length are hopeless. Without a central base, and completely isolated from our other strong-points and garrisons, how is it possible to hold out longer?"[29]

During the night Sean McLoughlin was called for by the leaders. "Sean MacDermott then spoke saying 'Now, Sean, you are going to have a big job. You will have to take charge now. You are the only one that is likely to get us out of here'. He added 'Mr. Connolly and the others have agreed that you take Mr. Connolly's place and all military commands will be given by you from now on' He continued, 'I don't know how long this will be'. I said a trifle foolishly 'While there's life there's hope.' Connolly said 'Well you seemed to be in at the beginning and in at the end…' I told them we must burrow as far as possible before daylight, that to evacuate Moore Street the men would have to be spread out over the widest possible front, that in any movement out of an enclosed position the close bunching of the men was a gift to the enemy as they could be mown down en masse. Scattered they presented a smaller target and offered a greater maximum of safety".[30]

Gilbert Lynch - Church Street

On Friday Gilbert was still receiving medical attention at Father Mathew Hall. "On Friday the machine gun firing was continuous and there were many explosions from bombs or hand grenades. We heard the heavy boom of cannon from the direction of the bay. This was Friday and owing to transport difficulties, food was running short, and it was difficult to obtain milk. The volunteers worked very hard to bring up provisions. And I should here recall the fearless conduct of the young Fianna who braved all danger and kept communications between various posts and rendered valuable assistance in maintaining supplies".[31]

Mrs Martin Conlon was in Father Mathew Hall. "That Friday night was terrible. The Church Street priests were with us and gave us general absolution and I think we received Holy Communion. The only lights we had in the hall were little night lights. The bombing and firing continued all the night and the next day until about 4 pm".[32]

Gilbert wrote, "One of the most interesting things was that on the Friday it was decided that everybody should go to confession and communion. I shared a mattress with a man - I don't know who he was - but when the priest came down to hear his confession he wouldn't go to confession. I asked him about it when the priest went away. He told me he was a Catholic. I talked and reasoned with him, and eventually before the priest went out he agreed that he would go to confession. I called over the priest and he went to confession. The priest told me I would have great grace for that - I hope I do.

It wasn't until about midnight on Friday night/Saturday morning, that the priests came in to give us Holy Communion. The firing in King Street was fairly heavy at that time, and stray bullets came along. All the lights were put out, and the priest had to feel with his finger for your mouth before he could put the host in. It was a most unique way of receiving communion. I hope we all got grace for it".[33]

"Another incident that happened in the Father Mathew Hall that I ought to relate: Just before the surrender Ned Daly, who was O/C of the area, came up from the Four Courts to bid the men goodbye. I did not know him and he didn't know me, but I happened to be lying near Liam Clarke, Shouldice, Sheils and a few more men that he seemed to know. He seemed very downhearted at the thought of surrender, and Liam Clarke, I think it was, who asked him, 'Well, what's going to happen now?'

'Well', he says, 'I think they will kick you fellows' backsides and send you home, possibly put a few of the leaders in jail'.

Liam Clarke said, 'Well, if they do that we will be a laughing stock for future generations. What will happen if they shoot any of you?'

'If they shoot any of us', he said, 'we will have won, but I don't think they will do that'. He was a better judge of the future history than I would have been".[34]

Redmond Cox - Church Street

On Friday, Redmond was guarding the area around Father Mathew Hall, either from a window in the building overlooking Nicholas Avenue, or from a barricade nearby. Sniping continued all day but, more frighteningly, he would have heard the heavy firing which was closing in on the streets a little further north of his position.

Early that morning the British troops were beginning to approach the Volunteers' positions at the junction of Church Street and North King Street. The soldiers, who had captured the length of Capel Street on Wednesday night, were now moving west along North King Street towards the top of Church Street. They were aiming to control the full length of North King Street and meet up with 2/5 South Staffordshire regiment who were planning to clear North King Street from the west. Their regimental history describes the terrain of the intended 'battlefield'. "Few visitors to Dublin and not all its inhabitants are deeply interested in North King Street. From a spectacular point of view in peacetime it was of little account, consisting as it did of innumerable houses of the smaller sort. If it was not actually a slum, it could certainly be described as a congested area, penetrated by infinite passages and alleys and more nearly resembling a rabbit warren than a battlefield".[35]

The two groups of British troops were advancing from opposite directions on 'Reilly's fort' at the crossroads of Church St and North King Street which was occupied by F or G Company of the 1st battalion of the Volunteers. This was barely a hundred yards north of the Father Mathew Hall where Redmond was stationed, and where Gilbert and many other injured were being tended. The junction itself was marked by a tricolour mounted on a captured lance which had been stuck in a manhole. It was defended by barricades at the junction and in streets around it. These were overlooked by Volunteers stationed in surrounding buildings, in particular Langans public house, on the corner of Caroline Street, and also Reilly's fort itself. This is often described as a pub, though Jack Shouldice called it an unoccupied corner house through the wall of which a hole was bored to the back of Lenihan's licenced premises. There were about 20 men guarding Reilly's Fort, mainly from F Company.[36]

Initially, soldiers advanced about 150 yards to the barricade outside Langans but retreated when they were met with a hail of bullets from the public house, and then from Jamiesons granary tower. However further attacks followed, resulting in heavy casualties on both sides, and to civilians. This area was beginning to experience some of the heaviest fighting of the whole week. During the afternoon as repeated attacks failed to dislodge or kill those defending Langans, the soldiers began to climb along the rooftops in order to use grenades on the pub and the barricades. However, climbing on the roofs made them targets for the defenders in Reilly's fort and they had to withdraw under heavy fire.

Observing the strength of the defence, the British commanding officer decided to use the improvised armoured personnel carriers. These set off on repeated journeys in which they would carry about 20 soldiers to the front of a house which was sprayed with bullets forcing the residents to lie down. The soldiers then smashed open the door and occupied the house, setting up firing positions in the upstairs windows. The lorries then returned with more soldiers to further houses overlooking Langans and its barricade. The personnel carrier could not advance closer to Church Street because of the barricade. Now, very violent and bitter fighting developed as British soldiers attacked the North King Street barricade using rifles and grenades. They were repulsed but only at cost of heavy casualties on both sides.

"Attacks by machine gun and rifle fire on our barricades became more intensive from the Capel Street and Smithfield ends. The barricades facing both ends became untenable for our men who fell back into Reilly's fort which commanded part of North King Street facing the Bolton Street or Capel Street end. Throughout the Friday night and Saturday morning the gunfire was practically continuous. We sustained casualties at the crossing losing a few who were killed outright and a number wounded. Volunteer Patrick O'Flanagan of C Coy, who was one of our defenders, was sent out for ammunition to Father Mathew Hall or wherever he could obtain it was, on his return, shot fatally coming into Reilly's".[37]

The Volunteer wounded were taken to Father Mathew Hall where they were looked after by members of Cumann na mBan who, however, felt they were only able to deal with more minor injuries as they had no trained doctor. Many had gunshot or shrapnel injuries, and the most seriously injured had to be carried at considerable risk by stretcher bearers up Church Street, past the fighting to Richmond hospital. The numbers of injured inside the hall continued to increase and Commandant Daly decided to release 24 policemen who had been held prisoner, and move his HQ to the Four Courts. He told the released prisoners to 'forget all you have seen'. He also moved the army pay corps prisoners to the Bridewell.

During the night the fighting continued. The sounds of rifle and machine gun fire would have been all pervasive in Father Mathew Hall. Outside it would have been less bright than previous days as the fire in Linenhall barracks subsided, but the darkness was broken by the light cast by 'Very Flares'.[38]

It was during that night that Redmond Cox was ordered to stop guarding the laneway in Church Street. "…and Friday evening I was sent into the Four Courts. We fought under the commander in the Four Courts".[39]

Many, who had been evacuated from other posts in the area, and including women from Cumann na mBan were now in the Four Courts buildings. Anna, Frank Fahy's wife had been in Father Mathew Hall for much of the week but on Friday was trapped inside the Four Courts on account of the intensity of the rifle fire. She said, "I helped with the cooking. On Friday a goat strayed into the green of the Courts. I milked it so we had grand tea that evening, a change from condensed milk".[40]

Sheila O'Hanlon - Marrowbone Lane

Friday morning began peacefully and optimistically at Marrowbone Lane. However, communication with the rest of the city was becoming increasingly difficult and it was now impossible to get to and from the South Dublin Union.[41]

"Up early for breakfast. We fried veal cutlets and gave the men a good feed. We had a meat dinner, meat and potatoes, etc. Live chickens commandeered. Captain tells us that the sounds we heard during the night was the Four Courts attack.

We had a few slight accidents to dress. The password for the night was 'I know you'. The green flag won at St Enda's college was hoisted over our fort. I was brought up to the firing lines to see two of the enemy soldiers lying dead on top of one another, just outside. Some of our men go outside and take their rifles off the bodies. We also saw the republican flag over Jacobs".[42]

Robert Holland said, "Friday morning broke. The weather was still quite summerlike and quite warm, even during the night. We thought the city must all be on fire as we saw the big red glow through clouds of smoke. The British soldiers were not so plentiful this morning… The Cumann na mBan girls then went to crush some wheat to make cake bread… I was brought down to kill another beast and I saw that a side of the beast I had previously killed had been used. I have, however, no recollection of getting any meat for my dinner and I asked for some. I was told it was Friday and handed a can of soup and some bread. We were all in good form and those on the ground floor were engaged in cleaning up the place. There was a feeling that we were going to be there for a long spell. I met Con Colbert and talked to him about our early days in the Fianna, our summer camps on the Strand at Malahide, and how we scraped up money to send the young boys to the circus that used to pull in at the green at Malahide…" [43]

Holland and Colbert then discussed who had responded to the Easter Monday mobilisation and listed the volunteers they knew. "It was easy to check up F Company as it consisted of practically a few families of brothers. There were four Hollands: Bob, Dan, Frank and Watty. There was Mick and Ned Neill. There was Tom and Martin Cavanagh, Bill, Liam and Arthur Power, Paddy and Christy Byrne, Joe Bowman, Con Butler, Joe Downey, Darcy, Peadar Doyle, Joe Gorman, Bill Kelly, Mick Liston, Tom Murphy, Dan and Billy Troy, M O'Callaghan, M Riordan, Mick White, Tom and Bob Young". [44]

(The three Power brothers are, as far as we know, unrelated to Liam Parr, though Liam was to cause considerable confusion by using the name William Power when he was arrested.)

"The majority of us were from 18 to 20 years of age. Colbert was then about 23. Colbert all the time seemed to think that we must win and said to me that we must come in at the peace negotiations when the European War had finished. But there was no mention of any of us surrendering at any time. The whole garrison more or less relaxed on this day…" [45]

"About four o'clock on Friday troops appeared on Rialto Bridge and we were all rushed into positions. It became evident from their movements that we were going to be routed if possible. They had field kitchens as far as we could see and were being fired upon from our garrison in the South Dublin Union. Some of these troops came down the canal and started to fire on us, others to spread into the fields and we started to reply to their fire. This continued until darkness and it eventually died down. I send down one of the girls to ask permission to go down to the main hall. I went down. This was about 10pm and the usual rosary had started. When this had finished, we had a talk with some of the girls as we all knew one another. During this chat some of the girls suggested that we should get some kind of music and have a ceilidh for Sunday night. Alice Corcoran said she would try and get her brother's violin if any of the Fianna boys would go for it. The main hall was lighted with candles but no light was visible from outside. When I got back to my post the city looked like an inferno; every place seemed to be burning and there was the usual firing and heavy explosions. We now knew that the British were using artillery and we expected that we would be the next to come under artillery fire. But we hoped that the Germans and the country volunteers would arrive in time".[46]

1 Henderson R. witness statement WS 1686 It is worth noting that Henderson's witness statements are intended to be a distillation of other first-hand evidence.
2 Henderson R. witness statement WS 1686 It is worth noting that Henderson's witness statements are intended to be a distillation of other first-hand evidence.
3 Humphreys, Dick. Easter week in the GPO. Nat lib Ireland MS18829 in Jeffery, Keith, The GPO and the Easter Rising. Irish Academic Press, Dublin. 2006
4 Humphreys, Dick. Easter week in the GPO. Nat lib Ireland MS18829 in Jeffery, Keith, The GPO and the Easter Rising. Irish Academic Press, Dublin. 2006
5 Henderson R. witness statement WS1686 It is worth noting that Henderson's witness statements are intended to be a distillation of other first-hand evidence.
6 Tannam. Liam. Witness statement WS 242
7 Ryan, Desmond. Witness statement WS 724
8 Ryan, Desmond. Witness statement WS 724
9 Good, Joe, Enchanted by dreams, the journal of a revolutionary. Brandon. Dingle. 1996
10 Ryan, Desmond. Witness statement WS 724
11 Daly, Denis. Witness statement WS 110
12 Henderson R. witness statement WS 1686 It is worth noting that Henderson's witness statements are intended to be a distillation of other first-hand evidence.
13 Humphreys, Dick. Easter week in the GPO. Nat lib Ireland MS18829 in Jeffery, Keith, The GPO and the Easter Rising. Irish Academic Press, Dublin. 2006
14 Henderson R. witness statement WS1686 It is worth noting that Henderson's witness statements are intended to be a distillation of other first-hand evidence.
15 McLoughlin. Sean witness statement WS 290
16 Ryan, Desmond. Witness statement WS 724
17 Tannam, Liam witness statement .WS 242
18 Tannam, Liam witness statement .WS 242
19 Good, Joe, Enchanted by dreams, the journal of a revolutionary. Brandon, Dingle,1996
20 Humphreys, Dick. Easter week in the GPO. Nat lib Ireland MS18829 in Jeffery, Keith, The GPO and the Easter Rising. Irish Academic Press, Dublin. 2006
21 Daly. Denis. Witness statement WS 110
22 Humphreys, Dick. Easter week in the GPO. Nat lib Ireland MS18829 in Jeffery, Keith, The GPO and the Easter Rising. Irish Academic Press, Dublin. 2006
23 McLoughlin witness statement WS 290
24 Tannam, Liam witness statement WS 242
25 Tannam, Liam witness statement WS 242
26 McLoughlin witness statement WS 290
27 Ryan, Desmond, witness statement WS 724
28 Tannam, Liam witness statement WS 242
29 Humphreys, Dick. Easter week in the GPO. Nat lib Ireland MS18829 in Jeffery, Keith, The GPO and the Easter Rising. Irish Academic Press, Dublin. 2006
30 McLoughlin witness statement WS 290
31 Aloysius, Father OFM. Witness statement WIT 200
32 Conlon, Mrs Martin. Witness statement WS 419.
33 Lynch, Gilbert; ed O Cathasaigh, Aindrias; The life and times of Gilbert Lynch; Irish Labour History society. 2011; Dublin

34 Lynch, Gilbert; ed O Cathasaigh, Aindrias; The life and times of Gilbert Lynch; Irish Labour History society. 2011;Dublin

35 The war history of the 2/6 South Staffordshire, William Heinemann, London

1924- quoted in O'Brien, Crossfire, the battle of the four courts 1916, New Island Dublin, 2012.

36 Shouldice, John. Witness statement. WS 162

37 Shouldice, John. Witness statement. WS 162

38 O'Brien, Crossfire, the battle of the four courts 1916, New Island Dublin, 2012.

39 Cox, Redmond. Pension application. MSP34REF1983

40 Fahy, Anna, witness statement WS 202

41 Henderson Ruaidhri. Witness statement 1686. This was written in 1945 for the purposes of distilling existing evidence for a military tattoo so is essentially secondary evidence.

42 Mc Namara, Rose. Witness statement. WS 482

43 Holland, Robert witness statement WS 280

44 Holland, Robert witness statement WS 280

45 Holland, Robert witness statement WS 280

46 Holland, Robert witness statement WS 280

Chapter Fourteen
Saturday 29th April

Liam Parr and Larry Ryan - Moore Street

Liam Parr and Larry Ryan were both in the houses on Moore Street.

"On Saturday morning I made my way through all the houses to the most advanced house in Moore Street. It was a good stretch up the street. I don't know what kind of rumours we heard then, but they were generally to the effect that we were finished. There was talk of surrender".[1]

Liam Parr was among those waiting in Moore Street. "My last recollection was seeing him in Moore Street after evacuation of GPO", wrote Brian MacMullan.[2]

While the volunteers were waiting for news, the leaders were discussing whether to try to break out and join their comrades in the Four Courts. Sean McLoughlin, to whom Connolly had so recently passed his military leadership, wrote: "I then decided that the only way left open now was to leave Moore Street in a frontal wave, cross to the opposite side and into the back lanes, re-form again in Denmark Street near to the top of Henry Street and that, for the moment, was as much planning as could be done in the circumstances where everything was in the nature of a gamble. I was quite convinced that we should never emerge from this place intact. It was only a question of hours with the British assuming activities later in the day when we would be completely smashed to pieces. The nerve of most would be broken: those who were not immediately killed would either be captured or surrender and only a small handful, of which I hoped to be one, would ever reach the objective - the markets in the Four Courts alive... I told him *(Connolly)* of the foregoing and what I proposed to do was we would now assemble a small body of men in Sackville Lane numbering from 20 to 30. Everyone else would be brought down to the doorways which would be open ready in all the houses in Moore Street. I proposed on a signal to rush the 20 or 30 men towards the barricade at the end of Moore Street. I would throw a bomb from the corner towards the British and immediately the whole body in Moore Street would dash across the street into the laneways on the opposite side and re-form. Only one wounded man would be taken, and that was Connolly himself. We could not be burdened with the prisoners or wounded. When we were re-formed we would do so at Denmark Street near the Henry Street Warehouse as the road turns at that point and we would be screened from Britain Street. We would make our way down a laneway at the back of Todd Burns. We would break through into Todd Burns, move towards Capel Street to enable us to make our way to the Markets and if possible to the Four Courts and fight it out with Daly there. There was less possibility in my opinion of us being burned out as there were more open spaces in that part of the town than around where we were and by keeping towards Henry Street in our retreat we would avoid the thickly populated areas of Lower Denmark

Street and Britain Street. Pearse said 'The only difficulty with this is that more innocent people would be killed'. I said 'I am sorry. I cannot help that. This is a military operation and I can only make it successful if I don't think about these things'. He agreed. I said the zero hour for the move would be at 12 o'clock as just about then the British being British and methodical would begin their operations and we must be prepared to leave before then. I then went out and formed the men into the 'Death or Glory Squad'.[3]

"Seemingly as if from nowhere, something I cannot understand, a rumour was wafted through the various buildings that we were about to surrender and I was hotly questioned. I said, quite truthfully at that moment that I knew nothing about any surrender and I then went back to Headquarters.

When I came back Julia Grennan was making arrangements with Elizabeth Farrell to leave. Pearse said to me: 'I am sending a message to the British to end this fight'; I said 'does it mean surrender?' He said: 'I don't know until we have heard from the British'. He then went out of the room, I believe with Julia Grennan to see her off. I went and sat with Tom Clarke and said somewhat bitterly: 'that's a curious way to act'. He patted me on the back and said: 'Don't take it like that, Sean, there are bigger things involved, you did your best'.

We were given a cup of tea each and then Connolly beckoned to me from the bed and said: 'You must not take it so hardly; you are young, you will see lots more struggles before you die'. I said, 'I know'. He said: 'There is no hope for me; all those who signed the Proclamation will be shot'. I said: 'Are you sure of that?' He said, 'Certain. The British can do no worse and we do not expect any mercy', and I said: 'What about the rest of us?' He said: 'The rank and file will probably be imprisoned and later released - You must keep quiet about the part you played. You will still be needed; you will have plenty to do in the future if you keep quiet about what you have done now'.

He said: 'We have tried our best; it was better than we hoped and it has not ended as it might have done, in disaster'".[4]

"A lull falls, deadly and ominous. A few snipers are heard in the distance. Finally, the Headquarters room where Connolly lies wounded and silent with Pearse and Plunkett conversing beside him gives orders for its last meal. 'Cheer up, boys', cries an officer passing through the room I am in, 'Good news soon'. The officers are reported to be tidying themselves up. I meet Willie Pearse and ask for news. 'Connolly has been asked out to negotiate', he says; 'they have decided to go to save the men from slaughter, for slaughter it is. But say nothing yet as it may not come to anything'. Orders are given that there is to be no shooting upon any account. Pearse passes out alone as firm as a rock. I went up to Headquarters room. Plunkett is calm. Tears are in McDermott's eyes. So too with Willie Pearse. Connolly stares in front of him. We are marched through the rooms in companies. Sean McDermott reads Pearse's letter and explains we have surrendered to save not ourselves but the citizens.

We are hopelessly outclassed in munitions but he is proud of us. Our work will tell some day, and this week of Easter will be remembered. He orders food, cheese, bread, and some fruit from cans to be served out, and recommends us to take a good meal as we may not get much where we are going to, and we may be there some time".[5]

"In the afternoon that day all Volunteers were assembled in a backyard in Moore Street and were addressed by Sean Mc Dermott, who informed us of the surrender that was to take place near Findlaters in O'Connell Street. There was a general cry from the men not to surrender but to fight on when Sean informed us it was an order from Volunteer HQ and must be obeyed, after which he praised the men for their noble stand and fight against the overwhelming arms of the British army. He then shook hands with each man and bade us all goodbye".[6]

"When some of the men were told of the surrender, they were furious, especially our London, Liverpool, Manchester and Glasgow men - the hard- core of the Kimmage garrison... They believed that if they surrendered they would be treated as deserters, most of them having English accents. They said that if they were in danger of being shot as deserters they would prefer to be killed still fighting the British army... Our hot tempered desperation was beginning to arouse a response from the Volunteers as a whole, and also from the few Citizen Army men who remained; tough nuts who would balk at nothing, whatever the consequences... Sean MacDermott was the mind of the revolution... Mac Dermott released his astonishing wide smile, cobalt blue eyes shining into every face.

'Now, what exactly is it', said he, leaning easy on his cane like any civil servant in his still entirely civilian suit, 'that you all want to do?'

There was a silence. And then he was assailed by all the arguments... And then he began to speak, very quietly, with enormous concentration. And total confidence.

He suggested we take a look along look at the dead civilians lying in the street outside our windows... He said we'd 'fought a gallant fight' and we'd only lose now by fighting further. He told us our only remaining duty now was to survive... 'The thing you must do, all of you, is to survive!' He ended by insisting quietly, and still smiling, that 'We, who will be shot, will die happy - knowing that there are still plenty of you around who will finish the job'".[7]

If Joe Good is accurate in saying that the Manchester Kimmage Volunteers were among the group who were incensed at the surrender order, then he is describing Liam or Larry as we have discovered no others in Moore Street at that time.

The surrender was signed at 3:45 pm.[8]

"At last we line up in Moore Street for the last march, as some Volunteers term it, Plunkett marches beside us, with Willie Pearse, carrying, both of them, white flags on small poles... Corpses lie here and there on the cobbles and pavements, waxen with red gashes in their heads - British soldiers, Volunteers, civilians, bloody, prostrate, strangely still and quiet. Around and as far as we can see the buildings smoulder still. We turn into O'Connell Street, and as we do, two British officers cover every pair of us as we pass the Henry St. corner with enormous revolvers and a grim look. The street is lined with troops. Our flags still fly even yet over the ruined Post Office and the huge shell of the Imperial".[9]

"We line up in front of the Gresham Hotel, and carry out the order to lay down our arms and equipment. Names and addresses are taken with the warning that false information will have serious consequences. A high- ranking British Officer, perhaps General Lowe snaps out in reply to a question, 'You will be watered and fed'. Second Lieutenants prowl behind him and loot the dumped Volunteer heaps of surrendered weapons for automatic revolvers, to low groans of rage from the ranks of the surrendered. An appalling outburst of lurid army language with lurid threats of what machine guns and bayonets will shortly do to the Etcetra-Etcetras, comes from the lips of an army of bluff and tough old sergeants, some of whom are very much ashamed of being disgraced by a lot of So and So's who call themselves so and so Irishmen. A sympathetic Tommy behind us says he wishes we had got more of his officers, that he was glad we had stopped but we wouldn't half catch what for. An old sergeant roars out as he waves a Howth bullet in our faces that the British Army wasn't a herd of elephants. Another that Old Casement had a bullet put through him down in Kerry and he would soon have company where he'd gone to. Angry officers roar at the old sergeants for talking to the damned rebels. Other contingents of Volunteers march into the street. A small crowd of curious folk on the Gresham steps is ordered inside. The peaceful sky darkens, and more and more surrendered Volunteers arrive beneath white flags looking preposterously small in numbers to the lines of khaki soldiers stretching from Parnell Street to Earl Street. The fires flicker against the sky. Armoured motors and the Red Cross wagons flit by. The rifles are taken off the street by the British. Dark descends upon this nightmare".[10]

Liam and Larry, and all the rest from the GPO, were arrested, and spent the night outside the Rotunda. When arrested, Liam said his name was William Power and that he was a plumber of 28, North Frederick Street.[11] This was used as a fake Dublin address by several English rebels and was the address of the Slaugh Emmett branch of Fianna Éireann, as well as various other nationalist organisations, and of course, where Gilbert had been staying.[12]

Larry Ryan surrendered with Liam Parr in Moore Street on Saturday. Like the others, he was marched to the Rotunda and kept there overnight. When he was interrogated, he told them that he was L. Ryan and his home address was 4 Portobello Harbour, Dublin.[13] He also knew not to admit to being from England.

"Finally we are marched to the grass plot in front of the Rotunda Gardens, rank and file, leaders, Cumann na mBan girls, all herded together there. A circle of bayonets surrounds us. We pass the night there. High above us on the Rotunda Hospital roof a party of snipers and machine gun are stationed. An officer arrives (Lee Wilson who was shot dead in Wexford later), a dark browed, florid, thick-lipped man, either drunk or mad with hysteria who behaves in a bullying, half-crazed manner. He strides around, yelling that no one must stand up, that no one must lie down, and as for the needs of nature, anyone who chooses the Rotunda Gardens for a bedroom can use it as a lavatory as well and, well, lie in both. He threatens his own men. He will have them shot in the morning as looters. He threatens the Volunteers in similar terms. He strikes matches and holds them in the Volunteer's faces, yelling at his men, 'Anyone want to see the animals?' A Volunteer snaps out at him, 'You are a nice specimen of an English gentleman'. He walks on and ignores the taunt. When the relief guard comes, he begins a litany of 'Who are the worst, the Germans or the Sinn Féiners?' 'The Sinn Féiners' chant the Tommies. 'What shall we do with them?' 'Shoot 'em, stick a bayonet in 'em' chorus the Tommies, or some of them, and their tone is rather one of humouring a maniac than real conviction".[14]

"I fell asleep, and on awakening, the first thing I saw was Winnie Carney putting her coat over Seán Mc Dermott".[15]

Gilbert Lynch - Church Street

On Saturday Gilbert was still incapacitated with an injured ankle in the Father Mathew Hall. The fighting near the junction of Church Street and North King Street continued all night. At about midnight, the garrison at Langan's public house, had retreated to Reilly's fort, and the British troops had moved into the houses which they had vacated. They then began to copy the volunteers' tactic of tunnelling from house to house to bring them closer to Reilly's fort without risking being under fire in the open. When they attacked they still had to cross open ground unprotected, including Beresford Road; in the first assault nine soldiers were killed and many more were left injured in the road. Despite their heavy losses, attacks continued, and by 9am the Volunteer's commanding officer had decided that Reilly's fort must be evacuated. By means of a ruse, the fourteen who were in the garrison were able to successfully run down Church Street to the next barricade.[16]

"Lieutenant Collins, in the course of his instructions to us, told us that we were to line up inside the shop of the fort on the ground floor and that when he gave an order to charge in a sufficiently loud voice which the enemy could hear we were to ignore that order. But when he gave a second order to charge we were to jump as one man through the window into the street and rush across to the barricade outside the Father Mathew Hall which was about 25 yards distant. On receiving the second order to charge, we all jumped and with the exception of one man, managed to

173

reach the comparative safety of the barricade referred to. This man, whose name I cannot at the moment recollect, was struck by a bullet on the heel of the boot and fell on the footpath. He remained lying still for a few seconds, and as soon as the enemy firing ceased, he jumped up and made a run for it and succeeded in reaching the barricade safely. In all about 14 men successfully crossed over".[17]

By late morning, the soldiers held North King Street, but were unable to safely use Reilly's fort as it was now being fired upon by Volunteers on barricades in Church Street and Beresford Road. However fighting was approaching the casualty centre at Father Mathew Hall. In the early afternoon, a section of the South Staffordshire regiment tried to storm the barricade on Upper Church Street, but they were repulsed by a counter attack from St Mary's lane. Now the front line was immediately outside the Hall. Fighting was still continuing around the Church Street, North King Street junction as volunteers were holding out, and firing from buildings north of the junction.[18]

Father Aloysius was in the Father Mathew Hall where he had spent most of the week. "The firing was very intense all through Friday night and without cessation until about 3 or 4 pm of Saturday afternoon. Many explosions and many buildings could be seen blazing. The number of wounded was increasing and many cases were brought to the Father Mathew Hall. By 4 pm the military were as far as the junction of King Street and Church Street and were firing on the Church Street barricades. The Cumann na mBan girls were very excited and naturally feared for the poor wounded under their care".[19]

"There were some very bad cases in the Hall and the girls of Cumann na mBan were getting nervous and excited, as it seemed certain the Hall would be shelled".[20]

"A message had been sent under a white flag to acquaint the military that the Hall was being used as a hospital but it had no effect… The reply was oral. The military would grant none of the amenities of war but would treat them as outlaws and rebels. The position was desperate and Father Augustine and myself decided that there was no option but to go ourselves and seek an interview with the officer in command. Accompanied by volunteer Doyle who carried a white flag, we passed a barrier and between two soldiers with fixed bayonets we went to North King Street until we reached opposite the new houses near Lurgan Street where we were told we should wait the arrival of Colonel Taylor who was in charge. While we waited there three large companies of soldiers marched by and an ambulance stood near. The colonel then arrived and listened to our statement: he made no answer but unceremoniously turned and walked off. A long time elapsed. To us it seemed an hour, so anxious were we for the poor patients in the Father Mathew Hall. Then we saw Col Taylor at the corner of Church Street, and we approached him. He very coolly informed us that a truce had been arranged. While with the Colonel, Miceal O'Foghludha came to complain that the soldiers had prevented him from going for a doctor. Just as he was speaking some shots rang out from a house between N King and N Brunswick streets; and turning to Foley Col Taylor brutally shouted at him to stop the firing or he would shoot him, and ordering him to the other side of the street he kept him covered with his revolver. Poor Foley, exhausted and hoarse, tried to tell the Volunteers that there was a truce, and asked them to cease firing. Father Augustine stepped forward and appealed to them too, and informed them that Col. Taylor had informed them that following advice to surrender from Pearse a truce had been made. The volunteers believed it was only a ruse of the military and would not believe it. However they agreed to keep the truce for the night on our undertaking to see Pearse in the morning at the earliest moment and satisfy ourselves of the genuineness of Pearse's message. We then returned to Father Mathew Hall and gave word to those in charge of the wounded. Arrangements were at once made to transfer the wounded to Richmond hospital".[21]

Mrs Conlon was in the Father Mathew Hall. "At about 4pm the surrender message came from Pearse. Nobody believed it for a long time. We were told that anyone who could should get home. All the wounded in the Hall were taken in stretchers to Richmond Hospital where beds were provided and they were well treated by the doctors and nurses… I went home the following day, but my husband went into the Richmond Hospital where he stayed for a couple of days. From that on he was on the run and he escaped to England to his people over there".[22]

Gilbert Lynch escaped arrest because he had been sent from the first aid station at Father Mathew Hall to Richmond hospital where he remained a few days.[23]

Gilbert said, "When the surrender took place we were all taken to the Richmond Hospital."

This was not an easy move because the Volunteers in Clarke's dairy, beyond North King Street, had not agreed to the surrender, saying they had heard nothing about it and had decided to fight to the finish. Despite that, the Cumann na mBan members, with help from medical students began carrying the wounded on stretchers to the Richmond hospital. This took much of the night.[24]

One of the Cumann na mBan members who escorted the wounded to hospital was Anna Fahy. "On the Saturday night of the surrender I helped to take some of the wounded to Richmond Hospital. Mrs Conlon and myself returned to the Hall as some of the younger girls were there and we feared they might be nervous, as British were surrounding the place".[25]

Gilbert safely arrived at the hospital. Martin Conlon said, "After the surrender on Saturday he was removed to Richmond Hospital. I with some others removed the wounded together with a supply of medical and surgical equipment to Richmond Hospital".[26]

Gilbert remembered being in hospital. "I was eventually put in the same ward as the others, and after a time one of the surgeons who was going around suggested that I should be put in another ward, and if any enquiries were made to tell them I was on holiday. I am not certain whether it was Surgeon Myles Keogh or Dr Thomas Myles, but they were all very good to us there. I don't remember the ward I was put into, but the nurse who was in charge when I was put in was a namesake of my own, Nurse Lynch from Roscommon. I have met her since, many years afterwards. They looked after us very well - in fact I think I was the top patient in the ward. The usual fare was bread and butter for breakfast and tea, unless something was sent in, but I had two boiled eggs every morning. I don't know who supplied them, but I had them. I was also allowed to say a decade of the rosary each night".[27]

Redmond Cox - Church Street

Redmond Cox had been in the Four Courts since Friday night. He said... "We fought under the commander in the Four Courts until the general surrender on Saturday afternoon. We surrendered to the British Military and marched to the Rotunda gardens".[28]

The order to surrender was met with incredulity in the Four Courts. Michael O'Flanagan had been asleep under the dome having spent the previous days in Reilly's fort. He was told that the order had come from Pearse, and that any who could escape arrest should do so.

"I then went to the toilet for a wash, and while there I met the vice commandant of the battalion, Piaras Beaslai, and informed him of the position. He knew nothing about the order to surrender and scoffed at the idea, pointing out that the position was 'impregnable and could be held for a month'. On looking through a window into the courtyard of the four courts I saw a number of the garrison lined up who were handing over their rifles through the railings to the enemy forces gathered in Chancery Street... Some short time afterwards, when all the rifles had been surrendered, Commandant Daly 'fell in' the Battalion in the courtyard of the Four courts and addressed the men. He told us of the order received, that he had no alternative but to obey, and that as far as he understood the ordinary rank and file would, after interrogation, be set free; but that as far as the officers were concerned he did not know what would become of them. He emphasised the fact that, while we were beaten by a superior military force, we were not, in fact, cowed and that we should carry ourselves with pride and conduct ourselves as true soldiers of the Republic... We then formed up into column of fours without any order and the Battalion, headed by commandant Ned Daly, Vice Commandant Piaras Beaslai, Captain Éamonn Duggan, adjutant, and Captain Frank Fahy, O/C Company took up position at the head of the column and marched out of the Four Courts by way of the Chancery Lane exit to the quayside. We then marched by way of the Quays, Capel Street and Parnell Street, and, on reaching the Parnell monument, we were lined up in O'Connell Street outside and facing Findlaters, the provision merchants. Just before turning into O'Connell Street our battalion was halted for a short period outside Mooney's public house facing the Rotunda Hospital where our officers were taken from us. After a half hour's delay outside Findlaters in O'Connell Street, we were turned about and marched back to a spot in Parnell Street facing the Rotunda Hospital... We were then interrogated by a British officer... As each man was interrogated he was passed over to the enclosed plot in front of the Rotunda hospital which was completely surrounded by a cordon of soldiers with fixed bayonets... This would have been about 7 o'clock on the Saturday evening. The number confined there comprised members of the volunteers and Cumann na mBan. The weather had been marvellously fine, but when I got into the enclosure I noticed that the ground was extremely wet, having apparently been hosed for our reception with a view to making conditions as uncomfortable as possible. The interrogation having ended about 8 pm, we were left there from that hour until about 7:30 o'clock on Sunday morning, during which time we got no food or water; nor were any arrangements made to segregate the sexes or provide sanitary arrangements".[29]

Sean Shouldice said. "We were marched off via Capel Street and O'Connell Street to the Rotunda and put inside the iron railing on the grass plot in front of the hospital. We were joined there by a number from the GPO garrison among them being Tom Clarke and Sean McDermott. The trials we had to undergo were beginning. We were kept throughout that night until the Sunday morning following in this confined space. The conduct of the military officers in charge of us was most aggressive and insulting, but there was no redress- a few who protested were hit with the butt end of rifles or pricked with bayonets."[30]

Sheila O'Hanlon - Marrowbone Lane

On Saturday morning at Marrowbone Lane, communications from the other Dublin garrisons had broken down but they did not seem to be under any particular threat. Rose McNamara remarked that a "Load of cabbage captured".[31] Otherwise nothing noteworthy happened.

"On Saturday morning all the British troops had been withdrawn out of range of our fire and appeared to be waiting for reinforcements. We were all warned to stand to our posts early on Saturday morning as a massed attack was expected... A few stray soldiers came within rifle range and got hit, but all Saturday was an uneventful day".[32]

1 Murphy, Fintan. Witness statement WS 370
2 Parr, William pension application II/RB/4077
3 Mc Loughlin, Sean witness statement WS 290
4 Mc Loughlin, Sean witness statement WS 290
5 Ryan, Desmond . witness statement WS 724
6 Donnelly, Charles, witness statement. WS 824
7 Good, Joe, Enchanted by dreams, the journal of a revolutionary. Brandon, Dingle 1996

8 Witness statements R. Henderson,1686; Mc Gallogly,244; Robinson,156; Gleeson,367; Daly,291 and Tannam, Liam wit 242

9 Ryan, Desmond, witness statement WS 724

10 Ryan, Desmond, witness statement WS 724

11 Sinn Fein rebellion handbook. Weekly Irish Times , Dublin 1917, page 70 .Power W, Plumber, 28 N Frederick Street in first batch of 200 arrested and sent to Knutsford. UK Nat archive HO 144/1455

12 Several of volunteers from mainland Britain when arrested gave their address as, 28 or 26 North Frederick street which was the address of Sluagh Emmett of Fianna Éireann and the Hibernian rifles. Lawlor, Damian, Na Fiana Éireann and the Irish revolution 1909-1923. Caolite books, Co Offaly. Undated. O Doherty witness statement 355 described it being used by English and Scottish "refugees". In the Sinn Fein rebellion handbook, 6 people gave it as their address, Mcmanus, Power, Clinch, Doyle, Derham and Redmond. An overlapping 6 names are listed at this address in Frongoch, University of Revolution, Mc Manus, Power, Clinch, Derham, Craven and Daly. Heuston lists 10 names as being in the North Frederick Street group. Thornton, Gleeson, Daly, Begley, Clinch, Donaghue, Mc Manus,, Mc Mullen, Mc Neive and Scullen. Robinson in witness statement 156 lists the following names from these lists as being among those at kimmage. These are, Daly, Mc Manus, Mc Neive, Scullen, Parr (Power), Clinch and Craven.

13 Laurence Ryan pension application. WS 291

14 Ryan, Desmond. Witness statement. WS 724

15 Cremen, Michael. Witness statement WS 563

16 O'Brien, Crossfire, the battle of the four courts 1916, New Island Dublin, 2012

17 O'Flanagan, Michael, witness statement WS 800

18 O'Brien, Crossfire, the battle of the four courts 1916, New Island Dublin, 2012.

19 Aloysius, Father OFM. Witness statement WS 200

20 Aloysius, Father OFM. Quoted in Connell, Joe, Rebels' Priests- ministering to republicans 1916-24, Kilmainham Tales, Dublin 2014

21 Aloysius, Father OFM. Witness statement WS 200

22 Conlon, Mrs Martin, Witness statement WS 419

23 Gilbert Lynch pension file MSP34REF41334

24 O'Brien, Crossfire, the battle of the four courts 1916, New Island Dublin, 2012.

25 Fahy, Anna, witness statement WS 202

26 Conlon, Martin in Lynch , Gilbert pension application.MSP 34 REF41334

27 Lynch, Gilbert; ed O Cathasaigh, Aindrias; The life and times of Gilbert Lynch; Irish Labour History society. 2011; Dublin

28 Cox, Redmond. Pension application. MSP34REF1983

29 O'Flanagan, Michael, witness statement WS 800

30 Shouldice, John, witness statement. WS 162

31 Mc Namara, Rose. Witness statement. WS 482

32 Holland, Robert witness statement WS 280

Chapter Fifteen
Sunday 30 April 1916

Sheila O'Hanlon in Marrowbone Lane

The next day also began peacefully for Sheila O Hanlon in the Marrowbone Lane distillery.

"Up early. Breakfast cooked for men as usual. Get style for Sunday (clean blouse); got ready for Mass".[1]

One of the male Volunteers, Robert Holland, the man who had butchered the cow, remembered that day. "Sunday morning found us in much the same way but the British troops appeared to have been completely withdrawn as none appeared to be in sight. We had an easy day and, apart for a few that remained on lookout duty, the rest of us could ramble all over the distillery". He estimated that there were about 100 men and 40 women in the distillery. "We were still in the best of spirits and the girls had baked some cakes and were getting ready for the ceilidh in the main hall which had previously been cleared".[2]

"Captain calls all the men together about 12 o'clock pm in the back yard; we all assemble too. He addressed us all in the most soul stirring manner. He asked if there were any complaints about food or sleep. All answered 'No', and if they were prepared to fight to the last, even though the old enemy we were fighting, playing her old game and starving us out. They all shouted, 'Yes'. He then quoted a passage from history - thus - 'Greater love no man hath than to lay down his life for his friend', and if all ended well, being Sunday, to have a sing song in the evening, to which the brave cailíní, were to be invited. Cheers from the men. All then disbursed to dinner. Not having a reply from the priest about Mass, prayers were said instead".[3]

Sheila's comrade, Annie Cooney, was enjoying the opportunity to relax. "On the Sunday things seemed to have quietened down and the shooting had diminished. It was so quiet in comparison to the rest of the week that we decided to relax, and we were to have a ceilidh that night. Seamus Murphy had given us permission for it if things continued to be all right.

We had no Mass on Sunday. Earlier in the week we had a visit from one of the Mount Argus priests who heard all our confessions and gave us his blessing".[4]

Robert Holland told what happened next. "We were looking forward to this *(the ceilidh)* when at about 6 pm a despatch came from Commandant Éamonn Ceannt at the South Dublin Union... We were told that this despatch had come from Ceannt and it was to the effect that no one was to fire on any British soldier he would see in uniform without first reporting to one of the officers. A rumour went round that a truce was being called...

Con Colbert explained. He said, 'Bobby I do not know what to say or think but if what I think comes true our cause is postponed to a future generation. We are to surrender unconditionally and I cannot forecast what that will mean. We must have been let down very badly as we have not had the support of our people that we expected'. This conversation occurred at 6:15 pm on Sunday evening. I went back up the building and as I came to each man that was left on guard who were all excited; I broke the news I had as easy as possible. They were all dumbfounded and a dejected appearance replaced the previous good spirit".[5]

Annie Cooney heard the news at the same time. "On Sunday afternoon a message came from Ceannt in the Union - to Seamus Murphy telling him to be ready to surrender. The news was received very badly and there was great disappointment. There was dreadful grousing. They were saying 'Was this what we were preparing for and living for all this time? Is this the end of all our hopes?' They were flinging their rifles around in temper and disgust. Then word went round the whole distillery that we were to assemble in front of the building for the surrender. There were a few who refused to surrender and they cleared off. It took some time to gather them from all points of the building and to persuade them to obey the order. It was finally brought home to most of them that as soldiers it was their duty to obey the order of their leader".[6]

Sheila's commanding officer was watching the arrivals: "Rev Father Augustine and Commandant McDonagh came in motor car to tell about surrender. Self and Miss Cosgrave gave priest some refreshments. He tells us all the sad news. McDonagh leaves crying: great commotion. Captain and Captain Con Colbert appear. We are told to go away home quietly. (But no), just then an accident occurs to one of the men to whom we rendered first aid".[7]

Annie Cooney was watching when Eamon Ceannt arrived to lead the garrison to the surrender. "While we were trying to get some of the last of them down I was standing at the window of the barley loft and saw the gate being opened by Sergeant O'Neill who had been in charge of it all the week - it was barricaded on the inside. When it opened who walked in but Eamon Ceannt who had come down from the Union. He was like a wild man; his tunic was open, his hair was standing on end and he looked awful. He evidently hated the task of asking the garrison to surrender. He put his two hands on the barricade, with his head bent, and presented a miserable appearance. With Ceannt was a British military officer to whom he had already surrendered. There was a third person, but I can't now recall exactly who it was." [8]

"...I saw a priest, a British army officer, with a volunteer officer in front marching in military formation. They passed our front gate entrance before they came to a halt. They had a white sheet on a flagpole... Ceannt shook hands with Colbert, Murphy and Murray and the six of them had a conversation lasting only a few moments. Colbert saluted Ceannt and walked back towards me in the yard. I asked him what was the news and he said it was all over. When I heard this I felt kind of sick in the stomach, to put it mildly. It came as a great shock. Colbert could hardly speak as he stood in the yard for a moment or two. He was completely stunned. The tears rolled down his cheeks..." The garrison were brought down to the yard and formed up.

"Colbert then announced that we were surrendering unconditionally and that anyone that wanted to go or escape could do so... Some left, over the wall, one saying, 'Toor-a loo, boys, I'm off!'" [9]

Ann Cooney continues: "Then the garrison surrendered through Seamus Murphy and prepared to leave. Ceannt had already gone away with his escort. I had a good view of the whole proceedings from the window at which I stood. Having induced the last unwilling man on the loft to obey orders, I was going down to assemble with the others when I met Lieutenant Sean O'Broin. I had a little set-to with him about his attitude towards the surrender and, while we were talking, Con Colbert came up to see whether the order had been obeyed and to ensure that nobody was left behind. He ordered O'Broin to go down and I asked Con what was going to happen to himself. He said he did not know, whatever the British authorities liked to do with him; but if he came through he would come back to our house. He went down to take his place with the others and I followed Seamus Murphy and he gave the order to move off. We Cumann na mBan fell in behind the Volunteers. They had tried to persuade us to go home, but we refused, saying that we would stick it out to the end. I certainly have the impression that we could have gone away home if we wanted to". [10]

Rose McNamara, Sheila's commanding officer led her and the twenty one Cumann ma mBan members out of the Distillery. "We (Cumann na mBan) all collected in front of the fort and shake the hands of all the men and give them 'God speed' and told them to be cheerful. Some were sad and some trying to be cheerful. After command from Captain to form fours all marched out the front gate through the city to St Patricks park (Ross Road), all the girls marching behind, singing; one of the girls picked up a rifle in the street, carried it on her shoulder. We all 22 of us gave ourselves up and marched down between two lines of our brave men. We waited until all the arms were taken away. The men gave each of us their small arms to do as we liked with, thinking we were going to go home, but we were not going to leave the men we had been with all week to their fate; we decided to go along with them and be with them to the end whatever our fate might be. Some of the girls had as many as three revolvers, some had more..." [11]

Although many volunteers have reported being jeered by bystanders after the Rising, some had more positive memories. Christopher Byrne was also in Marrowbone distillery when the garrison surrendered.

"When we came out of the distillery the crowd was cheering us. I think it took Ceannt all of his time to make up his mind to surrender when he saw the reception outside the distillery, but we did surrender and we were marched to Richmond barracks on Sunday evening".[12]

"Then Colbert reformed us up, numbered us off and we 'sloped arms' and we marched out of the front entrance of the distillery with Colbert at our head. A lot of men had gathered outside and I heard Éamonn Ceannt distinctly say, 'Where were you men when you were wanted.' We fell in behind the South Dublin Union ambulance which was in the rear of the South Dublin garrison. The Cumann na mBan girls were formed up in our rear... On our route we were subjected to very ugly remarks and cat calls from the poorer classes... We were put in double file facing what is known as Iveagh Baths and told to stand at ease. Colbert gave all military orders up to this. Then a military officer from the path in front of us gave the command for us all to lay down our arms on the road in front of us..."

They were then marched off.

"It would then be about 8pm and was falling dusk. At Kilmainham we were jeered at and as we passed by Murray's lane both men, women and children used filthy expressions at us... The British troops saved us from manhandling. This was the first time I ever appreciated the British troops as they undoubtedly saved us from being manhandled that evening and I was very glad as I walked in at the gates of Richmond barracks".[13]

Annie Cooney marched with the Cumann na mBan and followed Con Colbert and the Volunteers. "We marched from the Distillery to Ross Road beside St. Patrick's Cathedral. When we got there the whole 4th Battn. was lined up there and also the men from Jacob's. The British troops were there in force lined up on each side of Ross Road.

We took up our positions behind the rest of the 4th Battn. and the surrender took place there. The Volunteers had to lay down their arms and they had to take off their bandoliers and Sam Brown belts. The British officers asked us had we any arms or ammunition. We said no, though a few of us had small arms that some of the Volunteers had given us to keep safe for them, thinking that we would not be arrested or searched.

Thinking the men would be taken away and we would not see them again, I went forward to where Con Colbert was standing to see whether there was anything he wanted me to do for him and also to get some souvenir in case I should never see him again. He was standing in rank with the other Volunteers with one sock in one hand and piece of my mother's brown bread in the other. I asked him for a souvenir. 'Here' he said, 'these are all I have'. He had, like all the others, been stripped of all his accoutrements. I did not take either of the articles he offered me, as I thought he might need the brown bread and the sock. He abominated holes in his socks and I mended a pair for him.

We three *(had)* wondered why *(my father)* did not visit us again and we only found out about his arrest on the Sunday of the surrender as we were forming up outside the gate of the distillery. Somebody shouted the information to us... He was seen coming out of the Distillery by one of the 'separation' women and she trailed him up along until he came as far as Kilmainham Police Station - he did not know this. She reported him to the police who arrested him and kept him in the station for the night. The next day the police handed him over to the military in Richmond Barracks. He was removed from there to Kilmainham Gaol where he was detained until he was deported to Wakefield with the other prisoners after the surrender".[14]

Thomas Doyle was another who marched from Marrowbone Lane to surrender "...when we were marching from Marrowbone Lane to Bride Road, a fellow joined us who was fairly drunk. He staggered in amongst us as we marched on and arrived at Bride Road with us. Nobody bothered about him, but when he attempted to get out of Bride Road he was not allowed out. By the time we arrived at Richmond barracks he had sobered up and stated that he was a van driver for Easons. He said he was of the other way of thinking, but that when he saw the lads marching he joined in with them not knowing what they were. He tried to get out, and tried to get Easons on the job, but could not manage it... The Sergeant said to him, 'You are not a soldier, so you must be a Sinn Féiner. You have got to be either a soldier or a Sinn Féiner'. He was landed in Knutsford along with the rest of us".[15]

Annie Cooney continues. "The Volunteers were marched off and we were in ranks of four behind them, keeping step. There were two lines of armed soldiers marching at each side of us, for which we were presently thankful, as we would have been torn to pieces by the 'separation' women who followed us shouting out abuse and obscene language at us. They were kept at bay by the soldiers. The men asked us to sing all our marching songs in which they joined. They said this kept their hearts up. This went on the whole way till we reached Richmond Barracks. We marched right into the big square, where we were halted. There we were separated from the men who were put into a separate building. We were all - 22 of us - brought into a large building-up the stairs and we were first put into a rather small room, where we were divided up for the night, eleven of us in each of two rooms. A British military sergeant had charge of us and brought us tea in a bucket and some hard biscuits which we called dog biscuits. We ate and drank what we got, as we were hungry. The sergeant apologised for the sort of food he had to give us.

We spent the night there - not sleeping, as we had no mattresses or any sort of sleeping accommodation. In any case we thought it safer to remain awake, as we did not know what the soldiers might be like. We spent the night saying the rosary and talking. We wondered what was happening to the men.

There was a small, rather primitive lavatory attached to our room, for which we were thankful; we had not to go out at all to the corridors.

I should mention that we still had the guns in our possession that were given to us by the Volunteers to keep. During the night the sergeant asked us if we had any guns on us as we would be likely to be searched by the soldiers at some later stage. We foolishly said we hadn't, thinking we would be sent home and could hold on to them and not be searched. When he had gone out Miss McNamara, who was in charge of us, became a bit worried about the position. Eventually she decided we would say the Rosary for guidance as to what we should do. We noticed a fireplace in the room and somebody suggested that we should put them up the chimney. We found a couple of ledges at the side of the chimney and stuck them up there. We felt satisfied that we had not handed them over to the British anyway, and we had some faint, if silly, notion that they might be recovered some time".[16]

Gilbert Lynch - In Dublin

By about Sunday, Gilbert would have been discharged from hospital, but he was on the run in a devastated city controlled by the military.

"It was terrible in Dublin at that time. Every morning the stop press would come out in Dublin - 'One more executed', 'Two more executed'. At that time, Dublin was under martial law; you were not allowed on the streets after sundown; soldiers patrolled the streets; you were not allowed to show a light in a window after sundown. The soldiers were jittery. If they saw a light anywhere, they would shout, 'Put out that light'".[17]

Gilbert had left Richmond Hospital, though we don't know how well he could walk on his injured ankle. While in hospital he had given away his return ticket to England so that Martin Conlon could use it to travel to his family in Manchester. He had also given him his engraved pocket watch and identity papers, and hoped that he would be able to replace his permit and papers and return to Stockport himself.

He said, "During the week Mrs Fahy, Frank Fahy's wife, and another lady came in to see me. They asked me if I would try and get a permit to travel as Martin Conlon".[18]

"They asked me to give him my papers and would I get him a permit?"[19]

"The Red Cross man had not surrendered, and wanted to get away. I had met Martin Conlon during the week; in fact it was he who took me into the Father Mathew Hall to have my ankle attended to".

"I went with them to the police station in Brunswick Street, as it then was. I will never forget that day, because as we were going over O'Connell Bridge the newsboys came along with the express edition of the Evening Herald. We bought a Herald and the first thing we saw in it was that Frank Fahy had been sentenced to death. I think it said it was commuted to penal servitude, but Mrs Fahy took it very bravely. I went along and got the permit, but it only enabled one to travel in the city of Dublin - the one I wanted was to enable somebody to leave Dublin. I went with them to a house in Mountjoy Square - I don't know whose house it was".[20]

Redmond Cox - Under Arrest

Redmond Cox was sent to Richmond barracks.

"We were marched off at about 8 or 9am to Richmond barracks near Kilmainham. Our route passed through O'Connell Street and the quays. The appearance of O'Connell Street and the GPO, what was left of it was an unforgettable sight. From the GPO to O'Connell Street on both sides of the street the buildings were mostly burned out; a number of them were still smouldering, also a good portion of Lower and Middle Abbey Street. The bodies of some civilians shot during the week were lying about, also a few horses about O'Connell Bridge. The heart of the city presented a picture of utter desolation".[21]

"On arrival at Richmond barracks we were divided into groups. My group was put into the gymnasium with instructions to sit on one particular side of the room. There was already a number of other Volunteers confined in the room. It would have been 11 or about 12 midday when we were placed in the Gymnasium. While in the Gymnasium I noticed, among others, Tom Clarke, Willie Pearse, Eamon Ceannt and the brothers Bevan, one of whom - Thomas - had been in charge of the prisoners which we captured and confined in the Four Courts during the fight. Thomas, having been in charge of the prisoners, was regarded as of some importance by the British military although during the week he only held the rank of an ordinary Volunteer. After about two hours we were taken one by one out of the gymnasium into an adjoining annexe. At the door dividing the gymnasium from the annexe was placed a table at which a British officer sat with four well known members of the Detective Division, Dublin Metropolitan Police, whose function it was to identify each of us as we were passed through. Among them were Detectives Barton, Bruton and Hoey - two of whom were subsequently executed during the War of Independence, by the Republican Forces. As we were passing through the doorway, certain members of my party, having apparently been identified by the Detectives, were placed on one side under a special guard of soldiers with fixed bayonets. I, with about 23 others, having passed through the doorway, was escorted to another room in the barracks. Sometime after our confinement in the barrack room each of us was handed a tin of bully beef and 3 or 4 wartime biscuits, together with a mug of tea.

This was the first meal we had received since the surrender on Saturday afternoon. The room was not equipped with any facilities for sleeping, there being a complete absence of mattresses and blankets. I might mention that on our arrival at Richmond barracks we were thoroughly searched and all our personal belongings, such as money, watches and religious emblems including rosary beads, were taken from us. They made a special point of picking on the rosary beads..."[22]

Robert Holland, who had been with Sheila O'Hanlon in Marrowbone Lane, was also taken to Richmond Barracks that night so he would have been with Liam, Larry and Redmond. "Inside Richmond Barracks, we were packed choked full into a billet and three or four buckets were left in to act as latrines. The door was locked and we had barely room to sit down.

We were in this room all night. Everyone seemed to be in serious thought and no one wanted to converse as we were practically jammed tight together. Someone suggested that if one side of the room tightened the other half might get room to sit down and rest for a while. This was done… I opened the conversation with 'What will be the next British move?' Tom Young answered - 'The Lord only knows'. Martin Kavanagh said 'I would not be surprised if we were shipped to France', and elaborated on this. 'We are all trained men; they must be in a bad way on the various fronts in France as the Germans were beating them on all sides and I am not surprised, if the troops they have for replacement are of the same standard as those that have been sent against us… They may divide us into small groups so that we will not be in a position to be of any value to the Germans or detrimental to them'. Mick Liston was of the opinion that we would be shipped to some of the colonies as they had previously done so with other insurgents, or if not, that we would all be executed. After a pause Colbert spoke. He said that from his point of view he would prefer to be executed and said 'We are all ready to meet our God. We had hopes of coming out alive. Now that we are defeated, outside that barrack wall the people whom we have tried to emancipate have demonstrated nothing but hate and contempt for us. We would be better off dead as life would be a torture. We can thank the Mother of God for her kindness in her intercession for us that we have had the time to prepare ourselves to meet our Redeemer'. Colbert then called us all to recite the Rosary for the spiritual and temporal welfare of those who fought and died in the cause of Irish Freedom, past, present and future generations. We were in darkness and remembering no more, I fell asleep".[23]

Larry Ryan, Liam Parr and Redmond Cox - Deportation

That Sunday evening Larry, Liam and Redmond were all marched from Richmond barracks to the North Wall to be put on boats.

"At about 6 o'clock on Sunday evening a British officer came into the room and took us out, one by one, to the corridor where, with the assistance of a Dublin Detective, each of us was separately fingerprinted. As soon as the room had been emptied we were marched on to the barrack square and placed with other men who were already there. We were left standing on the barrack square for about 1½ hours until the occupants of the other rooms had been similarly dealt with. At about 7.30 or 8 o'clock, when dusk was falling, a heavily armed guard was marched on to the square under the command of an officer. We were then formed up in fours and, surrounded by an armed escort, we were marched out of Richmond barracks, down Kilmainham, Bow Lane, Stevens Lane, Kingsbridge and the North Quays to the North Wall where we were placed on a British War Department sloop. On our way from Richmond barracks to the North Wall all our men were in great spirits and sang the marching songs of the Volunteers.

On arrival at the North Wall we were marched directly on to the boat and we were left on deck surrounded by an armed escort. After about a half hour and as soon as the British military authorities had completed the ship's complement of prisoners, the sloop moved out en route for England.

The night being calm and the weather good, we enjoyed the crossing. Some of the men slept. As we were on deck, the passage was easier for us and during the night some of the sailors, who were sympathetic to us, handed us mugs of hot coffee or cocoa and bread which we greatly appreciated. As there were not enough mugs to go round we had to take turns in disposing of the food given to us".[24]

Not everyone had such a good crossing. Frank Robbins recorded his memories of that journey: "On Sunday night, April 30th, we were put aboard one of the L.M.S. boats. There were probably up to 300 or 400 prisoners all penned in the cargo hold of the ship. One bucket of water had been placed there, but before half of us had reached the cargo hold the supply of water was exhausted. We were a very tired and dishevelled group of men, very much in need of a wash up and a long rest. Before leaving Richmond Barracks we had been given some bully-beef, biscuits and water. The bully-beef created a great thirst on as all. Finding all the water used, I took the bucket with the intention of having it re-filled and made an effort to get up the gangway. On approaching the entrance to the gangway from the hold of the ship, I saw the top portion of the gangway well covered by British soldiers with fixed bayonets at the ready. Seeing my approach one of the soldiers immediately halted me. I told him I was seeking water as there was none in the hold, and his reply came quick and sharp, leaving no doubt of his intention, 'You dirty Irish pig, get back into the hold or you won't require any water'. This was rather a shock to me because, generally speaking, the ordinary British soldiers had shown a different attitude during the day towards their prisoners. Most of us then endeavoured to settle down with the object of having some rest, but there was very little space for this purpose. We made all kinds of attempts to be as comfortable as possible under the circumstances. A group of us managed in this way; two sat back to back, one at each side, and across our legs lay the heads or legs of other colleagues. In that position I went to sleep and did not awaken until the ship arrived at Holyhead early next day when I was stiff, cold and sore.

On looking around before we were taken from the hold of the ship some very revolting scenes met our eyes. During the trip some of the men had got sick and, having no room, actually vomited on their nearest colleagues or on themselves. This will give an idea of how closely packed we were, there being no room for the sick men to find, other accommodation".[25]

1 Mc Namara, Rose. Witness statement. WS 482

2 Holland, Robert witness statement WS 280

3 Mc Namara, Rose. Witness statement. WS 482

4 O'Brien, Anne (Cooney) witness statement WS 805

5 Holland, Robert witness statement WS 280

6 O'Brien, Anne (Cooney) witness statement WS 805

7 Mc Namara, Rose. Witness statement. WS 482

8 O'Brien, Anne (Cooney) witness statement WS 805

9 Holland, Robert witness statement WS 280

10 O'Brien, Anne (Cooney) witness statement WS 805

11 Mc Namara, Rose. Witness statement. WS 482

12 Byrne, Christopher,Witness statement WS 167

13 Holland, Robert witness statement WS 280

14 O'Brien, Anne (Cooney) witness statement WS 805

15 Doyle, Thomas. Witness statement WS 186

16 O'Brien, Annie (Cooney) witness statement WS 805

17 O'Brien, Nora, Connolly, Witness statement WS 286

18 Lynch, Gilbert;ed O Cathasaigh, Aindrias; The life and times of Gilbert Lynch; Irish Labour History society. 2011;Dublin pp

19 Lynch, Gilbert. Pension application. MSP34REF41334

20 Lynch, Gilbert;ed O Cathasaigh, Aindrias; The life and times of Gilbert Lynch; Irish Labour History society. 2011;Dublin pp

21 Shouldice, John F. witness statement WS 162

22 O'Flanagan, Michael. Witness statement WS 800

23 Holland, Robert. Witness statement WS 280

24 O'Flanagan, Michael. Witness statement WS 800

25 Robbins, frank. Witness statement WS 585

Chapter Sixteen
Monday May 1st

Monday was Mayday, the traditional day to celebrate the glories of summer and for the labour movement to meet and demonstrate its hopes for the future. Yet in 1916 there was little to celebrate; Europe was in the middle of the most destructive conflict it had ever seen with no sign of the carnage ending. In only two months was to be the beginning of the Battle of the Somme, which left 3,500 Irish soldiers killed and many more wounded.

In Glasgow the socialist John Maclean had just been sentenced to three years hard labour for sedition after making speeches against conscription. In Berlin Karl Liebknecht was arrested on May 1st for telling an anti-war rally, "Do not shout for me, shout rather 'We will have no more war. We will have peace - now!'"

Dublin woke to a devastated city with the rebels either in captivity or on the run.[1]

Liam Parr, Redmond Cox and Larry Ryan had already been shipped out of Ireland and were arriving at Holyhead that morning, on their way to prison in Knutsford or Stafford. It is ironic that the authorities, who were sending the men away from the scene of the insurrection, were putting them in prisons so close to their homes in Manchester.

Gilbert was the only one of the Manchester Volunteers still at large, his liberty only having been preserved because doctors and nurses had conspired to protect him. He was at risk of arrest, though, as he had given his papers and identity to Martin Conlon and had to spend the next days trying to replace these so he could return home to Stockport.

Sheila O Hanlon was moved that day to Kilmainham jail where she stayed with the rest of the Cumann na mBan women until they were released several weeks later. During that time most of the leaders were executed in the same prison. Sheila's comrades described hearing, every morning, the heavy footsteps of men going to the firing squad, followed by a volley of rifle fire. One of these was Con Colbert who had been the close friend of Annie Cooney.

Yet this was not the end of the story for the four men and one woman we have been following. The demoralisation that followed the defeat of the insurrection was short lived; even as they marched to prison many showed their defiance by singing republican songs. Very soon all the members of this group were working again with undiminished determination to achieve the Irish state they had fought for during Easter Week. This was not to be an easy struggle, and it was to continue in different forms until the end of 1923. Sheila and her sister Mollie continued as active members of Cumann na mBan. They concentrated on providing first aid, being couriers of messages and sometimes weapons, and most importantly perhaps, collecting and administering support to the families of executed and imprisoned Volunteers. It has been argued that the determined and disciplined presence of women collecting donations after Mass was a major factor in changing public opinion from the initial, often negative, perception of the rising to the almost universal support for Sinn Fein that was shown in the 1918 election results.[2] Sheila remained a courier all through the War of Independence as well as during the Civil War, being imprisoned in 1923.

Liam Parr and Larry Ryan were both interned until Christmas in a camp at Frongoch in Wales. Here the British authorities made the mistake of incarcerating together hundreds of the most determined nationalists who proceeded to set up what was afterwards described as a 'university of revolution'. Most of the future leaders of Ireland, such as Michael Collins, 'studied' here.

Larry Ryan never settled again in Manchester after his release from prison, but worked as a merchant seaman between Liverpool and the USA. He was imprisoned in New York on charges of smuggling weapons to Ireland. The time he spent in the Tombs prison had a disastrous effect on his health.

Redmond Cox was set free after about a fortnight. He returned to Dublin and worked in a mental hospital in the Dublin area whilst resuming his activities with the volunteers. He took part in jail escape plots, fought against the black and tans and was in the hospital during a raid when the only way to escape detection was for a Volunteer to be locked in the padded cell and pretend to be a patient.

Liam Parr also re-joined the Volunteers in Dublin, whilst working for the insurance company that was used as a cover for Michael Collins' intelligence activities. He played the Irish war pipes in the James Connolly pipe band and played in support of de Valera's 1917 election campaign where he was described as playing in the car with de Valera as he entered Clare. He was implicated in undercover activities when one of the IRA leaders' attaché cases was captured in a raid. As a result, he was advised to lie low and fled to Stockport on the morning of Bloody Sunday.

Gilbert was never arrested after the Rising so was able to return to Stockport once he had replaced his identity documents. Over the next few years he smuggled weapons to fight the black and tans, and campaigned around Manchester for Irish independence. He helped Irish prisoners to escape Strangeways in Manchester by carrying messages to them and gaining the trust of the prison authorities by using his police pocket watch to prove his respectability.

In 1920 he and Liam ran a by-election campaign to elect an imprisoned hunger striker as MP for Stockport. The election campaign was based in Liam's parent's house and one of the helpers was the daughter of Casey the fiddler. Casey had been performing in banned concerts in Dublin.

Gilbert was to retain all his life his deep commitment to socialism, Irish nationalism and Catholicism. When he was living in Stockport, between 1916 and 1920 he was a leading light in the Independent Labour Party. He worked tirelessly to support conscientious objectors and the Russian revolution. He joined with Liverpool dockers who were striking against carrying arms to Ireland and helped workers to sabotage Crossley tenders bound for the black and tans in Ireland. Eventually he was blacklisted by Manchester employers and returned to Ireland and to Sheila O'Hanlon. In Ireland he only avoided being shot by black and tans by using his Lancashire accent to convince them that he was not the man they were seeking.[3]

After the truce was signed none of the Manchester Volunteers took part in the Civil war, though Sheila became a courier for the IRA chief of staff and was imprisoned. As soon as the war was over, Sheila and Gilbert married in Dublin. Gilbert had been in digs before the wedding in the same house as the widow of James Connolly. One of the witnesses was Mollie O'Hanlon, Sheila's sister who had been with her in Marrowbone Lane. Mollie had a clerical job in a laundry in Dublin but her health deteriorated, as a result of the privations and stress of her service and she died in 1946, aged 48.

Larry Ryan never regained his health after being in prison in New York and died in Dublin in 1924 when he was 30.

Redmond Cox continued to work all his life in the hospital in Dublin, dying in 1956 aged 63.

Gilbert worked all his life in Ireland as a trade unionist, serving for a time as a Labour TD and president of the Irish TUC. He became something of an iconic figure in trade union circles. Others recall Lynch's bald head and Lancashire accent booming out his catchphrase 'You are the Union!' In the 1940s an Irish employer objected to negotiating with an English trade union official, to which Gilbert responded by producing his 1916 medal and asking how many of the bosses had one of those.[4] His family remained in Dublin and helped produce his memoirs.

Every Christmas Gilbert and Sheila went to Stockport. Here we can surely assume that they would have met Liam, the friend of both of them who had introduced them on the eve of the Rising.

Liam had returned to Stockport in 1920 on the day of Bloody Sunday, 21st November. His wife, Margaret said "He was knocked about from pillar to post. I had a good job at the time and we were married, as I could keep him until things quietened down. He was in a very bad nervous state as you can understand..."[5]

Margaret was a nationalist supporter who had met Liam through the Gaelic League. They married in 1923 and had three children, one being the daughter who has helped provide information so we can tell his story. He was an enthusiastic singer, often playing the leading man in performances at the local Catholic Church. However, he was never in good health after his involvement in the war of independence, struggling with his memories, and dying when he was only 41. Although Margaret had to fight with tenacity to preserve Liam's memory and to bring up three children without their father, her daughter Bernadette was protected from any knowledge of the struggles her mother went through. Liam died when she was very small so she doesn't remember him. Instead she remembers the honour he was held in and the lupins he used to grow when they lived in Manchester.

"Perhaps if my father hadn't died so young he would have written a memoir, but my mother said the memories of what had happened troubled him a lot, but time can bring about healing".[6]

This book highlights the experiences of just some of the people who took part in the rebellion of 1916. I hope that this account does justice to all the courageous men and women who fought for freedom in Dublin a hundred years ago. I hope it helps to keep their memories alive.

1 This section is an abbreviated précis of the author's unpublished manuscript, The Manchester Volunteers and the Irish War of Independence. It follows the five main individuals through the rest of their lives. Main sources continue to be pension applications , witness statements., family memories and Ó Cathasaigh's , Life and Times of Gilbert Lynch

2 Caoimhe nic Dhaibheid (2012), the Irish national aid association and the radicalization of public opinion in Ireland. 1916 to 1918. The Historical journal.. September 2012. 55.pp705-729.

3 Gilbert Lynch pension application MSP34REF41334

4 Quoted in Lynch, Gilbert; ed O Cathasaigh, Aindrias; The life and times of Gilbert Lynch; Irish Labour History society. 2011;Dublin

5 Pension application, Pension administration section. Department of defence . Ireland. Documents re Parr DP9542. Letter to de Valera

6 Wall, Bernadette, personal communication 24 November 2014

Appendix
Liam Parr learning the pipes

There are no documents which prove where and when Liam learnt the pipes. There are a number of pieces of circumstantial evidence which suggest that this probably happened in some way that was connected with Andy Dunne and the first Fianna Éireann Sluagh in Camden Street.

We know that he was brought up as a child to have broadly nationalist sympathies; we have heard the stories of the children in his family spitting on the statue of King Billy.

We know that Liam had become a proficient piper and a committed nationalist, ready to take up arms by 1916 and 1917. He appears on lists at Kimmage garrison and the GPO at the beginning of the Easter Rising.[1] His pension application mentions him playing the pipes for de Valera during the East Clare election of 1917.[2]

What we do not know is how he progressed from one position to the other. We do however have a number of snippets of information which allow us to make an informed decision.

We have heard no stories of there being any other pipers in the family who could have taught him, so it is pretty certain that he chose to learn the pipes as a youth and he probably did this through contacts with nationalist organisations in Dublin. The Irish war pipes were a recently resurrected tradition, so he must have learnt from others in the movement. A boy like Liam, brought up in nationalist circles in Dublin, would have had little difficulty finding an opportunity to learn the pipes, particularly as he had musical talent and seemed to have been a serious and determined individual.

It is, of course, theoretically possible that he learnt the pipes after moving to Manchester, but this seems very unlikely as he would have had far more opportunity to learn in Dublin, at the centre of Irish cultural and political nationalism, than in Manchester where I have discovered no mention of any pipe bands at this time.[3]

Although Liam must have known members of the Dublin Pipers' Club and the St Laurence O'Toole Pipe Band, I think it most likely that his main piping activity was in connection with Andy Dunne and the Fianna Éireann. Although Liam's name does not appear in any surviving records of the Fianna, this is not surprising as its membership lists were actively destroyed after the Rising. Nor is he mentioned in any witness statements of former members of the Fianna. This could be explained by his involvement being peripheral, as he was older than most members and he would have been involved for a relatively short period, as he was to move to Manchester in 1911. This shortage of evidence is not uncommon, and it is interesting to note how rare it is to find mentions of any of the Manchester Volunteers in witness statements.

Liam's pension application was completed by his widow twenty years after the events described. In this she provided the names of Liam's commanding officers, so that his service could be checked to justify her claim to receive a pension. Her evidence must have been considered to be reasonably accurate, as the pension authority issued a 'Certificate of Service' for Liam. The names of the officers she mentioned are; Thos Weafer, Geo and Jack Plunkett, (Dempsey) Wm McDonagh, 55 Lr Dorset St. and Andy Dunne. Almost all these are credible and agree with other evidence.[4]

The exception is Andy Dunne. Dunne was never to be in a position to command Liam in the Volunteers or any other military organisation. He was very active in the first Fianna branch and a singer and drummer in the Fianna Pipe Band. He is commonly mentioned as one of 'Madame's boys' and taking part in musical activities at Markievicz's and at Liberty Hall. Dunne did become an officer in the Fianna, but only after Liam had moved to England. Dunne took part in the Easter Rising in St. Stephen's Green, where he would not have come into contact with Liam. Dunne did not remain militarily active after the Rising because his damaged sight rendered this impossible. It therefore appears clear that his connections with Liam were undoubtedly musical rather than military. This suggests that Liam's links with Dunne were important enough for his widow to remember and mistakenly describe him as a commanding officer. The most obvious conclusion would be that both Liam and Dunne were associated with the Fianna pipe band that was formed shortly after the inauguration of the first Sluagh of the Fianna in Camden Street in 1909.[5]

There are other pieces of evidence that would fit with Liam being associated with the Fianna band, though none are proof on their own.

In later life, Liam was photographed in piper's uniform with a set of war pipes. His family remember the kilt as being green, and have preserved a kilt pin from the uniform. The green kilt was part of a number of uniforms, including some of the Fianna, though it is interesting to note that the Camden Street Sluagh was one of the few that retained the kilt rather than changing to shorts.

The kilt pin that Liam was photographed wearing, and that has been preserved in his family, was very commonly worn by members of various nationalist organisations. There are photos of other people wearing this pin, (including a member of the Dublin Pipers' Club) but it was very commonly worn by Markievicz and Con Colbert, members of the first Fianna.

A particularly interesting element of the uniform was that Liam wore a very unusual badger's head sporran which was unique to the James Connolly Pipe Band. The pipe major of this band was Tom O'Donoghue, another member of that first Fianna Pipe Band.

It is reasonable to conclude that Liam did join, or have links with, the Fianna

Pipe Band from 1909-1911, and later the James Connolly Pipe Band. This is the most likely scenario which can explain Liam learning to play the pipes, his connections with Andy Dunne, the photographic evidence of his uniform and the surviving medallion.

Unless further evidence is discovered to justify any other conclusion, I believe it is reasonable to assume that this is what happened.

1   Heuston, John M. O.P, Headquarters Battalion: Easter Week 1916. Joannes Carolus. Dublin. 1966; Also Robinson, Seumas witness statement 1721; MA/MSPC/RO/607 Kimmage garrison 1916 military service pensions collection

2 Parr, William pension application DP 7542; Parr Margaret pension application II/RB/4077

3 He must have been involved in and trusted by republicans in Manchester to have known to go to Kimmage. It seems more likely that he developed his commitment to Irish nationalism over a longer period of his youth in Dublin though it is possible that his political development happened rapidly after he had arrived in Manchester.

4 Parr, William pension application DP 7542;Parr Margaret pension application II/RB/4077

5 Parr, William pension application DP 7542. Andy Dunne was involved in the first Fianna Branch in Camden St from 1909 when he was only 11, and is mentioned in a number of witness statements. Later, after 1911 he is mentioned as one of 'Madame's boys' at Surrey House. Most mention his singing ability. He became branch commander in 1915 and fought in St Stephens Green. He was imprisoned in Knutsford and Frongoch but was in camp hospital with eye infection. He said his eyesight was too poor for him to resume the struggle in 1917. No witness statements list him in a position of authority after Easter week. Liam would have been 17 at the formation of Fianna so may have been involved and known Dunne at the time. It is also possible that they also knew each other, possibly musically between 1917 and 1920 when both were in Dublin.

Sources

The main written sources for this work are the wonderful resources of the Irish Bureau of Military History.

Witness statements and pension files are specified in the chapter notes.

Witness statements are available at: http://www.bureauofmilitaryhistory.ie/bmhsearch/search.jsp

Pension documents that have been released are at: http://www.militaryarchives.ie/collections/online-collections/military- service-pensions-collection

Books and Websites

Allen, Kieran; The politics of James Connolly. Pluto press. London. 1990

Andrews, C S; Dublin Made me. The Lilliput press, Dublin 2001

Arrowsmith, Peter; Stockport: a history. Stockport Metropolitan Borough Council; Stockport. 1997

Askwith, Lord, Industrial problems and disputes, London 1920 quoted in Brown, Geoff, ed. The industrial syndicalist. Spokesman books. Nottingham. 1974

Bielenberg, Andrew, Coach Building. In Connolly, SJ ed The oxford companion to Irish history. Oxford University Press, Oxford.2002.

Big Jim Haywood; Wikipedia article accessed July 8 2015 at http://en.wikipedia.org/wiki/Bill_Haywood

Blatchford, Robert (as Nunquam); Merrie England. Journeyman Press. London. 1976

Brennan-Whitmore, W.J. With the Irish in Frongoch. Mercier Press, Dublin,2013

Brown, Geoff, ed. The industrial syndicalist. Spokesman books. Nottingham. 1974

Callow, John. James Connolly and the re-conquest of Ireland. GMB and RMT. London. 2013

Caoimhe nic Dhaibheid (2012), the Irish national aid association and the radicalization of public opinion in Ireland. 1916-1918. The Historical journal.55.pp705-729.

Casey, Christine, Dublin: the city within the Grand and Royal canals and the Circular Road. Yale University Press 2005

Caulfield, Max; the Easter rebellion; Gill and Macmillan; Dublin 1995

Cavendish, Richard, the foundation of Sinn Féin. History Today. Vol 55. Iss.11. 2005

Challinor, Raymond; the origins of British Bolshevism; Croom Helm, London, 1977

Clarion March 31 1916

Connell, Joe; Rebels' Priests- ministering to republicans 1916-24, Kilmainham Tales, Dublin , 2014.

Connell, Joseph E.A. Jnr; Where's where in Dublin. Dublin City Council. Dublin. 2006

Connolly papers. Marx memorial library. Éamon de Valera's recollections of
Connolly. 27 Dec 1960

Connolly, James, The re-conquest of Ireland, in Callow, John, James Connolly and the
Re-conquest of Ireland. Evans Mitchell Books, London ,2013

Connolly, James; James Connolly: Selected writings. Pluto press. London. 1997

Coogan, Tim Pat. De Valera. Long fellow, long shadow. Arrow. London 1995

Coogan, Tim Pat. Michael Collins, a biography. Hutchinson, London, 1990

Coogan, Tim Pat. The IRA. Harper Collins. London 2000

Coogan, Tim Pat; 1916: the Easter rising. Phoenix. London. 2005

Dangerfield, George. The strange death of liberal England. Serif. London. 2012.

De Bovet, Anne, Three months in Ireland, London 1891, quoted in Pakenham, Thomas
and Valerie; A traveller's companion to Dublin, Robinson, London, 2003.

DeCourcey Ireland, John, The Sea and the Easter Rising- 1916. Maritime Institute of
Ireland. Dublin 1966

Devine, Francis. Casey! Will the real Walter Hampson please stand up? Saothar Vol
33 (2008) pp 115-118

Digital Salford. Accessed 8 Aug. 2015 at http://www.salford.photos/2015/06/armed-
police-march-in-salford-1911/

Dowling, Martin. Traditional Music in Irish Society- Historical perspectives. Ashgate.
Farnham, Surrey. 2014

Ebenezer, Lyn; Frongoch Camp 1916; Gwasg Carreg Gwalch, Llanrwst. 2006

Ferriter, Diarmaid- Ireland 1900-2000 Profile books. London,2004

Fintan Lalor Pipe band, History. Web site. Not signed or dated. Retrieved Nov 2013 .at
http://flpb.ie/index.php/history/

Gibbs, Philip, The pageant of the years. London 1946 quoted in Brown, Geoff, ed. The
industrial syndicalist. Spokesman books. Nottingham, 1974

Good, Joe, Enchanted by Dreams, the Journal of a revolutionary. Brandon. Dingle,
1996.

Greaves, C. Desmond. The life and times of James Connolly. Lawrence and Wishart.
London 1986

Griffith, Kenneth and O'Grady Timothy E. Curious Journey. An oral history of
Ireland's unfinished revolution. Hutchinson, London 2007.

Hampson, Walter (Casey) A wandering Minstrel I. 2nd ed Deveron Press, Turriff.
Undated.

Harker, Dave. Tressell, the real story of the Ragged Trousered Philanthropists. Zeb
book. London 2003

Hart, Peter; Mick, the real Michael Collins. Macmillan. London 2005

Haverty, Anne, Constance Markievicz; Pandora, London 1988

Heath, Nick, Anarchists against World War I: two little known events- Abertillery and Stockport at libcom.org accessed 8 Aug. 2015 at https://libcom.org/history/anarchists-against-world-war-one-two-little- known-events-abertillery-stockport

Henry, William, Supreme sacrifice, the story of Éamonn Ceannt. Mercier press, Cork, 2005.

Herbert, Michael, The wearing of the green. A political history of the Irish in Manchester, Irish in Britain Representation Group. London 2001.

Heuston, John M. O.P.; Headquarters Battalion: Easter Week 1916.Joannes Carolus. Dublin.1966

Hinton, James. The first Shop stewards' Movement. George Allen and Unwin. London 1973.

Horton Jim. War on the home front- class struggles in Britain. Socialism today. Issue 180. July/Aug 2014

IRB Wikipedia article at http://en.wikipedia.org/wiki/Irish_Republican_Brotherhood

Irish genealogy.ie website accessed march 2015 at http:// churchrecords.irishgenealogy.ie/churchrecords/

Irish-American (newspaper May 9 1863.

Jeffery, Keith, The GPO and the Easter Rising. Irish Academic Press, Dublin. 2006

Kearns, Kevin, C, Dublin Tenement Life, an oral history, gill and Macmillan. Dublin. 1996

Lawlor, Damian;Na Fianna Éireann and the Irish Revolution 1909 to 1923.caoillte books; Rhode, Ireland. undated

Lissadell hall website. Accessed January 2015. http://www.constancemarkievicz.ie/politics.php

Lockout centenary 1913-2013 website. Accessed Jan 2015. http:// www.lockout1913.ie/the-history

Lynch, Gilbert; ed O Cathasaigh, Aindrias; The life and times of Gilbert Lynch; Irish Labour History society.; Dublin, 2011

Lyons,F S L. Ireland since the famine, Fontana, London,1985, Manchester Guardian 13 April 1910

Manchester Guardian Mar 16 1910

Manchester Guardian May 16 1911

Manchester Guardian 13 Sept 1913

Manchester Guardian 17 Nov 1913

Manchester Guardian 17 Nov 1913

Manchester Guardian 17 Nov 1913

Manchester Guardian Mar 19 1906

Manchester guardian March 21 1914.

Manchester Guardian Nov 15 1910

Manchester Guardian22 April 1908 Markievicz, Constance, Eire, June 9, 1923. Retrieved on 20 Nov 2014 from https:// fiannaeireannhistory.wordpress.com/2014/05/18/countess- markievicz-recalls-the-founding-of-na-fianna-eireann-in-1909/

Marrenco, Anne; The rebel countess. Phoenix, London 1967

Matthews, Ann. The Kimmage garrison 1916. Making billy cans at Larkfield. Four courts press. Dublin 2010.

McCoole. Sinéad; No ordinary Women. Irish female activists in the revolutionary years.1900-1923. O'Brien Press, Dublin .2008

McGarry, Fearghal; The rising, Ireland Easter 1916, Oxford, Oxford. 2010

McGuire, Charlie. Sean Mc Loughlin. Ireland's forgotten revolutionary. Merlin Press. Pontypool. 2011

Merthyr pioneer 17 Feb 1917

Merthyr pioneer 5 Feb 1916.

Nat library of Ireland. Website. The 1916 Rising- personalities and perspectives. http://www.nli.ie/1916/

Newsinger, John; Jim Larkin and the great Dublin Lockout. Bookmarks. London .2013

Norman, Diana; Terrible Beauty, A life of Constance Markievicz. Hodder and Stoughton, London 1987

O Mahony, Sean. Frongoch. University of revolution. FDR Teoranta, Dublin, 1987

Ó Muiri, Pol; Look West in Dublin review of books Issue 69, July 2015

O'Bracken, Fergus; Irish freedom Fighter: Peadar Bracken. TAF publishing.2009

O'Brien, Paul. Crossfire- the battle of the four courts 1916. New Island Dublin, 1912.

O'Brolchain, Honor,.Joseph Plunkett-16 Lives. The O'Brien Press. Dublin, 2012

O'Casey, Sean, Autobiographies 1. Papermac London 1992.

O'Casey; Autobiographies.II. Macmillan, London ,1963

O'Faolain.Sean; Constance Markievicz; Cresset Women's Voices.. London, 1987

O'Malley, Ernie. On another man's wound. Mercier press.. Cork. 2013

Pakenham, Thomas and Valerie; A traveller's companion to Dublin; Robinson , London, 2003

Pearce, Cyril. Comrades in Conscience. Francis Boutle, London 2014

Plunkett Dillon, Geraldine. (ed O Brolchain, Honor) All in the Blood. , A and A Farmar. Dubin. 2006.

Pollitt, Harry. Serving my time. Laurence and Wishart. London. 1976.

Pye, Denis; fellowship is life- the story of the national clarion Cycling club, National Clarion Publishing. 2004

Reid, Naomi; Hampson, Walter (Casey). In Bellamy, Joyce and Saville, John; Dictionary of Labour Biography. Vol VI; Macmillan. London, 1982

Salveson, Paul; Socialism with a Northern accent: Radical traditions for modern times. Lawrence and Wishart. London 2012.

Sebestyen, Amanda, (ed); Prison letters of Countess Markievicz; Virago, London 1987.

St Laurence O'Toole pipe band website accessed April 2015 at https://web.archive.org/web/20130616042956/http://www.slotpb.com/histor y.shtml

St. Laurence O'Toole Pipe band. Ui Tuatail Abu. 1910-2010-, St Laurence O'Toole Pipe band. Celebrating 100 years. Dublin, undated – probably 2010.

Sunday Independent, Dublin, 23 April 1916 by mac Neill, Chief of Staff of the Irish Volunteer Force.

Tiernan, Sonja, Eva Gore-Booth, an image of such politics. Manchester university press. Manchester 2012

Townshend, Charles. Easter 1916. The Irish rebellion. Penguin, London, 2005

Townshend. The republic, Penguin, London 2013

Tressell, Robert; the Ragged Trousered Philanthropists. Granada. London. 1965

Viny, Tomas letter to Benjamin Franklin. May 6th 1785, in franklin papers website accessed March 2015. *franklinpapers.org/franklin/yale?vol=43&page=099*

Watts, John R. Na Fianna Eireann, A case study of a political youth organisation. University of Glasgow 1981

Weekly Irish times, Sinn Fein rebellion handbook. Weekly Irish Times, Dublin 1917

Whitehead, Peter J; The industrial Heritage of Britain- the Ashton canal. Accessed 8 Aug. 2015 at http://www.pittdixon.go-plus.net/ac-basin- ancoats/ac-basin-ancoats.htm

www.nli.ie/1916/1916_main.html

Picture credits

Thanks for the use of pictures to:

1, 40, 41, 42, 44; Courtesy of Bernadette Wall

43; Courtesy of Christopher Wall

2, 3, 4, 5, 6, 13, 19, 22, 23, 24, 28, 30, 31, 35, 36; Courtesy of Wikimedia Creative Commons and National Library of Ireland

11, 39; Courtesy of Kate Hayes and Aindrias Ó Cathasaigh

14; Courtesy of Marx Memorial Library and Workers' School, London

12; Courtesy of Charles H Carr and Working Class Movement Library

17; Courtesy of Gerry Kavanagh

20, 25; Courtesy of Honor O Brolchain

27; IE/MA/BMH/P42- also D125/11 (Air Corps Rising sites of Action collection) Marrowbone Lane Distillery, Bureau of Military History, Military Archives, Cathal Brugha Barracks

32; © Irish Capuchin Provincial Archives, Dublin,Ireland

34; © Royal Mail Group Ltd 1916, courtesy of the British Postal Museum and Archive

38; Courtesy of Lyn Ebenezer

8, 9, 10, 40; Courtesy of the Earle family

33; Reproduced courtesy of Trinity College Dublin

15; Courtesy of University of Brighton , Hastings

All other pictures are the property of the author and his family.

Index

Agnew, Arthur; 93, 94, 97, 99, 100
Aloysius, Father ; 98, 100, 126, 131, 150, 153, 167, 174, 178
Alright; 113
American Civil war; 1, 15, 25, 34-37
Askwith, George; 59, 66
Augustine, Father; 174, 175, 180
Baden Powell; 18, 20, 23, 24
Barrett, Seamus; 69
Béaslai, Piaras; 112, 176
Belcamp Park; 28
Beresford Place; iii, 26, 111, 145, 146
Bevin, Ernest; 59
Blatchford, Robert; 61, 85, 86
Boer War ; 9, 17, 18, 61
Boland, Lieutenant; 156
Bonham, Alice; 13, 38
Bonham, Gus; 13, 15, 37, 38
Bonham, Margaret; 13, 37, 38
Breen, Liam, Captain; 109, 128, 135
British Socialist Party (BSP); 72, 73
Brooklyn; 35, 37
Bulfin, Éamonn; 156
Burke, Joan; 98
Byrne, Christy/Christopher; 88, 89, 166, 181, 188
Byrne, Sean; 115
Callendar, Brian; 22, 24
Casement, Roger; 81, 172
Casey the fiddler; 19, 31, 63, 64, 65, 67, 190
Ceannt, Aine; 17, 31, 93, 94
Ceannt, Éamonn; 12, 17, 18, 29, 31, 89, 105, 117, 121, 152, 179-182, 185, 199
Cheetham; 1, 79
Childers, Erskine and Molly; 123
Clarion; 52, 53, 60-63, 65, 72, 75, 85
Clarke, Liam; 88, 163
Clarke, Tom; 12, 38, 57, 86, 104, 105, 108, 124, 161, 163, 170, 177, 185
Collins, Maurice; 93, 115, 142, 145, 175
Collins, Michael; i, iii, 79, 82-84, 86, 190
Con Colbert; 23, 27, 88, 118, 130, 152, 166, 179-182, 186, 189, 194
Conlon, Martin, and Mrs Conlon; 72, 79, 80, 89, 92-94, 98, 113, 122, 141, 142, 144, 150, 153, 162, 167, 175, 178, 184, 189
Connolly, James; 3, 5, 14, 20, 24, 26, 28, 32, 38, 48, 53, 55-57, 60-63, 74-76, 79, 83-85, 87, 89-92, 95, 101, 102, 104-106, 125, 129, 138, 142, 145, 146, 149, 157, 160, 161, 162, 169, 170, 190, 191, 194, 195
Connolly, Joe; 26
Connolly, Nora, /O'Brian; 83, 93, 96, 188
Connolly, Roddy; 101

Cooney, Annie; 88, 94, 118, 122, 130, 133, 142, 146, 179-183, 188, 189
Corcoran, Alice; 166
Cosgrave Miss; 142, 180
Cosgrave, Phil; 88
Costello, Alfred; 38
Costello, Edward; 116
Costello, Florence see Earle, Florence
Costello, George; 14, 15, 34, 38, 43
Costello, Mary Sen Ne Murphy; 13, 34, 38
Costello, Mary/Stella see Parr, Mary/Stella
Cowan, Colonel; 91
Cox, Miss; 71
Cox, Redmond; iii, iv, v, 1, 38, 51, 69, 72, 75, To Dublin; 79, 89, 93. Sunday; 98. Monday; 113-116. Tuesday; 126-127. Wednesday; 141-142. Thursday; 150-151. Friday; 163-165. Saturday; 185-186. Deportation; 185-186. After Easter; 189-191
Crossley, Jim; 62, 72
Cullen, Liam; 136
Cullen, Nancy; 5
Cumann na mBan; iv, 29, 30, 83, 87, 88, 101, 108, 111, 113, 116-120, 126, 133, 136, 141, 151, 156, 165, 173-177, 181, 182, 189
Cumiskey, Miss; 120
Daly, Denis; 99, 127, 131, 159, 167
Daly, Edward, Commandant; 113, 115, 126, 141, 146, 151, 163, 165, 169, 176
Daly, William; 12, 15, 79, 85, 87, 93, 94, 97, 100, 109, 121, 122, 131, 134, 136, 143, 178
Dangerfield, George; 58, 66
Darrow, Clarence; 53
De Burca, Fergus; 125
De Coeur, Robert; 25
Delaunty, Mr; 39
DeValera, Eamonn; iii, 15, 43, 76, 90, 94, 120, 190, 192, 193
Devereaux; 30
Dillon, John; 74
Dillon, Tommy; 80, 81, 99, 106
Dolphins Barn; 17, 18, 29, 95-98, 117, 143
Doyle, Tommy; 174, 183, 188
Drinán, Frank (Frank Thornton); 109, 180
Dublin Lockout; 12, 25, 50-57
Dublin Pipers'Club; 17-18, 193-194
Duggan, Éamonn, Captain; 176
Dunne, Andy; 22, 24-27, 29, 32, 95, 96, 193-195
Earle, Florence; 34
Earle, Hannibal, Ernest; 33
Earle, William; 14, 33, 34, 43
Ennis, Peter; 145,146
Fagan, Madge; 159

Fahy, Anna; 165, 168, 175, 178, 184
Fahy, Frank; 176, 184
Farrell, Elizabeth; 170
Faulder's Chocolate; 34
Feis Ceoil Association; 11
Fenains see Irish Republican Brotherhood
Fhoghudha, Bridghid; 124
Fianna Éireann; 12, 14, 17, 18-32, 48, 74, 83,
89, 113, 116, 151, 162, 166, 172, 178, 193-195
Fintan Lalor Pipe Band; 25, 57, 66
Fisher, Harry; 62
Fitzgerald, Desmond; 124, 136, 159
Flynn, Ignatius; 135
Fox, Tom; 51
Foy, F J Dr; 39,40
Franklin, Benjamin; 2
French, Percy; 19
Gaelic Athletic association; 9, 10, 27, 70
Gaelic League; 12, 20, 21, 27, 39-43, 45, 47,
48, 69, 70, 76, 98, 119, 126, 191
Gallagher; 158
Gibbs, Brian; 59, 66
Gibson J M; 39
Gifford, Grace; 99, 101
Gifford Donnelly, Nellie; 87
Ginnell, Larry; 25, 37
Glasgow; iii, 75, 81, 101, 171, 189
Glasier, Bruce; 65
Gleeson, Joseph; 76, 81, 86, 93, 94, 178
Gonne, Maud; 9
Good, Joe; 83, 86, 93, 94, 99, 100, 103, 121,
167, 171, 177
Gore-Booth, Constance see Markievicz, Con-
stance
Gore-Booth, Eva; 19, 31, 32, 49
GPO- General Post office; iii. Monday; 101-
108. Tues; 123-125. Weds; 136-140. Thurs; 145
-150. Fri; 155-162. After Evacuation; 169, 172,
177, 185, 193
Grant, Ulysses, S, General; 37
Great Southern and Western Railway Company;
1, 151, 152
Gregory, Lady ; 40
Grennan, Julie; 160, 170
Griffith, Arthur; 17, 20, 21
Hampson, Walter see Casey the fiddler
Haywood, Jim, Big; 53, 56
Hegarty, Liam; 114
Henderson, Fred; 85
Henderson, Leo; 129
Henderson, Ruaidri; 100, 111, 119, 120, 134
Henratty, John; 150
Hill, John; 60
Hobson, Bulmer; 21-22, 27, 30, 89-93, 97, 98,
113, 142

Holland, Robert; 118, 119, 122, 144, 151, 153,
165, 166, 168, 178, 179, 185, 188
Humphries, Dick; 124
Hyde, Douglas; 11, 15
Inchicore; 1, 14, 88, 142, 151
Independent Labour Party (ILP); 60, 61, 63, 79,
191
Industrial workers of the World (IWW); 53
Inghínídhe na hÉireann; 9, 20, 30
Irish Citizen Army; 12, 20, 23, 25-28, 57, 89,
102, 104, 108, 120, 121, 125, 138, 139, 171
Irish Republican Brotherhood (IRB); 10, 11, 17,
20, 21, 27, 28, 30, 57, 69-72, 75, 79-82, 86, 89-
93, 104
Irish Transport and General Workers Union,
(ITGWU); 25, 26, 50-57
Kavanagh, Ernest; 145
Kavanagh, Martin; 186
Kavanagh, Seamus; 22, 31
Kearney, Peadar; 22, 24, 25
Keating Con; 81, 99
Keating, Annie; 29
Kelly, Pat; 47
Kelly, Patrick; 76,
Kelly, Tom; 87
Kennedy, Margaret; 29, 32, 87, 94, 99, 100,
117, 122, 130, 131, 153
Kennedy, Phelim; 71
Kilgannon, John A; 108
Kimmage /Larkfield Mill; iii, v, 80-85, 91, 93,
96-103, 108, 109, 116, 123, 129, 136, 171
Laffan, G; 115
Larkin , Delia; 57
Larkin, Jim; 21, 25, 26, 38, 48, 50-57, 60-62,
80, 108
Lavin , Peter; 48
Lee, Robert E, General, 37
Liberal; 19, 41, 42, 46-48, 60
Liberties, 1-5
Liberty Hall, iii, 26, 52, 86, 91, 95, 101, 102,
111, 112, 120, 133, 137, 138, 145, 146, 194
Lincoln, Abraham; 37
Liston, Mick; 143, 151, 166, 186
Lively, Paddy; 70
Liverpool; iii, 38, 54, 59, 63, 69, 70, 73, 75, 81,
99, 111, 171, 190, 191
Lloyd George, David; 59, 60, 66
London; iii, 2, 3, 12, 19, 38, 51, 54, 69, 76, 79,
81-83, 86, 87, 90, 109, 136, 171
Lowe, General; 172
Lower Camden Street; 21, 23-26, 29, 30, 193-
195
Lyme Hall; 64
Lynch, Fionan, Captain; 112, 114
Lynch, Gilbert; i, iii, iv, 1, 38, 39. Manchester;
43-65. Volunteers; 69-72. War; 72-79. To Dub-

lin; 85-87. Weekend; 95-100. Mon; 111-113.
Tues; 125-126. Wed; 140-141. Thu; 150. Fri;
162-163. Sat; 173-176. Sun; 184. After the
Rising; 189-191.
Lynch, Michael; 142
Lynch, Nurse; 176
Lyons Madame; 39
Mac Diarmada , Sean see MacDermott, John
MacDermott, Seán, John; 70, 90, 98, 106, 147,
160-162, 170, 171
MacDonagh, Thomas; 101, 105
MacMullan, Brian/Bernard; 86, 87, 102, 169
MacNeill, Eoin; 71, 81, 89, 90, 97-99.
Madden, Margaret see Parr Margaret
Mallin, Michael; 120
Manchester; i, iii, iv, v, 1, 19, 22, 26 Liam; 33-
43. Gilbert; 43-78. 79, 80, 81, 85, 86, 113, 116,
171, 184, 189-193
Markievicz, Constance; 18-28, 48, 52, 57, 95,
121, 194
Martin, Ellen; 33
Mathew, Theobald, Father; 126
McBride, John; 106
McGrath, P.; 120
McCabe, Frank; 115
McGarry, Sean; 110
McGrath Paddy; 129, 159
McGrath, Joe; 88
McHale, John, Dr, Archbishop of Tuam; 45
McHugh, Patrick; 47
McLoughlin, Sean; 101, 159, 160, 162, 169
McMahon, Liam; 69
McNamara, Rose; 30, 118, 120, 151, 177, 181,
184
Mellows, Liam; 24, 27, 38
Minstrel Boy; 25, 36, 37, 98
Mitchell, Paddy; 135
Molony, Helena; 20, 22, 24, 27
Morel. E.D; 74
Morris, William; 61, 65
Muirthuile, Sean; 71
Mulvey; 130
Murphy, Seamus; 118, 120, 179-181
Murphy, William Martin; 50, 52, 57
Murphy, Barney; 25
Murphy, Fintan; 129, 138, 149
Murphy, Margaret see Bonham, Margaret
Murphy, Mary see Costello, Mary
Murphy, Mrs; 120, 142
Murphy, William; 126
Murray; 119, 180
Myles Keogh, surgeon or Dr Thomas Myles;
176
Na Fianna Éireann see Fianna Éireann
New Jersey; 35, 37, 38
New York; 35, 36, 53, 190, 191

Ni Cheallaigh, Mairead, (O'Kelly); 141
No Conscription Fellowship; 73
Nolan, Michael; 29
North Frederick Street; i, 80, 85-87, 95-98, 100,
111, 172
Nunan, Sean; 103
Ó Ríain, Miceál see Ryan,
Ó Ríain, Máire; 70
O'Broin, Sean, Lieutenant; 181
O'Callaghan, Dinny; 140
O'Casey, Sean; 7, 8, 12, 14, 17, 31
O'Connell, Murt; 93
O'Connor, Blimey; 130
O'Connor, Rory; 81, 99, 106
O'Donoghue, Miss; 47
O'Donoghue, Patrick; iii, 128
O'Donoghue, Tom; 22, 24, 25, 128, 136, 194
O'Dwyer; iii, iv
O'Flanagan, Father; 137, 138
O'Flanagan, Michael; 176
O'Flanagan, Patrick; 164
O'Foghludha/Foley, Miceal; 174, 175
O'Gorman, Christina; 111
O'Growney; 39, 40, 42, 43, 48, 69
O'Hanlon, Connie; 26
O'Hanlon, James; 18, 29
O'Hanlon, Julia see O'Hanlon, Sheila
O'Hanlon, Mary Margaret see O'Hanlon,
Mollie
O'Hanlon, Mollie; 29, 87, 88, 95, 116, 118,
120, 152, 189, 191
O'Hanlon, Patrick; 29
O'Hanlon, Sheila; i, iv, 87, 95, 96, 97. Week-
end; 98-99. Mon; 116-120. Tues; 130. Wed;
142-143. Thurs; 151-153. Fri; 165-167. Sat;
177. Sun; 179-184. After the rising; 191.
O'Higgins, Brian; 25
O'Holahan, Gary; 24
O'Keefe, Josie; 119
O'Kelly, Michael; 126
O'Neill, Sergeant; 180
O'Shannon, Cathal; 75
O'Shea, M; 103
ÓBriain, Eoghan; 125
O'Brien brothers, Larry, Paddy and Denis; 130
O'Rahilly , Michael, Joseph, The; 98, 104, 124,
127, 145, 157-160
Parr, Christopher; 1, 4
Parr, Liam; iii, iv, 48, 51. Childhood; 1-16.
Youth; 17-30. To Manchester; 33-43. War; 75-
76. To Dublin; 79-85, weekend; 95-100. Mon;
101-111. Tues; 127-130. Wed; 133-136. Thurs;
145-146. Fri; 155-162. Sat; 169-173. Sun; 186-
187. After the rising; 189-192. Appendix; 193-
195.
Parr, Mary ne Costello; 1, 14

Parr, Stella see Parr Mary
Parr, William – see Parr, Liam
Partridge, Mr; 51
Pearse, Pádraig (or Patrick); 12, 23, 57, 84, 90, 92, 98, 102, 104, 105-107, 111, 125, 127, 139, 142, 146, 155, 156, 158-161, 170, 175, 176
Pearse, Willie; 104, 106, 139, 172, 185
Plunkett family; i, 80, 82
Plunkett, George jun; 84, 101, 102, 134
Plunkett, George, Noble,/Count; 80
Plunkett, Geraldine; 81, 82, 99, 106
Plunkett, Jack; 194
Plunkett, Joe; 90, 92, 99, 101, 102, 104, 105, 134, 155, 158, 161, 170, 172
Plunkett, Josephine; 80
Pollitt, Harry; 62, 72, 73
Pounch, Seamus; 30
Power, brothers Bill, Liam and Arthur; 168
Powers, Liam/Billy see Liam Parr
Prendergast, Sean; 26, 113
Price, Leslie; 111
Ragged Trousered Philanthropists; 60, 61
Reddish; 45-47, 86
Redmond, John; 41, 42, 48, 52, 69, 73, 74
Reilly, Joe; 136
Reynolds, Brian; 25
Reynolds, Joseph; 151
Robbins, Frank; 145, 187
Rooney, Catherine (Byrne); 108, 111
Roper, Esther; 19
Roscoe, J and sons; 71
Roscommon; 1, 79, 93, 176
Ryan , Larry; iii, iv, 1, 39, 51. Volunteers; 69-72. War; 75. To Dublin; 79-85. Mon; 101-108, 116. Tues; 123-125. Wed; 136-140. Thurs; 146-150. Fri; 155-162. Sat; 169-173. Deportation; 186-187. After the rising; 189-191.
Ryan, Desmond; 137, 138, 161
Ryan, Laurence- see Ryan, Larry
Ryan, Michael Sen; 70, 71
Ryan, Michael, Jun; 70
Salford; 1, 19, 49, 51, 60, 71
Sammon, Eugene; 50
Saul, Jack; 152
Shaw, George Bernard; 11
Sheehy Skeffington; 128
Sheerin, Tom; 126
Shelley; 55
Shouldice, Sean; 91, 114, 115, 163, 164, 177
Sinn Féin; 17, 20, 37, 91, 173, 183, 190
St Joseph's Industrial school; 39, 40, 45
St Laurence O'Toole Pipe Band; 12, 193
Stockport, Theatre Royal; 34, 65
Stockport; i, iii, iv, 1, 13, 30, 33, 34, 35, 38, 39, 42, 43, 45, 46, 50, 51, 60, 62-65, 71, 73, 76, 79, 85, 184, 189-191

Synge, J.M; 11, 19, 41
Tannam, Liam; 103, 107, 129, 133, 134, 156, 160
Taylor, Colonel; 174, 175
Thornton, Frank see Frank Drinán
Tillet /Tillett, Ben; 54, 56
Tobin, Sean; 92
Touhy, Dr; 133
Tressell, Robert; 60
United Irish League; 39, 41, 43, 47, 48
Victoria, Queen; 9
Walsh, Bridie; 136
Walsh, Eily; 30
Walter Hampson see Casey the fiddler
Weafer, Tom; 12, 109-111, 116, 127, 129, 133-135, 138, 194
Webb, F J D; 39
White, Jack, Captain; 57, 125, 138
White, Jack; 125, 138, 139
Wilde Oscar; 11
William III; 8
Wilson, Lee; 173
Yeats, W.B; 11, 19, 40, 41, 48
Young Ireland; 36, 40
Young, Tom; 186